005.5 O322o
Office 2010 /
33090014630141
LOSA 03/11

W9-BZC-916

Microsoft®
Office® 2010
Digital
Classroom

Microsoft®
Office® 2010
Digital
Classroom

The AGI Training Team

WILEY

Wiley Publishing, Inc.

Microsoft® Office® 2010 Digital Classroom

Published by
Wiley Publishing, Inc.
10475 Crosspoint Boulevard
Indianapolis, IN 46256

Copyright © 2011 by Wiley Publishing, Inc., Indianapolis, Indiana
Published by Wiley Publishing, Inc., Indianapolis, Indiana
Published simultaneously in Canada
ISBN: **978-0-470-57777-6**
Manufactured in the United States of America
10987654321

No part of this publication may be reproduced, stored in a retrieval system or transmitted in any form or by any means, electronic, mechanical, photocopying, recording, scanning or otherwise, except as permitted under Sections 107 or 108 of the 1976 United States Copyright Act, without either the prior written permission of the Publisher, or authorization through payment of the appropriate per-copy fee to the Copyright Clearance Center, 222 Rosewood Drive, Danvers, MA 01923, (978) 750-8400, fax (978) 646-8600. Requests to the Publisher for permission should be addressed to the Legal Department, Wiley Publishing, Inc., 10475 Crosspoint Blvd., Indianapolis, IN 46256, (317) 572-3447, fax (317) 572-4355, or online at **http://www.wiley.com/go/permissions**.

Limit of Liability/Disclaimer of Warranty: The publisher and the author make no representations or warranties with respect to the accuracy or completeness of the contents of this work and specifically disclaim all warranties, including without limitation warranties of fitness for a particular purpose. No warranty may be created or extended by sales or promotional materials. The advice and strategies contained herein may not be suitable for every situation. This work is sold with the understanding that the publisher is not engaged in rendering legal, accounting, or other professional services. If professional assistance is required, the services of a competent professional person should be sought. Neither the publisher nor the author shall be liable for damages arising herefrom. The fact that an organization or Website is referred to in this work as a citation and/or a potential source of further information does not mean that the author or the publisher endorses the information the organization or Website may provide or recommendations it may make. Further, readers should be aware that Internet Websites listed in this work may have changed or disappeared between when this work was written and when it is read.

For general information on our other products and services or to obtain technical support, please contact our Customer Care Department within the U.S. at (800) 762-2974, outside the U.S. at (317) 572-3993 or fax (317) 572-4002.

Please report any errors by sending a message to errata@agitraining.com

Library of Congress Control Number: 2010928467

Trademarks: Wiley and related trade dress are registered trademarks of Wiley Publishing, Inc., in the United States and other countries, and may not be used without written permission. The AGI logos are trademarks of American Graphics Institute, LLC in the United States and other countries, and may not be used without written permission. All other trademarks are the property of their respective owners. Wiley Publishing, Inc. is not associated with any product or vendor mentioned in this book.

Wiley also publishes its books in a variety of electronic formats. Some content that appears in print may not be available in electronic books.

About the Authors

The AGI Creative Team is composed of Adobe Certified Experts and Adobe Certified Instructors from American Graphics Institute (AGI). They work with many of the world's most prominent companies, helping them use creative software to communicate more effectively and creatively. They work with design, creative, and marketing teams around the world, delivering private customized training programs, and teach regularly scheduled classes at AGI's locations. The Digital Classroom authors are available for professional development sessions at companies, schools and universities. More information is available at *agitraining.com*.

Acknowledgments

Thanks to our many friends at Microsoft who made this book possible and assisted with questions and feedback during the writing process. To the many clients of American Graphics Institute who have helped us better understand how they use the Microsoft Office software programs and provided us with many of the tips and suggestions found in this book. A special thanks to the instructional team at AGI for their input and assistance in the review process and for making this book such a team effort.

Credits

Writing
Sandi Hoffman, Christopher Smith,
Michael Stillman, Greg Heald

**President, American Graphics Institute and
Digital Classroom Series Publisher**
Christopher Smith

Executive Editor
Jody Lefevere

Senior Acquisitions Editor
Stephanie McComb

Technical Editors
Barbara Holbrook, Rebekah Blizzard,
Cheri White

Editor
Marylouise Wiack

Editorial Director
Robyn Siesky

Business Manager
Amy Knies

Senior Marketing Manager
Sandy Smith

Director of Content
Jeremy Osborn

**Vice President and Executive Group
Publisher**
Richard Swadley

Vice President and Executive Publisher
Barry Pruett

Senior Project Coordinator
Lynsey Stanford

Project Manager
Cheri White

Graphics and Production Specialist
Lauren Mickol

Media Development Project Supervisor
Chris Leavey

Proofreading
Jay Donahue

Indexing
Michael Ferreira

Contents

Word Lesson 3: Editing the Document

Word Lesson 4: Formatting Paragraphs

Word Lesson 5: Working with Pages

Word Lesson 6: Working with Styles and Themes

Word Lesson 7: Working with Tables

Word Lesson 8: Working with Graphics

Excel Lesson 1: Microsoft Excel 2010 Jumpstart

Excel Lesson 2: Getting Started with Microsoft Excel 2010

Excel Lesson 3: Editing Cells

Excel Lesson 4: Formatting Cell Ranges

Excel Lesson 5: Building Formulas and Functions

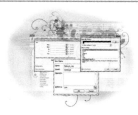

Excel Lesson 6: Displaying Data with Charts

Excel Lesson 7: Analyzing Excel Data

Excel Lesson 8: Adding Graphic Objects

PowerPoint Lesson 1: Microsoft PowerPoint 2010 Jumpstart

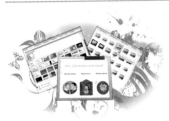

PowerPoint Lesson 2: Getting Started with Microsoft PowerPoint 2010

PowerPoint Lesson 3: Working with Tables and Charts

PowerPoint Lesson 4: Working with Graphic Elements

Access Lesson 1: Microsoft Access 2010 Jumpstart

Access Lesson 2: Getting Started with Microsoft Access 2010

OneNote Lesson 1: Microsoft OneNote 2010 Jumpstart

OneNote Lesson 2: Getting Started with Microsoft OneNote 2010

Publisher Lesson 1: Microsoft Publisher 2010 Jumpstart

Publisher Lesson 2: Getting Started with Microsoft Publisher 2010

Outlook Lesson 1: Microsoft Outlook Essentials

Starting up

About Microsoft Office 2010 Digital Classroom

Microsoft Office 2010 is the leading software package for communicating and organizing everything you need for work, school, or home. Microsoft Office 2010 is available in three versions: Home and Student, Home and Business, and Professional. This book covers all three versions of Microsoft Office 2010, so you can use it with any of these three versions. This book includes sections that cover the Office 2010 versions of Microsoft Word, Excel, PowerPoint, OneNote, Outlook, Access, and Publisher.

You can use the *Microsoft Office 2010 Digital Classroom* to discover how to create professional looking documents with Word, impactful presentations using PowerPoint, and high-quality publications with Publisher. You'll also discover how to use powerful analytical tools with Excel, Track information using Access, Stay connected and organized using Outlook, and keep your data organized using OneNote.

The *Microsoft Office 2010 Digital Classroom* helps you to understand the capabilities of these software tools so you can get the most out of Microsoft Office and get up-and-running right away. You can work through all the lessons in this book, or complete only specific lessons that you need right now. Each lesson includes detailed, step-by-step instructions, along with lesson files. Many lessons also contain useful background information and video tutorials available online.

Microsoft Office 2010 Digital Classroom is like having your own expert instructor guiding you through each lesson while you work at your own pace. This book includes 27 self-paced lessons that let you discover essential skills, explore new features, and understand capabilities that save you time and let you work more efficiently. You'll be productive in Microsoft Office 2010 right away with real-world exercises and simple explanations. Each lesson includes step-by-step instructions that use lesson files that are available for download from the Digital Classroom website. There are also video tutorials online that enhance the materials covered in the book The *Microsoft Office 2010 Digital Classroom* lessons are developed by a team of experts that have created many of the official training guides for companies such as Adobe Systems and Microsoft. The lessons in this book cover the essential skills for using the software programs that are part of the Microsoft Office 2010.

Prerequisites

Before you start the *Microsoft Office 2010 Digital Classroom* lessons, you should have a working knowledge of your computer and Microsoft Windows. You should know how to use the directory system of your computer so that you can navigate through folders. You also need to understand how to locate, save, and open files, and you should also know how to use your mouse to access menus and commands. If you need help with the basics of operating Microsoft Windows, explore the *Microsoft Windows 7 Digital Classroom* book and DVD combination, available from your favorite bookseller.

Before starting the lessons files in the *Microsoft Office 2010 Digital Classroom* make sure that you have installed Microsoft Office 2010. The software is sold separately, and not included with this book. You may use the free trial version of the Microsoft Office applications available at *www.microsoft.com/office/try* web site, subject to the terms of its license agreement.

System requirements

Before installing the Microsoft Office 2010 software make sure that your computer is equipped for running it. Remember that you must purchase the software separately. You can find the minimum system requirements for using Microsoft Office 2010 here *www.microsoft.com/office/try* by clicking the System Requirements link. Note that the system requirements vary for each of the three versions of Microsoft Office 2010: Home & Student, Home & Business, and Professional.

Menus and commands are identified throughout the book by using the greater-than symbol (>). For example, the command to print a document could be identified as File > Print.

Fonts used in this book

Microsoft Office 2010 Digital Classroom includes lessons that refer to fonts that were installed with your copy of Windows or Microsoft Office 2010. If you did not install the fonts, or have removed them from your computer, you may substitute different fonts for the exercises or re-install the software to access the fonts.

If you receive a Missing Font warning, replace the font with one available on your computer and proceed with the lesson.

Loading lesson files

The *Microsoft Office 2010 Digital Classroom* uses files for the exercises with each of the lessons. These files are available for download at *www.DigitalClassroomBooks.com/Office2010*. You may download all the lessons at one time or you may choose to download and work with specific lessons.

For each lesson in the book, the files are referenced by the file name of each file. The exact location of each file on your computer is not used, as you may have placed the files in a unique location on your hard drive. We suggest placing the lesson files in the My Documents folder or the Desktop so you can easily access them.

Downloading and copying the lesson files to your hard drive:

1 Using your web browser, navigate to *www.DigitalClassroomBooks.com/Office2010*. Follow the instructions on the web page to download the lesson files to your computer.

2 On your computer, navigate to the location where you downloaded the files and right-click the .zip file you downloaded, then choose Extract All.

3 In the Extract Compressed (Zipped) Folders window, specify the location where you want to save the files, and click Show Extracted Files When Complete.

Video tutorials

The *www.DigitalClassroomBooks.com/Office2010* site provides *Office 2010 Digital Classroom* book readers with many video tutorials that enhance the content of this book. The videos use the popular Silverlight player for viewing on your desktop or notebook computer, or use iPad compatible video if you are using an iPad to read an electronic version of this book. Most other ePub devices are not optimized for playing video, and you should use a notebook, desktop, or tablet computer for viewing the video tutorials. An Internet connection is necessary for viewing the supplemental video files.

The videos enhance your learning as key concepts and features are discussed by the book's authors. The video tutorials supplement the book's contents, and do not replace the book. They are not intended to cover every items discussed in the book, but will help you gain a better or more clear understanding of topics discussed in many lessons of the book.

Additional resources

The Digital Classroom series goes beyond the training books. You can continue your learning online, with training videos, at seminars and conferences, and in-person training events.

DigitalClassroomBooks.com

You can contact the authors, discover any errors, omissions, or clarifications, and read excerpts from the other Digital Classroom books in the Digital Classroom series at *digitalclassroombooks.com*.

Seminars, conferences, and training

The authors of the Digital Classroom seminar series frequently conduct in-person seminars and speak at conferences, including the annual CRE8 Conference. Learn more about their upcoming speaking engagements and training classes at *agitraining.com* and *cre8summit.com*.

Resources for educators

If you are an educator, contact your Wiley education representative to access resources for this book designed just for you, including instructors' guides for incorporating Digital Classroom books into your curriculum. If you don't know who your educational representative is, you can contact the Digital Classroom books team using the form at *DigitalClassroomBooks.com*.

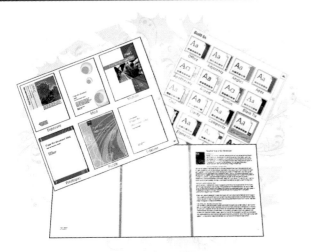

What you'll learn in this lesson:

- Creating a new blank document

- Copying and pasting text from one document to another

- Customizing the Quick Access Toolbar

- Inserting background color and margins

Microsoft Word 2010 Jumpstart

In this lesson, you will get a general introduction to Microsoft Word 2010. This lesson is intended to provide a quick introduction, so you can jump right in and get your feet wet. If you aren't ready for a quick overview, feel free to skip this lesson and move to Lesson 2, "Getting Started with Microsoft Word 2010," and then return to this lesson later.

Starting up

You will work with several files from the Word01lessons folder in this lesson. Make sure that you have loaded the OfficeLessons folder onto your hard drive from *www.DigitalClassroomBooks.com/Office2010*. See "Loading lesson files" on page XXIV.

See Lesson 1 in action!

Use the accompanying video to gain a better understanding of how to use some of the features shown in this lesson. The video tutorial for this lesson can be found at www.DigitalClassroomBooks.com/Office2010.

The project

In this lesson, you will create a document from scratch. Using the most popular features of Word 2010, you will compose a document that contains an article, a blank page, and a cover page.

1 Launch Microsoft Word 2010.

2 Choose File > Open. Navigate to the Word01lessons folder located in the OfficeLessons folder that you copied to your computer from the DVD that came with this book, then double click word0101_done to open the file.

A Word document opens to the first page in a document; the cover page. In this exercise, you will reproduce this document from a blank page. You can keep this file open as you work, or, after examining it, close the file by choosing File > Close.

The completed Word document.

The Word workspace is similar to other Microsoft Office applications, and the tools are conveniently located on the Ribbon, across the top of the window for whenever you need them.

The Ribbon displays different options depending on the tab you click. Here, the Home tab displays the most commonly accessed tools and options.

The Ribbon is divided into tabs, and within each tab there are groups. The Ribbon replaces traditional menus that existed across the top of the screen and toolbars which were found in older versions of Microsoft Office. The primary tabs of Word 2010 are File, Home, Insert, Page Layout, References, Mailings, Review, View and Acrobat.

The Ribbon is context sensitive, meaning that its appearance changes depending on your current task. Some tabs appear only in certain contexts and change depending upon where your cursor is located or what item you have selected.

Creating a new document

You'll start by creating a blank document and adding elements to it.

1   Choose File > New > Blank Document > Create.

2   Choose File > Save As. Even though you haven't added anything to the document, saving a file right after you create it is good practice. It makes it easy to save modifications as you build the document, and helps Microsoft Word recover your file should your computer or software stop working correctly.

3   Navigate to your Word01lessons folder, then in the File name text field, type **word0101**. Click Save. The dialog box closes, and the blank document is on your screen.

    You will now open another document that contains information you will copy into your blank document.

4   Choose File > Open.

5   Navigate to your Word01lessons folder, and then double-click word0102 to open this file.

6   In the word0102 file, click to place your cursor at the beginning of the document before the first paragraph. At the top of your screen, make certain that the Home tab is selected.

7   In the Editing group of the Ribbon, which is located to the far right of the screen by default, choose Select > Select All.

Editing Group of the Ribbon Select Menu.

8   In the Clipboard group of the Ribbon, click Copy.

    Now that you've copied the content, you can close the word0102 document by clicking the X in the upper-right corner of the document window.

9   Return to the original document, word0101, and click Paste.

You can press Alt+Tab to toggle between documents at any time.

10 Choose File > Save. It's important to save your document often, and it is a good habit to develop in order to keep your documents safe.

Customizing the Quick Access Toolbar

The Quick Access Toolbar places many commands at your fingertips. It's located in the top left of the Word workspace, and you'll need to know a bit more about it before we move on with this lesson.

In this part of the lesson, you will learn how to use and customize the toolbar.

The Quick Access Toolbar helps save time.

By default, the toolbar displays Undo, Repeat, and Save. You will add Open and Spellcheck to your customized toolbar.

1   Click the Customize Quick Access Toolbar icon (▾) on the toolbar. You can locate the toolbar above the Ribbon tabs in the upper-left hand corner of the window.

2   On the Customize Quick Access Toolbar menu, select Open. When the menu closes, click the Customize Quick Access Toolbar icon again and select Spelling and Grammar.

Select any of the options on the Customize Quick Access Toolbar menu to make working in Word easier.

Now you can simply click an icon to open a document or activate a spell check. For all lessons from now on, use the Quick Access Toolbar for opening, undoing, repeating, saving, and spell checking. If you want other options to be visible on the toolbar, use the same procedure to add new commands.

Applying Styles

You can use preset styles to instantly format your work. You can also create your own styles, which you'll cover later in this book.

You will now apply styles to the text in the document using the Quick Style Gallery.

Use the Quick Style Gallery to choose styles for your text.

1   With the word0101 document still open, select the text *Haunted Tours of San Francisco*.

2   From the Quick Style Gallery on the Home tab, click the Heading 1 style.

3   Click and drag over the text *Introduction* to select it, and then click the Heading 2 style.

4   Click anywhere in the paragraph under *Introduction*, and then click the Normal style to apply the style to the paragraph.

Now you'll select three headings and apply the Heading 2 style to them.

5   While holding the Ctrl key down, select *The San Francisco Ghost Hunt*, *Haunted Haight Walking Tour*, and *San Francisco Chinatown Ghost Tour*, and then click Heading 2 to apply this style to the selected text.

6   Click anywhere in the paragraph under *The San Francisco Ghost Hunt*, and then click Normal.

7   Repeat this procedure for both paragraphs under *Haunted Haight Walking Tour* and text under *San Francisco Chinatown Ghost Tour* to apply the normal style to the text.

8   Click the Save icon (💾) on the Quick Access Toolbar.

Applying a theme

If you would like more color or style in your document, you can quickly assign a theme to create more professional-looking pages. Themes have certain color schemes, fonts, and other decorative accents to brighten up your work.

In this exercise, you will apply a theme to the document.

1   Click Page Layout, and then choose Themes. The Built-In themes are displayed.

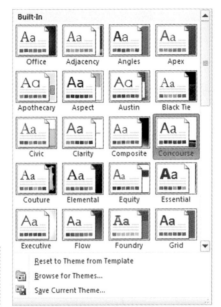

Scroll to see the Built-In theme options.

2   Click the Austin theme. Notice that the font style changes to Century Gothic and the Heading 2 colors change to green.

3   Click Save.

Adding and positioning a graphic

Graphics add visual elements to your work. Here, you'll see how to add a picture to this article.

1   Place your cursor before the title of the article and click Insert > Picture.

2   Navigate to the Word01lessons folder in your OfficeLessons folder.

3   Select the word0110 image and click Insert. The picture sits at the top of the page.

4   With the picture selected, click Wrap Text > Square to push the text away from the picture.

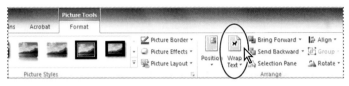

Click Wrap Text to view the Wrap Text options.

Now you'll put a soft edge around the perimeter of the picture.

5   If it is not already selected, click the Picture Tools tab to display the picture tools.

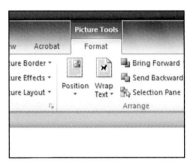

The Picture Tools tab becomes visible when a graphic is selected.

6   In the Picture Tools tab, select Soft Edge Rectangle. Depending on your screen's resolution, you may need to expand the Picture Styles section by clicking the More symbol (⋅) to the right of Picture Styles.

Select the Soft Edge Rectangle Picture Style.

7   Choose File > Save or use the Save button found on your customized Quick Access Toolbar.

Changing background color and margins

You can apply a background color to a paragraph or to an entire page. In this exercise, you will apply a background color to the whole page.

1   Place your cursor anywhere on the page and click Page Layout > Page Color > White, Background 1, Darker 5%.

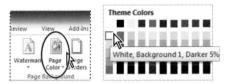

Select the first color under white for White, Background 1, Darker 5%.

2   In the same Page Layout tab, choose Margins > Narrow.

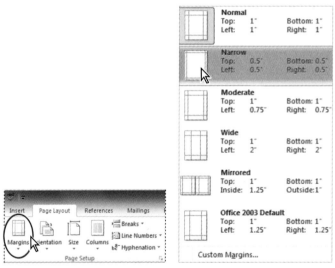

Select Narrow for a narrow margin.

3   Click Save. When you select a narrow margin, there may be a blank page remaining at the end of the document. If there is a blank page, you can move on to complete the following exercise.

Deleting a blank page

To delete a blank page:

1   Click View on the Ribbon.

2   In the Document Views group, click Draft.

3 Scroll down to the end of the document where you see the fine dotted line.

4 Place the cursor below the line and press Delete until the line disappears.

Inserting additional pages

In this exercise, you will insert additional pages into the document. The first page will be a cover page, followed by a page that will remain blank.

Inserting a blank page

1 From View, select Print Layout to view the document as it will appear on the printed page. Place your cursor before the title of the article.

2 Click Insert > Pages > Blank Page. The page appears in front of the article.

The title may shift to the left when you insert the blank page. You can correct this by placing the cursor to the left of the title and pressing Enter.

Inserting a cover page

Now you'll select a cover page for your document.

1 Click Insert > Pages > Cover Page.

Word displays a menu with several built-in cover page options.

Word includes several cover pages you can use in your documents, or you can make your own.

2   Click Sideline to select this cover page style.

3   In the Type the company name box, type **Spirits USA**.

4   Click Type the document title, and type **Haunted Tours**.

5   Click Type the document subtitle, and type **Famous Ghostly Places**.

6   Click anywhere in the document but outside of the text field and click the Save button located in the Quick Access Toolbar.

Adding page numbers

Next, you will add automatic page numbers to the packet. As you add additional articles or pages, the page numbers will automatically appear for each new page. As you add and delete pages, Word keeps track of the sequence and numbering of the pages.

1   Click Insert > Page Number > Bottom of Page.

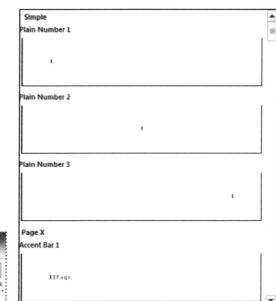

Word provides several options for styling and the placement of the page numbers.

2   From the Page Number menu, select Plain Number 3 to display the page number on the right-hand side in the footer of the document.

3   To exit the footer section of the pages, double click outside of the footers anywhere in the document.

Protecting the document

To keep the document from being changed, you will restrict editing to control the changes people can make.

1   Click the File tab and Word displays the File menu and detailed information about the document. You also find a list of commands you can use to manage files. Among these file management options are commands that can protect the document from unwanted editing.

2   Click File > Info > Protect Document. Word presents options for protecting the document from editing.

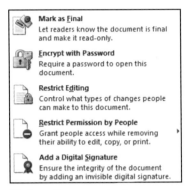

The Protect Document options let you secure your files.

3   Click Restrict Editing. Word displays a sidebar to the right of the document for restricting changes and edits to the document.

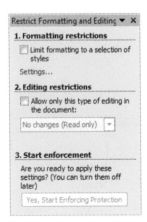

Use Restrict Formatting and Editing to specify which restrictions will be applied to a document.

4   Under Editing restrictions, click Allow only this type of editing in the document. From the drop-down menu, click Comments. This means the document cannot be modified, but comments can be added.

5   Under Start enforcement, click Yes, Start Enforcing Protection.

Word displays the Start Enforcing Protection dialog box.

You can enforce protection using the Start Enforcing Protection dialog box.

6   Type a password.

7   Retype the password and click OK.

8   Click Save. Word protects the document and saves the protection.

Congratulations! You have started to see some of what Microsoft Word 2010 has to offer with this quick tour of several significant features. Throughout the book, you will learn these features in greater depth.

Self study

1   Add the following commands to the Quick Access Toolbar: Insert Picture from File, Copy, and Paste.

2   Change the theme of the document from Austin to Aspect.

3   Open the document word0102. Copy and paste the contents into a new document and apply the Heading 2 style to Haunted Tours of San Francisco and the Heading 3 style to Introduction, The San Francisco Ghost Hunt, Haunted Haight Walking Tour, and San Francisco Chinatown Ghost Tour.

Review

Questions

1 How do you apply the same heading style to three nonconsecutive headings?

2 When working with a graphic, when does the Picture Tools tab become visible?

3 What is the name of the tab that appears on the Ribbon when you select a graphic in the document?

Answers

1 Click Ctrl then select the heading text. The headings remain selected, so you can apply the style to all three headings at once.

2 A graphic has to be selected for the Picture Tools tab to be visible. Click the Picture Tools tab for the tools to be visible.

3 The Picture Tools tab appears on the Ribbon when you insert a graphic or when you have selected a graphic.

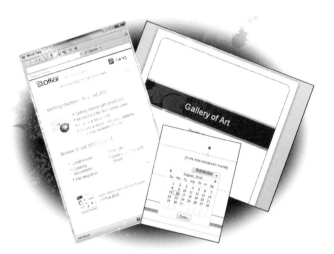

What you'll learn in this lesson:

- Creating new documents from a template
- Customizing tools and commands
- Using the scroll bar, zoom settings and viewing options
- Making documents compatible with earlier versions of Word

Getting Started with Microsoft Word 2010

In this lesson, you will discover the basics of Word and how to use the Word workspace area. You will begin by creating a new document from a template and gain an understanding of the Word workspace. You will customize your work area and use the zoom settings and viewing options.

Starting up

You will work with several files from the Word02lessons folder in this lesson. Make sure that you have loaded the OfficeLessons folder onto your hard drive from *www.DigitalClassroomBooks.com/Office2010*. See "Loading lesson files" on page XXIV.

See Lesson 2 in action!

Use the accompanying video to gain a better understanding of how to use some of the features shown in this lesson. The video tutorial for this lesson can be found at www.DigitalClassroomBooks.com/Office2010.

Understanding Microsoft Word

Microsoft Word is an application for creating, editing, formatting, and sharing professional looking documents. Word 2010 also includes tools for editing and revising your work, as well as collaborating with others to create great documents to share in print or online. Your documents can include text and graphics, and you can use Microsoft Word to adjust the formatting and appearance of them through a variety of layout controls.

Creating a new document from template

When creating a new document, you can select a template from several choices that are included within Word, or from templates that are available online. All documents are built on templates. The template controls the appearance of the final document—such as the number of columns, whether page numbers are included on the bottom, and the overall size and width of the pages in a document. You can choose a template from the Available Templates page, or create a blank document. Blank documents are also based on a template called the Normal template. The Normal template offers styles to help you format your pages and control the look of a blank document.

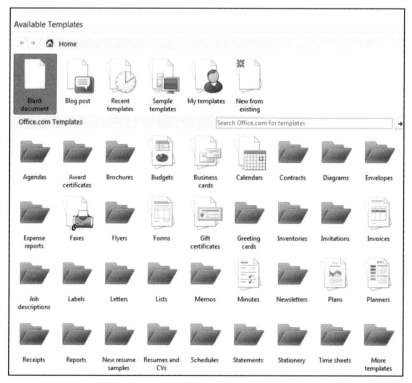

Choose a template to apply a predefined format to your documents.

In this exercise, you will create a new document from a template and save it to a folder.

To create a new document from template:

1   Launch Word.

2   Choose File > New > Sample Templates > Equity Report > Create.

3   Choose File > Save As and navigate to the Word02lessons folder.

4   Type the name **word0201** in the filename text field, and click Save. Keep this file open to use later in the lesson.

Customizing the workspace

To work efficiently in Word, you can customize the workspace to display or hide elements. This lets you display the most common items you use for working on your documents. In this exercise, you will:

- Adjust the status bar to display what is visible while you work, such as the page number and the location of the insertion point.

- Revise the Quick Access Toolbar to show the icons for the commands you use most often, such as Save.

- Arrange the ribbon for your editing convenience.

Status bar

Use the status bar to display options you want to use throughout this lesson. The status bar is located along the bottom of the Word window. The left side of the status bar displays information that helps you better understand the status of documents on which you are working. The right part of the status bar shows the view and zoom options.

The Microsoft Word status bar before it is customized.

In this exercise, you will customize the status bar to display formatted page numbers, the view shortcuts, and the zoom slider.

To customize the status bar:

1   Right click the status bar.

You can customize the status bar to display information you want visible while you work.

2   Be sure that the following options are checked:

- Formatted page number

- Page number

- Word count

- View shortcuts

- Zoom

- Zoom slider

3   Click anywhere outside of the menu to close it.

The Status Bar after customizing.

Quick Access Toolbar

The Quick Access Toolbar is used to quickly access tools that you use most often when working within Word. This toolbar is located at the top-left corner of the Word window. For the Quick Access Toolbar, you can modify many settings, such as what is displayed on the toolbar and whether it is displayed over or under the ribbon.

You will display the toolbar under the ribbon and add the Spelling and Grammar icon to it.

To customize the Quick Access Toolbar:

1 Click the Customize Quick Access Toolbar icon (⬇).

2 Check the following options, if they are not already selected:

- New

- Save

- Spelling & Grammar

- Undo

- Redo

- Show Below the Ribbon

Customizing the Quick Access Toolbar lets you add commands that you use often.

3 Click anywhere outside of the menu to close it.

If you do not see the option you want on the list, click More Commands. Word displays a list of commands that you can select and add to the Quick Access Toolbar.

Ribbon

Use the ribbon to access commands, such as copy and paste. The ribbon is divided into tabs, such as Home, and the commands within each tab are separated into groups, such as Clipboard.

A. Tab. B. Commands. C. Group.

You can minimize the ribbon if you want to focus more on your documents. The ribbon is displayed by default. If you hide the ribbon, the tabs remain visible so you can still access any commands you need.

In this exercise, you will discover how to hide the ribbon, and work within the word0201 document using basic ribbon commands.

To hide the ribbon and work with some commands:

1 Click the Minimize the Ribbon icon (⌄) in the upper-right corner; Word hides the ribbon.

Another way to display the hidden ribbon is to press Ctrl+F1.

2 In the word0201 document, type **Gallery of Art** in the Type the document title text box. Press Tab and, in the Type the document subtitle text box, type **Monthly Report**.

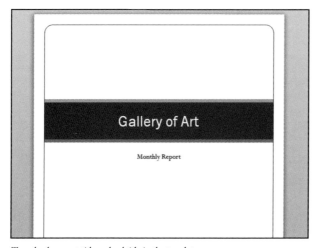

Type the document title and subtitle in the template.

3 Move to the bottom of the page, click inside the Type the Company Name text box, and type **Classic Galleries**.

4 Click on Pick the date text box and select the date from the Date drop-down menu.

Click the down arrow to display the calendar.

5 In the Authored By text box, type **Your Name**.

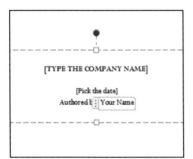

Enter your name in the Authored by Text Box.

Word fills-in the author according to your login name, by default. You can leave this name, or change it.

Formatting using the Ribbon

Now that you have entered the information, you will format the title and subtitle using the Ribbon commands. You will then save and close the document. First, you will redisplay the ribbon.

1 To redisplay the ribbon, click the Expand the Ribbon icon (⌄) located above the Ribbon on the far right.

2 Click anywhere inside the Monthly Report text to select it. On the Ribbon, in Font group on the Home tab, select bold and then italics.

Select Bold and Italics from the Font group
to format the subtitle in bold italics.

3 On the Quick Access Toolbar, click Save to save the document.

 It is best to keep the ribbon visible throughout the lessons.

Using the View options

The View options are located on the bottom right side of the status bar.

Use the View options to change between Print Layout, Full Screen Reading, Web Layout, Outline, and Draft.

View options allow you to display your document
in different modes.

VIEW OPTION	DESCRIPTION
Print Layout	Displays the whole page of text, graphics, and columns in the window just as it would look when printed or if converted to a PDF file.
Full Screen Reading	Uses the entire screen to display the document, including print options and controls, to move through the document for online reading.
Web Layout	Shows how your document will look as a web page.
Outline	Displays outline symbols and indentations to show you how a document is organized and to make it easy to quickly restructure it.
Draft	Displays only basic text and none of the formatting like graphics, columns, and page breaks, so it is easier to concentrate on what you are writing.

In this exercise, you will change how you view the document from the default view, Print Layout to Draft view. You will then increase the magnification.

To switch to Draft view and change the zoom:

1   Click the Draft icon (≣).

2   Click the plus or minus control to adjust the zoom to 120%.

 You can also use the zoom lever, located between the minus and plus signs, for zooming in and out.

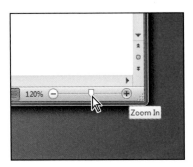

The zoom lever allows you to control the magnification of the document.

3   Click File > Save and then File > Close to close the document.

Getting help

You can always find help when you need it if you are working in a Word document. You can click the Help button (❷) located in the upper-right corner of the window, or you can select Help from the File menu. Use the File menu if you need additional help beyond what you find by searching. The File menu gives you access to the Microsoft Help Desk by email, chat or phone.

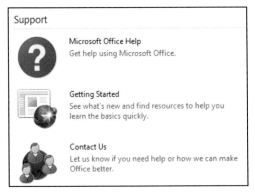

You can access the Help Desk by email, chat or phone to answer questions not resolved in your search.

In this exercise, you will use the search option to find information on how to insert a graphic.

To use the search option for help on Word:

1   Select File > Help and click Microsoft Office Help under Support. Word displays the Help window.

Search by entering a keyword in the Help window.

2 Type **insert graphic** in the Search box, and then press Enter. Word displays titles of articles matching the search criteria.

Word displays the search results for the topic you entered.

By default, the Word Help window remains on top. If you'd prefer to have it in a different location, click and hold the Word Help title bar and drag to move it to a more convenient location.

3 Click Add a drawing to a document to view an article. Word displays the article in the Word Help window.

4 Click the X in the upper-right corner to exit Help.

Converting Word documents from prior versions to Word 2010

If you have older Word documents, you can easily convert them to the new Word 2010 format. In this exercise, you will convert a document saved in a previous version of Word to Word 2010.

To convert an old Word document:

1   Navigate to Word02lessons and double-click to open the file named word0202. In this example, we use a Word 2003 document. Notice that the title bar shows that the document is open in Compatibility Mode.

Compatibility Mode allows you to work on documents created in versions of Word prior to 2010. When working in Compatibility Mode, some new Word 2010 functions may be disabled. As soon as you convert a document to the current version of Word, Compatibility Mode disappears from the title bar, and the new functions become available to you.

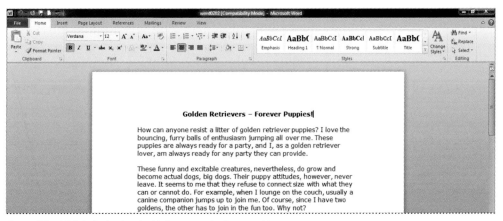

Compatibility Mode is displayed in the title bar next to the document title.

2   Click File > Info > Convert. Word displays a dialog box.

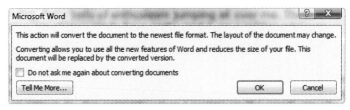

Click the checkbox if you do not want Word to display the conversion message again.

3   Click OK. Notice that Compatibility Mode is no longer visible on the title bar.

4   Choose File > Save As. Word displays the Save as dialog box. Make sure that file name is still word0202 and the location is the Word02lessons folder and click Save.

5   Choose File > Close.

Self study

1   Create a new document, and choose a different template this time. Peruse the different templates on the Available Templates page.

2   Customize the Quick Access Toolbar by adding Quick Print and Open Recent File.

3   Click the Help button and type **lists** in the Search box and review the results.

Review

Questions

1   Name two ways to create a new document in Word 2010.

2   Which View option on the Status Bar does not display the graphics in a document?

3   What displays in the title bar when you open a document to alert you that it was created in an earlier version of Word?

Answers

1   You can either create a blank document or choose a template from the Available Templates page.

2   The Draft view does not show graphics.

3   The words *Compatibility Mode* appear in the title bar.

What you'll learn in this lesson:

- Opening and editing an existing document

- Switching between documents

- Selecting, copying, pasting and manipulating text

- Protecting a document from editing

Editing the Document

In this lesson, you will open and edit an existing document by cutting and pasting text from one part of the document into another. You will also apply fonts to text.

Starting up

You will work with several files from the Word03lessons folder in this lesson. Make sure that you have loaded the OfficeLessons folder onto your hard drive from *www.DigitalClassroomBooks.com/Office2010*. See "Loading lesson files" on page XXIV.

See Lesson 3 in action!

Use the accompanying video to gain a better understanding of how to use some of the features shown in this lesson. The video tutorial for this lesson can be found at www.DigitalClassroomBooks.com/Office2010.

Opening and editing an existing document

In this exercise, you will open and modify two existing documents located in the Word03lessons folder. One document contains text that you will be copying from and the other contains a document into which you will be pasting the text and creating the finished document.

To open the documents you need for this lesson:

1 Launch Word.

2 Choose File > Open, and navigate to the Word03lessons folder.

3 Press the Ctrl key while you click on the files word0301 and word0302 to select both. With both files selected, click Open.

Keep both documents open, as you will be working with them in the next part of this exercise.

 Word remembers the 25 most recently opened documents. To open any of these documents at a later point if you decide to stop working or accidentally close the files, click File > Recent and select the file you want to open.

Working with text

Entering and manipulating text is a central part of using Microsoft Word. In this set of exercises, you will work within two documents. You will discover clipboard options available when you paste from a source document, and you will change fonts and learn how to emphasize text. The two documents you opened in the previous steps, word0301 and word0302, should now be open. You will be working with both of these documents.

Viewing documents

When you need to switch between two open documents, you can use any of three methods:

• Press Alt +Tab to switch between open documents.

- On the Ribbon, Click View > Window > Switch Windows and click a document.

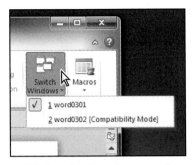

Word displays a list of open documents under the Switch Windows option.

- Click the document you want to view on the Word task bar located on the bottom of the window under the Status bar.

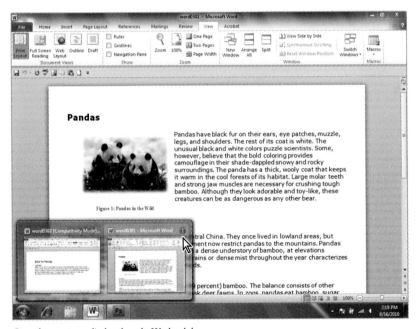

Open documents are displayed on the Word task bar.

When you need to view more than one document at a time, use the Window group on the View tab.

- Press Arrange All to view the documents one above the other.

- Press View Side by Side to view the documents beside each other.

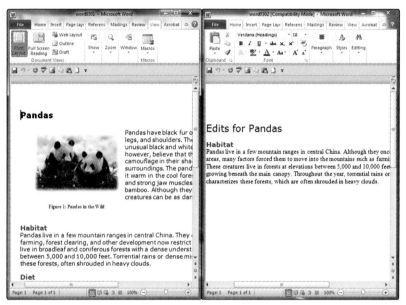

Use the View tab to easily arrange multiple open windows.

Selecting text

When you want to format or edit text, you must first select it. After it is selected, you can format and modify it to meet your needs. Word uses several easy methods to select sections of text such as words, sentences, entire documents, and even nonconsecutive text. You will be selecting and editing text later in this lesson.

Each time you select text, a faded, mini toolbar appears. Place the cursor over the mini toolbar so you can see it more clearly.

Use the mini toolbar to apply formatting to selected text.

 If the mini toolbar disappears before you can select what you need, right-click the text you wish to edit, and the toolbar reappears.

A word about selecting

Block of Text: Position the mouse pointer to the left of the text you want to select. Click and drag to make the selection.

Single Word: Position the mouse pointer anywhere within the word you want to select. Double-click to make the selection.

Sentence: Press and hold Ctrl. Click anywhere within the sentence you want to select.

Paragraph: Position the mouse anywhere within the paragraph and triple click.

Entire Document: Choose Home > Select > Select All or move the pointer to the left of any text until it changes to a right-pointing arrow, and then triple-click.

Nonconsecutive Text: Make a selection. Press Ctrl and hold it down as you select the other areas you want.

Copying and pasting

In this exercise, you will add words to the title of the article. Then, you will select a block of text so that you can copy a paragraph from one document and paste into another one.

While you are learning about how to move text between documents, it's important to note that Microsoft Word also has features that automate the process of merging edits from multiple documents into one complete file. Because the edits for this lesson only apply to a portion of the text, and because this lesson is focused on fundamental skills, we'll focus on copying and pasting at this time.

1 In the word0301.docx document, place your cursor after the letter *s* in Pandas and type **of China**, so the title reads *Pandas of China*.

2 Place your cursor anywhere in the paragraph below the title *Habitat*.

3 Click three times to select the paragraph beginning with *Pandas* and ending with *clouds*, and click Cut in the Ribbon's Clipboard group.

4 Switch to the document word0302 by pressing Alt Tab. Place your cursor in the paragraph located under *Habitat*.

5 Triple-click to select the entire paragraph.

6 Click Copy on the Clipboard in the Home tab, and switch back to the document word0301, with the title *Pandas of China*.

7   Place your cursor after the *t* in the title Habitat and press Enter.

Paste options

Habitat

Pandas live in a few mountain ranges in central China. Although they once lived in lowland areas, many factors forced them to move into the mountains such as farming and forest clearing. These creatures live in forests at elevations between 5,000 and 10,000 feet with dense bamboo growing beneath the main canopy. Throughout the year, torrential rains or dense mist characterizes these forests, which are often shrouded in heavy clouds.

Paste Option options.

When you paste text, the Paste Options icon () appears after the pasted block of text. Click the down arrow to select paste options.

ICON	OPTION NAME	DESCRIPTION
	Keep Source Formatting	Uses the formatting of the original text you copied or cut.
	Merge Formatting	Uses the formatting of the destination where you are pasting the text.
A	Keep Text Only	Applies no formatting; only plain text is pasted.
None	Set Default Paste	Displays the Word Options dialog box so you can set the default paste settings which will be applied when you use the paste command.

Clipboard options

When you cut or copy a selection, Windows places the copied or cut selection on the Windows clipboard, which is a storage area that holds the selection until you are ready to do something with it such as pasting it. In Word, several selections can reside on the clipboard at the same time and you can selectively paste the items you have previously cut and put them into your documents.

You can easily view the items that are stored on the Clipboard so you know what is available to paste into your documents. To view what is on the Clipboard, go to the Home tab, then click the dialog box launcher in the bottom-right corner of the Clipboard group.

Dialog box launcher displays items on the clipboard.

The Clipboard task pane contains the items that you have copied or cut from a document.

Copy and Paste feature

Copying

You can use the Copy command several times in a row to copy many items.

Word's Clipboard can hold 24 items. Once you copy the 25th item, the oldest selection is removed from the Clipboard and replaced by the newest item.

Pasting

To paste an item from the Clipboard, place your cursor where you want to insert the copied item and click the item on the Clipboard you wish to insert. Word inserts the text at the insertion point.

Be sure to click only once. If you click multiple times, multiple copies will be inserted.

To insert all items on the Clipboard, click the Paste All button located on the top of the Clipboard.

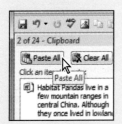

The Paste All button.

Deleting and closing

When you click the down arrow on the right side of an item on the Clipboard, Word displays a shortcut menu. Click Delete to remove the items from the Clipboard.

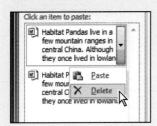

Deleting an item from the clipboard.

Click Clear All at the top of the task pane to delete all items in the Clipboard, but be careful because you cannot undo the deletion.

Click the X in the upper-right corner of the task pane to close the pane.

Working with fonts

Word gives you control of text formatting used in your documents. The Font group in the Home tab is the place to look for most of the text formatting options you will need.

Use the Font group to apply text formatting.

The Font group helps you quickly apply formatting to your text. You can:

- Change the font face, which changes the overall text style
- Make text smaller or larger
- Change the case and the color
- Apply formatting, such as bold or italics
- Highlight certain words or phrases

In this exercise, you will work within the word0301 document and make some changes to the fonts. You will start by changing the font face then change the size and color of the headline.

1 If it isn't still open from the previous exercise, open word0301.docx and scroll down to the final section, entitled *Conserving the Panda*, which has no formatting applied to it.

2 Select the heading and the two paragraphs following it. You will change the font face to Verdana for all the text.

 In this lesson you're choosing Verdana, a sans-serif font, because this document will be distributed online. Sans-serif fonts, like Arial and Helvetica, are easier to read online. If you were distributing this in a printed format, you would have been more likely to choose a font like Times New Roman, a font with serifs, that is better for printed documents.

3 In the Ribbon in the Font group, click the down arrow after the label of the current font Times New Roman and select Verdana from the drop-down menu.

4 Select the headline, *Conserving the Panda*, and move the cursor so it hovers over the mini toolbar that appears after you have selected the text.

Mini toolbar appears to the right of a selected item.

5   For font size, type **13** and click the Bold icon (**B**).

6   For color, click the down-arrow to the right of the Font Color button (**A**), and select the orange color in the Theme Colors called Orange Accent 1.

Reducing font size

The remainder of the section of text needs to match the style of the rest of the article. The text in the article uses Verdana at 11 points, so you will change the text in this section to match this format.

1   Place your cursor before the word *Early*, then click and drag to the word *monitoring* at the end of the second paragraph, selecting the rest of the section.

2   On the mini toolbar, click the Shrink Font icon (ᴀ) reducing the font from 12 points to 11 points in size.

Changing the case

You will now discover how Word can help change the case of text that is incorrectly formatted.

1   Place your cursor before the word *Figure* under the graphic and click three times, selecting all the text in the caption *(Figure 1: Pandas in the Wild)*.

2   On the Ribbon in the Font group, click the Change Case icon (Aa▾). Word displays the Change Case menu.

Use the Change Case menu to: apply sentence case, change to lowercase or uppercase, toggle the case, or to capitalize each word.

3   Click UPPERCASE. The caption appears in all uppercase letters.

4   Select File > Save As and name the document **word0301_done**. Select File > Close to close the document.

5   In the document word0302, select File > Close.

Emphasizing text

In this exercise, you will practice using Word's character formatting tools to make some text stand out from the rest of the text in a paragraph. You'll discover that you can emphasize text in many ways. You can make a heading bold, italicize the title of a book, or underline a word. You might even need to use the subscript and superscript features, so you can write things like CO_2 or 42nd street. You can also use the highlight and strikethrough options when sharing editing ideas. You will also find ways to easily remove formatting using the Clear Formatting tool.

When you want to apply formatting to a character, you must first select the character. Refer to "A Word about Selecting," discussed earlier in this lesson. After selecting the text to be formatted, you can apply a special format to a single character, a word, or a phrase.

In this exercise, you will use the word0303 document to practice working with the character formatting tools. The Font group on the Home tab displays the icons you can use.

Use the Font group on the Ribbon to change the font in many ways.

1 Select File > Open.

2 Navigate to word0303, and then double-click to open the file.

3 In sentence number one, place your cursor before *Tom Sawyer*, then click and drag to select these two words.

4 On the Ribbon, click Home, and in the Font group, click the Italics icon to apply italics to the book title Tom Sawyer.

5 Place your cursor before the *2* in e=mc2, located in the same sentence, and drag to select the 2.

6 In the Font group, click the Superscript icon (x‘) to apply a superscript to the 2 in e=mc2.

7 Place your cursor before the 2 in H2O, located in sentence number 2, and drag to select the 2.

8 In the Font group, click the Subscript icon (x,) to apply a subscript to the 2 in H2O.

9 Place your cursor before the word *This* in sentence number 3, and triple-click to select the sentence.

10 In the Font group, click the Strikethrough icon (abc) to apply a strikethrough to the sentence.

11 Place your cursor before the word *alpaca* in sentence number 4, and double-click to select the word.

12 In the Font group, click the Underline icon (**U**) to underline the word.

13 Place your cursor before the word *Figure* in the caption under the picture, and triple-click to select the whole caption.

14 In the Font group, click the Bold icon (**B**) to apply bold to the caption.

15 Click the Save icon on the Customize Quick Access Toolbar to save the changes. Keep this document open as you will use it to practice setting document protections.

Character Formatting tools

ICON	TOOL	SHORTCUT	EXAMPLE
B	Bold	Ctrl+B	**Bold**
I	Italic	Ctrl+I	*Italic*
U	Underline	Ctrl+U	Underline
abc	Strikethrough	N/A	~~Strikethrough~~
x₂	Subscript	Ctrl+=	Subscript$_1$
x²	Superscript	Ctrl+Shift+(plus sign)	Superscript^1
aby	Highlight	Select the highlight color from the menu.	Highlight
Aa	Clear Formatting	N/A	***Formatted*** Cleared

Protecting a document from editing

You can protect your document so that other people are not able to make changes to it.

To set protections:

1 With word0303 open, click File > Info to display information about the open file.

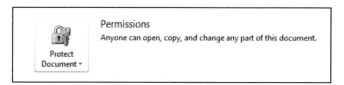

> Permissions
> Anyone can open, copy, and change any part of this document.
>
> Protect Document ▾

Use the Protect Document option to set permissions on your file, restricting opening or editing.

2   Click Protect Document in the Permissions group. The Protect Document menu is displayed.

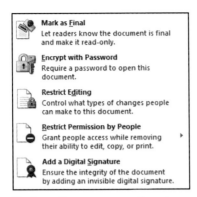

The Protect Document menu provides options for securing your file.

3   Click Restrict Editing to display the Restrict Formatting and Editing window.

Use the Restrict Formatting and Editing window to set formatting and editing restrictions for the file.

4   Under Formatting restrictions, select Limit formatting to a selection of styles if it is not already checked, then click Settings. The Formatting Restrictions dialog box is displayed.

Use the Formatting Restrictions dialog box to limit the styles people can change.

5   Click Block Theme or Scheme switching from the Formatting section at the bottom, and then click OK. Word displays a dialog box. Click No as a response. This means that the look and feel of the document cannot be changed. Later, in Lesson 4, you will learn more about using themes.

6   Under Editing restrictions, click the *Allow only this type of editing in the document* checkbox, and select Comments from the drop-down menu. This lets reviewers add comments but not change other items.

7   Under Start enforcement, click Yes, Start Enforcing Protection. Word displays a dialog box allowing you to set an optional password. Click OK.

8   Save your changes and close the file.

Protect Document options

Other options to protect your document appear on the Protect Document menu.

OPTION	DESCRIPTION
Mark as Final	Sets the document to read only.
Encrypt with Password	Requires a password for anyone attempting to open the document.
Restrict Editing	Controls the type of changes people can make.
Restrict Permission by People	Grants people access without giving them permission to edit, copy, or print.
Add a Digital Signature	Ensures the integrity of the document by adding an invisible digital signature.

Self study

1   Open word0301 and word0302. Try different methods of switching between documents:

  •   Press Alt+Tab to toggle between documents.

  •   Click View > Switch Windows and click a document.

  •   Click the document you want to view on the Word task bar.

2   Practice selecting a paragraph, a single word, a sentence, an entire document, and some nonconsecutive text by clicking multiple times in the same location or by clicking and dragging.

3   Select the entire word0301 document and change the font face first to Arial, then to Times New Roman, and finally back to Verdana.

4   On the Home tab in the Clipboard group, click the dialog box launcher located on the lower-right corner of the Clipboard group to make the Clipboard visible. With word0301 open, make several different selections and copy them, then observe how they are collected on the Clipboard.

Review

Questions

1 What command lets you easily open a recent Word file from inside a Word document.

2 What are some of the ways you can select a sentence?

3 How can you remove everything from the Clipboard?

Answers

1 File > Recent.

2 The three ways to select a sentence are:

- Press and hold Ctrl. Click anywhere within the sentence you want to select.

- Click at the beginning of the sentence and drag to the end.

- Click three times before the sentence and Word selects the sentence.

3 On the Clipboard, click Clear All.

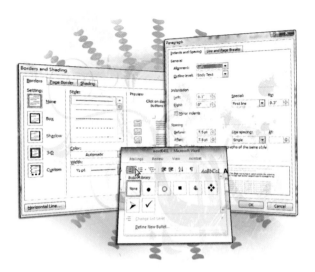

What you'll learn in this lesson:

- Creating space within or between paragraphs
- Applying paragraph alignment
- Creating bulleted, numbered and multilevel lists
- Indenting paragraphs
- Applying a border

Formatting Paragraphs

In this lesson, you will apply formatting to paragraphs using the spacing, indentation, alignment, border and list tools.

Starting up

You will work with several files from the Word04lessons folder in this lesson. Make sure that you have loaded the OfficeLessons folder onto your hard drive from *www.DigitalClassroomBooks.com/Office2010*. See "Loading lesson files" on page XXIV.

See Lesson 4 in action!

Use the accompanying video to gain a better understanding of how to use some of the features shown in this lesson. The video tutorial for this lesson can be found at www.DigitalClassroomBooks.com/Office2010.

Working with paragraphs

You probably remember from basic grammar classes that a paragraph is a collection of related sentences dealing with a single topic. Microsoft Word considers a paragraph anything on the page where the Enter key has been pressed before and after. So it could be a single sentence, or several sentences. Microsoft Word lets you apply separate left and right margins—the space along the left and right side of the text, to each paragraph. It also lets you apply space on top of and below a paragraph—known as space before and after the paragraph. You can also control alignment, tab stops, and line spacing separately for each paragraph.

As you type a document using Microsoft Word, it creates new paragraphs each time you press the Enter key.

The Paragraph group in the Home tab is where you can find the tools for applying paragraph formatting.

The Paragraph group..

The Paragraph group helps you quickly format a paragraph. You can:

- Apply paragraph alignment
- Change line spacing within and between paragraphs
- Create bulleted, numbered and multilevel lists
- Decrease and increase indent to a paragraph
- Apply paragraph borders

Use the Dialog Box Launcher to display the Paragraph dialog box.

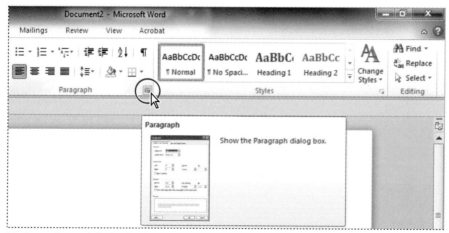

The Paragraph group dialog box launcher.

The Paragraph dialog box gives you options to set indents, spacing, line and page breaks. You also can preview the paragraph's appearance.

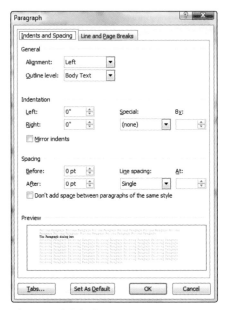

The Paragraph dialog box.

Applying paragraph alignment

In this exercise, you will open a document located in the Word04lessons folder and align each paragraph to enhance the look of the document.

To open the document you need for this lesson:

1   Launch Word.

2   Choose File > Open, and navigate to Word04lessons.

3   Locate the word0401 file, then press Open.

To change paragraph alignment:

1   In word0401, click anywhere within the first paragraph.

2   Click the Home tab. In the Paragraph group, click the Justify icon(▤).

3   Click anywhere within the second paragraph.

4   Click the Justify icon again in the Paragraph group.

5 Select the paragraph under the heading *Behave this way:* by clicking anywhere between the words *Safe* and *books*. Be certain to not click within the headline above this text. Because you are applying formatting to the paragraph, you don't need to select the entire paragraph—Microsoft Word knows to apply formatting to the entire paragraph where your cursor is inserted.

6 Click the Align Text Left icon (≣) in the Paragraph group.

7 Insert your cursor in the paragraph below the title, *Do not behave that way* by clicking anywhere within that paragraph.

8 Click the Align Text Right icon (≣).

9 Click anywhere in the paragraph with the sentence *Your best bet*, then click the Center icon (≣).

10 Click on the picture of the road, then click the Center icon.

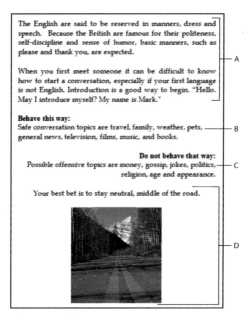

The English are said to be reserved in manners, dress and speech. Because the British are famous for their politeness, self-discipline and sense of humor, basic manners, such as please and thank you, are expected. — A

When you first meet someone it can be difficult to know how to start a conversation, especially if your first language is not English. Introduction is a good way to begin. "Hello. May I introduce myself? My name is Mark."

Behave this way:
Safe conversation topics are travel, family, weather, pets, — B
general news, television, films, music, and books.

Do not behave that way:
Possible offensive topics are money, gossip, jokes, politics, — C
religion, age and appearance.

Your best bet is to stay neutral, middle of the road.

— D

The document after adjusting the paragraph alignment. **A**. *Justified.* **B**. *Left aligned.* **C**. *Right aligned.* **D**. *Center aligned.*

Changing line spacing

This exercise covers setting line spacing between paragraphs and within a paragraph.

 One line of space is equal to approximately 12 points.

Within a paragraph

To set line spacing within a paragraph:

1 In word0401, click anywhere within the first paragraph.

2 On the Home tab in the Paragraph group, click the Line and Paragraph Spacing icon (‡≡) to display the various spacing options.

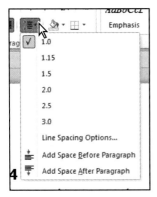

The Line and Paragraph Spacing menu.

3 Select 1.5 for the paragraph to spread out the lines within it by one and a half spaces.

Options for line spacing

OPTION	DESCRIPTION	SHORTCUT
1.0	Single space	Ctrl+1
1.15	Word 2010's default spacing	
1.5	1 ½ spaces	Ctrl+5
2.0	Double space	Ctrl+2
2.5	2 ½ spaces	
3.0	Triple space	

Between paragraphs

You can also change the amount of space Word places between paragraphs. This is a much better option than pressing the Enter key several times between paragraphs. By using the space before or space after options you can specify the exact amount of space to apply. If at any point you want to change the space between the paragraphs, you can easily make one adjustment rather than searching throughout the document to remove or apply extra returns to adjust spacing.

To set line spacing between paragraphs:

1   In word0401, select the first and second paragraphs by clicking before the first word of the first paragraph and dragging to the last word in the second paragraph and release.

2   Click Home > Paragraph dialog box launcher.

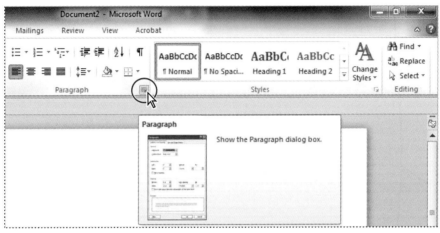

The Paragraph dialog box launcher.

3   In the Spacing section, select 6 from the Before drop-down menu and 6 from the After drop-down menu. You can also type **6 pt** in each field to make the selections. This applies an additional 6 points of spacing between paragraphs. Remember that there are 72 points per inch, so this extra space is a fraction of an inch: 1/12 of an inch to be precise.

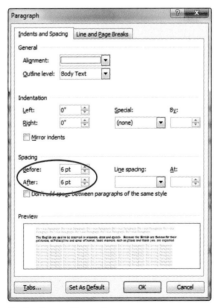

Spacing Between Paragraphs.

4 Click OK to make the spacing change between the two paragraphs.

To add or remove one line space preceding a paragraph, press CTRL+0 (zero)

Creating lists

In your document, you can use bullets and numbers for items in a list. Use numbers when there is a sequential order, and bullets are appropriate for an unordered list. The list tools are located on the top row of the Ribbon in the Paragraph group.

List items.

In some cases, such as outlines, you might want to use multilevel lists to separate a list into more than one level.

You can choose from a variety of style for bullets and numbers that are applied to lists.

Click the down arrow to the right of the Bullets icon to display the Bullet Library.

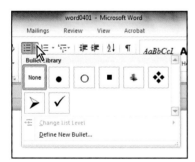

Use the Bullet Library to choose the style of bullets applied to a list.

Clicking the down arrow to the right of the Numbering icon displays the Numbering Library.

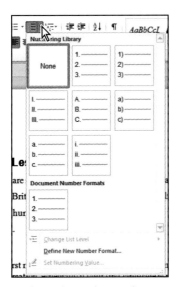

Use the Numbering Library to select a format for numbered lists.

Clicking the down arrow to the right of the Multilevel icon displays the List Library.

Use the List Library to select a style for a list.

Numbered and bulleted

In this section, you will create a numbered and bulleted list.

1 In word0401 at the bottom of page 1, click and drag from *Hold the fork*, in the second line, to the end of the list. When you select the text, you may scroll to the top of the next page; this should not concern you, as long as the text is selected.

2 Click Home > Paragraph group > Numbering icon (⋮≣).

3 Click outside the selection to deselect the text and continue working.

4 Under the heading British Desserts and Puddings, beginning with Apple cake, select the entire list of desserts.

5 Click Home > Paragraph group > Bullets icon (⋮≣). Then click anywhere outside the list to deselect the text.

Multilevel lists

In this exercise, you will recreate the multilevel list on page 3 in word0401.

To create a multilevel list:

1 Continuing to work in the document word0401, place your cursor at least two lines below the multilevel list on page 3 and press Enter.

2 Type **British desserts** and press Enter.

3 Click Home > Paragraph group > Multilevel List icon (≒).

4 Select the bulleted list from the List Library.

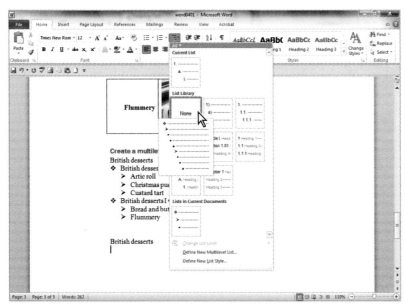

Select the bulleted list option.

5 Type **British desserts I would take:**

6 Press Enter, then press Tab.

7 Type the following list items pressing Enter after each one:

- **Arctic roll**
- **Christmas pudding**
- **Custard tart**

8 Press the Decrease Indent icon (▦). Word inserts the first level bullet.

9 Type **British desserts I would leave:**

10 Press Enter, then press Tab.

11 Type the following list items pressing enter after each one:

- **Bread and butter pudding**
- **Flummery**

12 Press Enter three times to end the bullet list typing format. You have created a multilevel bullet list. Notice that each level of the list contains a unique symbol. This exercise recreates the list above it.

13 Select File > Save, then File > Close, to save and close the file.

Displaying formatting marks and rulers

You can display formatting marks that do not print but help you identify the formatting in your Word document. Spaces, tabs, hidden text, and paragraphs are some of the marks you can display.

Display formatting marks

In this part of the lesson you'll work on displaying formatting marks in your document:

1 Start by opening the document word0402. Choose File > Open, and navigate to Word04lessons. Select word0402 and click Open.

2 Click Home > Paragraph group > Show/Hide icon (¶). Word displays the formatting marks within this document.

Formatting marks

WORD DISPLAYS...	WHEN YOU PRESS...
Single dot ·	Spacebar
Paragraph mark ¶	Enter
Arrows →	Tab
Hidden text underlined with dots ····	
Optional hyphens —	Ctrl+-

3 Click the Show/Hide icon to hide the formatting marks.

Display rulers

You can also hide or display horizontal and vertical rulers to help you identify the position of the insertion point, to align text or to set tabs.

To display rulers in your document, if it is not already showing:

1 In word0402, click View tab found above the Ribbon bar. In the Show group on the Ribbon, click Ruler.

In the Show group on the Ribbon you can choose to display the ruler by clicking the Ruler checkbox.

Word displays a ruler at the top and left side of the document. If you do not need the rulers and want to give yourself more writing space, click the Ruler checkbox again to hide the rulers.

Indenting paragraphs

You can indent paragraphs from the left and right margins, providing more or less space along the left and right edge of your text. You can also indent only the first line of a paragraph or all lines except the first line of the paragraph.

To indent paragraphs:

1 In word0402, click and drag to select the paragraph under Nature. Click Home > Paragraph group dialog box launcher.

2 In the Indentation group of the Paragraph dialog box, select 0.1 in the Left menu and select 0.1 in the Right menu. An easy way to do this is by clicking the up arrow once for each selection or you can type **.1** in the text fields. In North America, the default measurement system is inches, so the indent values and rulers are displayed using inches.

3 In the Special drop-down menu, select First Line, and in the By menu, select 0.3 by clicking the down arrow twice or typing in .3.

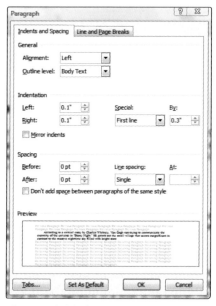

The Paragraph dialog box.

4 Click OK. You can now see the changes you have made to the paragraph titled *Nature*. You have indented the first line by 0.3 inches and indented the entire paragraph on the left and right sides by 0.1 inches.

5 Click File > Save, then File > Close, to save and close the document.

Special Indentation options

OPTION	DESCRIPTION
First Line	Indents only the first line of the paragraph
Hanging	Indents all line except the first line of the paragraph

Setting tabs

Tabs help you organize information in a structured way across a page. You can use them to align data such as the times listed in a train or ferry schedule.

Tabs can help you:

- Line up text
- Create lists
- Format tables

You can use left, center, right, decimal, or bar tabs to line up information in columns and control how the text aligns in relation to other text. Using tabs ensures that the information lines up correctly.

 Word places tabs every .5 inches across the page between the left and right margins, although you can easily customize the location of the tabs.

1   Choose File > Open, and navigate to word04lesson.

2   Locate the file word0403, then press Open.

3   Click View. In the Show group section of the Ribbon, select Ruler if the ruler checkbox is not already selected.

4   Click the tab indicator (⌊) on the top left of the document to select the type of tab you want to set. Each time you click the tab indicator, a new tab option becomes visible.

5   Select Left tab.

Tab types

ICON	TYPE	DESCRIPTION
⌊	Left tab	Traditional tab stop
⊥	Center tab	Centers text, frequently used for titles or headings
⌐	Right tab	Right justifies the text
⊥	Decimal tab	Aligns the decimals in numbers regardless of the numbers to the left or right of the decimal
▯	Bar tab	Inserts a vertical bar at the tab position

6   Place your cursor after the title, then press Enter twice.

7   Click the horizontal ruler on the 2 inch mark to add a tab. Word displays a tab where you clicked.

8   Type **Mandy and Jim**.

9   Press Tab, type **112-3334**, and press Enter.

10 Add the following names and numbers to your list, pressing Enter after each entry:

- **Jon and Marge**, press **Tab**, **223–4445**
- **Ken and Barb**, press **Tab**, **334–5556**
- **Keith and Kim**, press **Tab**, **445–6667**
- **Scott and Kris**, press **Tab**, **556–7778**

Party Invitation List

Mandy and Jim	112-3334
Jon and Marge	223-4445
Ken and Barb	334-5556
Keith and Kim	445-6667
Scott and Kris	556-7778

The completed text.

To delete a tab, place your cursor in the paragraph containing the tab and in the ruler drag the tab up and off the ruler.

Adding paragraph borders

You can accentuate a paragraph by adding a border to it.

1 In word0403, select the title and the sentence beginning with *Yogi-ism*.

2 Click Home. In the Paragraph group, choose the down arrow next to the Borders icon (⊞).

3 Select Borders and Shading from the Borders menu to display the Borders and Shading dialog box.

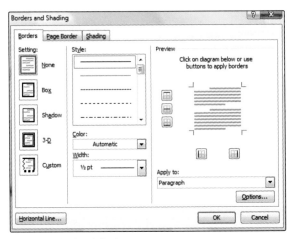

Borders and Shading dialog box.

4 Make the following selections:

- On the Borders tab, and under Setting options, click Box.
- For Style, click the second choice for a dotted line.
- For Color, click the first gray color, which is the third from the left in the top row.
- For Width, click 1 pt.

5 Click OK.

To remove a border, select the text containing the border, and click No Border on the Borders and Shading menu.

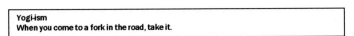

| Yogi-ism |
| When you come to a fork in the road, take it. |

The completed text.

6 Save the document and close.

Congratulations! You have completed the lesson.

Self study

1   Open word0401. After selecting the first paragraph, align the paragraph in the center. Using the same paragraph:

- Create a 1 pt. border around it.
- Place a double space between each line in the paragraph.

2   In the word0401 document:

- Display the formatting marks and rulers.
- Hide the formatting marks and the rulers again.
- Delete the border around the paragraph.

Review

Questions

1   What does a point measure?

2   How do you delete a tab?

3   What is the center tab used for mostly?

Answers

1   A point is a unit of measurement used for type and also in print design; there are 72 points per inch.

2   Place your cursor in the line containing the tab then drag the tab off of the ruler.

3   The center tab is used primarily for titles and headers.

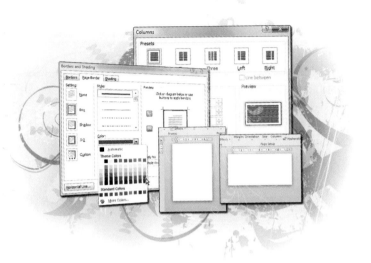

What you'll learn in this lesson:

- Introducing page tools
- Setting the page size and choosing a layout
- Setting page margins
- Working with columns and column breaks
- Adding headers and footers

Working with Pages

In this lesson, you will set up a page incorporating some important elements of page layout, such as margins, columns, background color, and other components of page design.

Starting up

You will work with several files from the Word05lessons folder in this lesson. Make sure that you have loaded the OfficeLessons folder onto your hard drive from *www.DigitalClassroomBooks.com/Office2010*. See "Loading lesson files" on page XXIV.

See Lesson 5 in action!

Use the accompanying video to gain a better understanding of how to use some of the features shown in this lesson. The video tutorial for this lesson can be found at www.DigitalClassroomBooks.com/Office2010.

Introducing the page tools

When planning the page layout for a project, you must consider some basic page design principles. The design must appeal to your target audience. You must balance your text, graphics, and white space to create a pleasing layout, and also use a background that contrasts with the text color for increased readability. You should also use color consistently to please the eye and add interest to the page contents. Word provides the tools so you can design each page to fit your needs.

The Page Layout tab on the Ribbon contains the tools you need to apply formatting to a page.

The Page Layout tab displays tools to set up and design pages.

The Page Layout tab helps you quickly format a page. From this tab, you can:

- Apply themes for consistent color and font style
- Set margins, page size, and page orientation
- Create columns and add page breaks
- Apply a watermark, background color, and border
- Insert page and section breaks
- Add line numbers in the margin
- Turn on hyphenation so Word breaks lines between the syllables of words

Setting the page size

In Word, the default page size is 8.5 x 11 inches and the default page orientation is portrait. If you need any other setting for a document, such as Executive 7.25 x 10.5 inches or Legal 8.5 x 14 inches, you have to change the page size manually.

In this exercise, you will work with an existing document and set the page size to 8.5 x 14 inches with landscape orientation.

To open the document you need for this lesson:

1 Launch Word.

2 Choose File > Open. Word displays the Open dialog box.

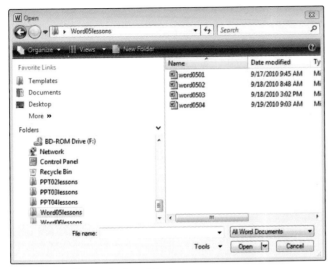

You can open a file using the Open dialog box.

3 Navigate to the Word05lessons folder. Click word0501 and then click the Open button.

4 Choose File > Save As. Word displays the Save As dialog box. In the Save As text box, type **word0501_done** and then click OK.

5 Click the Page Layout tab on the Ribbon. In the Page Setup group, click Size.

6 Select Legal 8.5" x 14".

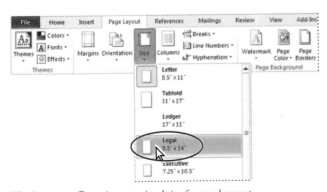

The Size menu offers various page size choices for your document.

Word applies the page size you set here to all pages in your document unless you divide the document into sections. You can then use a different page size for each section. To apply a particular paper size to all sections in the document, click More Paper Sizes.

Choosing a layout

When you select a layout for your document, you have two choices: portrait or landscape. Portrait, which is the default setting, is longer than it is wide. The landscape setting is wider than it is long.

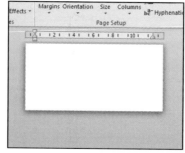

The portrait layout is tall.   *The landscape layout is wide.*

You'll now set the layout for this document to be landscape.

1 In the document, on the Page Layout tab in the Page Setup group, click Orientation.

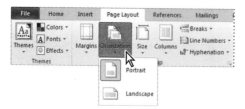

Although the portrait layout is best for most documents, landscape orientation is more suited to documents that require columns, such as a brochure or newsletter.

2 Select Landscape. Word displays the page in landscape layout.

Setting margins

A margin is the white space that surrounds the text on a page. By default, Word provides one inch from each edge as a margin. You can adjust the right, left, top, and bottom margin sizes to suit your document's needs.

1 On the Page Layout tab in the Page Setup group, click Margins.

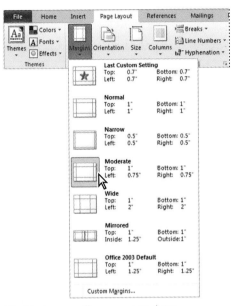

The Margins menu offers many margin choices.

2 Select Moderate. Word moves the content to accommodate moderate settings.

> *If you need to create margins that do not appear on the Margins menu, select Custom Margins. Word displays the Page Setup dialog box where you can customize the margin settings.*

Working with columns

You can format the text in your document to appear in columns. Column formatting is effective for brochures, newspaper articles, and newsletters. Word also offers the tools to mix column formats so that part of your document can be in one format and the rest of the document can be in another.

1 In the word0501_done document, on the Page Layout tab in the Page Setup group, click Columns.

2 Click More Columns. Word displays the Columns dialog box.

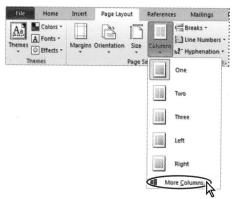

You can select a column format from the Columns menu.

3 In the Presets group, click Left.

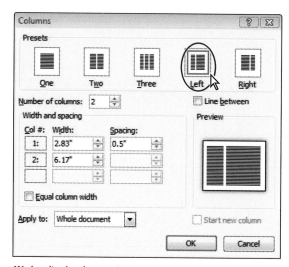

Word applies the column settings.

4 Click the Line between checkbox. Ensure that Whole Document is selected in the Apply to drop-down list and click OK.

If you want to apply columns to only part of the document, it is important to place your cursor where you want the columns to begin.

Inserting column breaks

Word gives you the tools to insert a column break where you want it. For example, you might want to break a column to begin the next column in a different place from where Word has automatically separated the first from the second column.

In this exercise, you'll insert a column break.

1   In the word0501_done document, place the cursor in the bottom of the first column to the left of the word *In*, in the sentence beginning "*In an exciting, yet somewhat unexplained series of events…*"

2   On the Page Layout tab, in the Page Setup group, click the down arrow to the right of the Breaks icon.

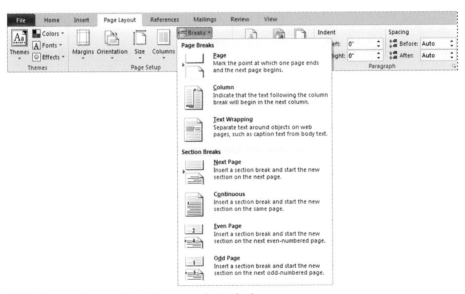

The Breaks menu gives you options to insert page and section breaks.

3   Select Column. Word breaks the column at the insertion point.

4   Click File > Save, and then click File > Close.

Adding a page border

Now let's open a different document and add some interest to the page. In this exercise, you'll add a border.

1 In Word, choose File > Open, and navigate to the Word05lessons folder.

2 Click word0502, and then click the Open button.

3 Choose File > Save As. In the Save As text box, type **word0502_done**, and then click Save.

4 Click the Page Layout tab on the Ribbon. In the Page Background group, click Page Borders.

5 The Borders and Shading dialogue box will appear. From the Setting group, click Box.

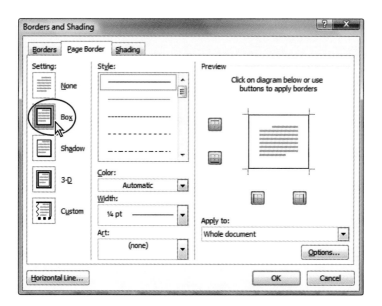

6 Click the Color drop-down arrow. Word displays the Color menu.

7 Select Orange Accent 6 Darker 25%, the second color from the bottom in the last row.

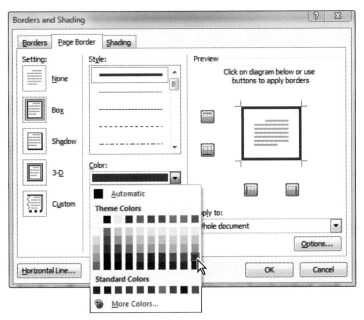

The Color menu displays various colors.

8   Click the Width drop-down arrow, select 6 pt, and click OK.

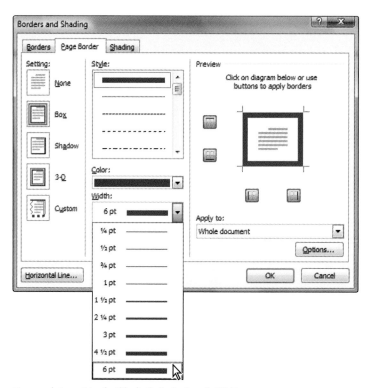

You can select a variety of widths for the border from the Width menu.

You have just added a decorative orange border around the entire document.

Adding headers and footers

A header is text that appears at the top of every page, and a footer is text that appears at the bottom of every page. Both reside in special areas and are not affected by what you do within the document. Text elements such as a document name, date, and page number are commonly added as headers or footers.

In this exercise, you'll add a header and footer to the word0502_done document.

To add a header:

1 In word0502_done, click the Insert tab on the Ribbon. In the Header & Footer group, click Header.

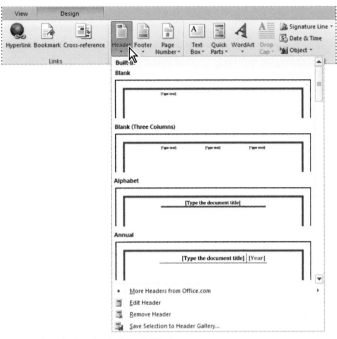

You can select a built-in header from the Header menu.

2 Select Blank, the top choice. Word displays the header in the document and the Header & Footer Tools tab on the Ribbon.

3 In the Type text box in the header, type **Let's Talk Coffee Newsletter**.

4   Place the cursor to the left of Let's and triple-click to select the header you just typed. Move the cursor over the mini-toolbar that displayed when you selected the header.

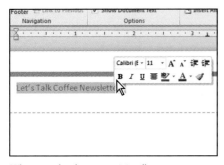

When you select the text, a mini-toolbar appears.

5   Click the down arrow to the right of the Font color icon on the mini-toolbar and select the second color from the bottom in the last column to match the orange in the border.

To add a footer:

1   Click the Header & Footer Tools tab and in the Navigation group, click Go to Footer.

2   In the Header & Footer group found in the Insert tab, click Footer.

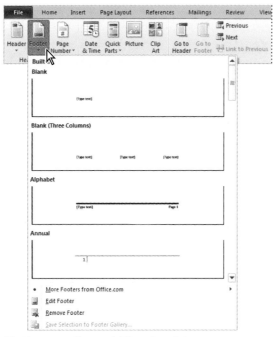

The Footer menu offers several different footer choices.

3   Select Blank (Three Columns) from the Footer menu. Word inserts three placeholders where you can insert text.

4   Place the cursor anywhere within the placeholder on the right. In the Insert group on the Ribbon, click Date & Time to display format options.

Word displays the Date & Time menu.

5   Select the first format, mm/dd/yyyy. Word inserts your choice in the placeholder.

6   In the footer, click the middle placeholder and type **Let's Talk Coffee**.

7   Click the placeholder on the left and type **Coffee Corner**.

8   In the Close group in the Design tab, click Close Header and Footer.

Adding a background color

Word provides tools to add a background color to a document page. When you add a color to the background of the page, be sure that it contrasts with the color of the text. For example, if you have a dark background, such as dark brown or navy blue, you'll need a light text color.

In this exercise, you'll change the background color of the page.

1   Click the Page Layout tab on the Ribbon. In the Page Background group, click Page Color.

2   Select the third color from the left in the top row, Tan Background 2.

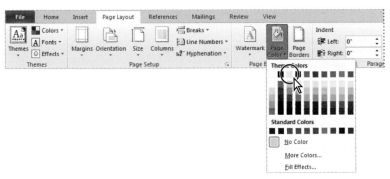

You can choose from a variety of colors for the page background.

Word applies a light tan color to the background.

3   Choose File > Save. It is always a good idea to regularly save your work.

Adding a watermark

A watermark is an image that is imbedded into paper. Word lets you simulate a watermark on a document page. You can add text as a watermark, such as Confidential, or you can add an image, such as a company logo. In this exercise, you'll add the image of a coffee cup.

1   In the Page Layout tab on the Ribbon, click Watermark in the Page Background group.

2   Select Custom Watermark.

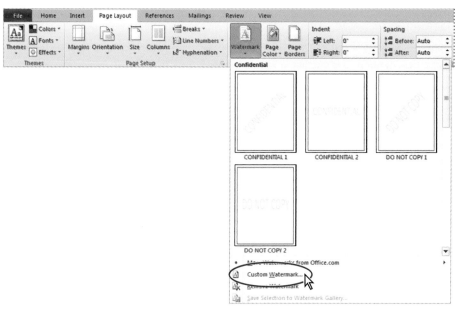

You can mark the page with text or a custom watermark.

Word displays the Printed Watermark dialog box.

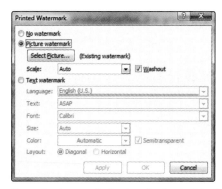

You can insert a customized watermark using the Printed Watermark dialog box.

3 Click Picture Watermark and then click Select Picture. Word displays the Insert Picture dialog box.

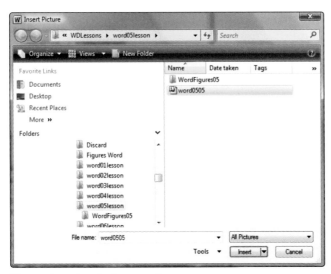

You can select a picture for the watermark.

4 Navigate to the Word05lessons folder; click word0505, click Insert, and then click OK.

Word places the watermark on the page background.

If you want to remove the watermark, select Remove Watermark from the Watermark menu.

Adding pages and page numbers

In this exercise, you'll add a cover page to the word0502_done document. Then you'll append another Word document to it and add page numbers.

To add a cover page:

1 Click the Insert tab on the Ribbon. In the Pages group, click Cover Page.

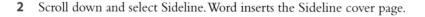

2   Scroll down and select Sideline. Word inserts the Sideline cover page.

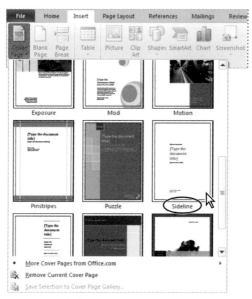

You can insert a built-in cover page.

3   In the Company text box, type **Coffee Corner**; in the Title text box, type **Coffee Reviews**; in the Subtitle text box, type **Volcano Roast and Verona Blend**. Type your name in the Author text box, and then click the down arrow to the right of the date and select a date from the calendar.

To insert a Word file:

1   Position the cursor on a new line at the bottom of page 2.

2   On the Insert tab, in the Text group, click the down arrow to the right of the Object icon.

3   Select Object. Word displays the Object dialog box.

The object menu lets you insert an object or text from a file.

4   Click the Create from File tab.

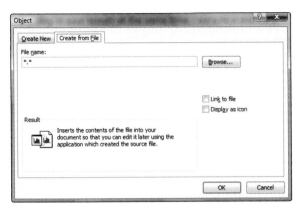

Word gives you options to create a new object or create an object from an existing file.

5   Click the Browse button to the right of the File name text box. Word displays the Browse dialog box.

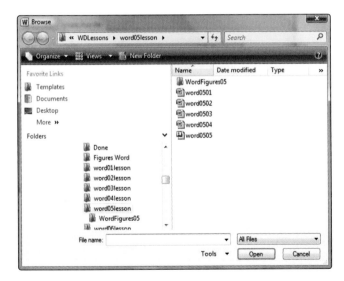

6   Navigate to the Word05lessons folder, click word0503 and Insert. In the Object dialogue box, click OK to insert the file as a new page.

To add page numbers:

1   On the Insert tab, and in the Header & Footer group, click the down arrow to the right of the Page Number icon.

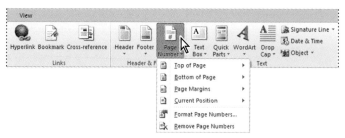

You can select the location of the page number on the Page Number menu.

2   Select Top of Page and then select Plain Number 3.

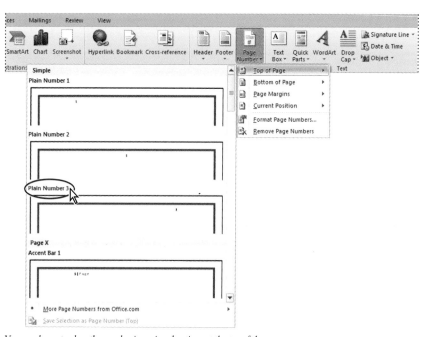

You can choose to place the number in various locations at the top of the page.

Word inserts a page number on every page except the cover page.

3   Select File > Save, and then select File > Close.

Inserting a section break

Generally, page-formatting commands affect every page in a Word document. For example, the settings for margins, page orientation, and other types of formatting apply not only to a single page but to every page in the document. You might want a section of a document to behave differently from the rest. This is when sections come in handy.

In this exercise, you'll add a section break to allow a single-column format for the title of the document and a three-column format for the rest.

1 Choose File > Open and navigate to Word05lessons folder.

2 Select word0504 and click Open.

3 Choose File > Save As and type **word0504_done** in the File name text field, and click Save.

4 Place the cursor to the left of the title *Lorem ipsum dolor* and triple-click to select it.

5 Click the Page Layout tab on the Ribbon. In the Page Setup group, click Columns and select One from the Columns menu. Word moves the title along the top of the page and inserts a section break after it.

   You cannot see the section break in Page Layout view.

6 Click View. In the Document Views group, click Draft. Word displays the document in Draft view. Notice the section break below the title. Click Print Layout to return to the previous view.

Controlling text flow

Word lets you control text flow and pagination. There are many times when the page or column breaks leave words or sentences dangling at the beginning (orphans) or end of a page.

You might encounter the following situations that can distract from readability and disrupt the continuity of a document:

* A word or two at the top of a column that belongs with the paragraph at the bottom of the previous column

* The start of a paragraph at the bottom of a column when the rest of the sentence continues on the next column

* Subheads that appear at the bottom of a column or the end of a page, without at least two to three lines of the associated text

In this exercise, you'll continue working in a three-column document and correct text flow that detracts from the continuity and readability of the document.

1 Place the cursor to the left of *Titulus Duos*, at the bottom of the first column.

2 On the Page Layout tab, click the dialog box launcher in the bottom-right corner of the Paragraph group.

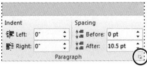

The dialog box launcher displays the Paragraph dialog box.

The Paragraph dialog box lets you control the text flow in the document.

3 Click the Line and Page Breaks tab.

4 In the Paragraph dialog box, select the Keep with next checkbox, and then click OK. The subtitle moves to the top of the next column.

5 Near the top of the third column, place the cursor to the left of the red word *Suspendisse*.

6 Click Breaks in the Page Setup group. Word displays the Breaks menu.

7 Select Column. Word moves the text to the top of the third column.

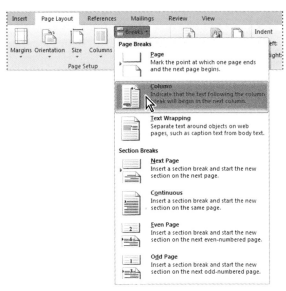

The Breaks menu lets you insert page, column, and section breaks.

8 Select File > Save, and then select File > Close.

Congratulations! In this lesson you have discovered how to control the look and feel of a page using the Page Layout tools that Word provides.

Self study

Open Word and create a blank document (select File > New > Blank Document > Create). In the document, try to complete the following tasks:

- Insert narrow margins on the page.

- Add a blue border with a 3-point width.

- Change the page size to Executive 7.25 x 10.5.

- Add a light-green color of your choice as a background.

- Insert a page number in the bottom-right corner of the page.

Review

Questions

1 When would you insert a section into a document?

2 You can control the text flow of a document if it distracts from readability and disrupts the continuity of a document. Give three situations where you would need to do this.

3 What is a watermark? Give an example of one.

Answers

1 When you format a page in Word, Word automatically applies the formatting to the entire document. You would insert a section when you want that section of the document to behave differently from the rest of the document.

2 Three situations where you would need to control the text flow of a document include:

- A word or two at the top of a column that belongs with the paragraph at the bottom of the previous column

- The start of a paragraph at the bottom of a column when the rest of the sentence continues on the next column

- Subheads that appear at the bottom of a column or the end of a page, without at least two to three lines of the associated text

3 A watermark is an image that is imbedded into paper. Some examples of watermarks are text such as Confidential or Draft, or an image such as a company logo.

What you'll learn in this lesson:

- Understanding styles
- Introducing the styles tools
- Switching between style sets
- Customizing the Quick Styles Gallery
- Applying a document theme

Working with Styles and Themes

In this lesson, you will work with styles and themes to improve and enhance the appearance of a document.

Starting up

You will work with several files from the Word06lessons folder in this lesson. Make sure that you have loaded the OfficeLessons folder onto your hard drive from *www.DigitalClassroomBooks.com/Office2010*. See "Loading lesson files" on page XXIV.

See Lesson 6 in action!

Use the accompanying video to gain a better understanding of how to use some of the features shown in this lesson. The video tutorial for this lesson can be found at www.DigitalClassroomBooks.com/Office2010.

Understanding styles

A style is a set of pre-defined formatting instructions that you can use throughout a document. Styles ensure that the elements in your document remain consistent.

For example, if you wanted each heading in a document to have a navy blue color and 16-point bold centered text, you would need to perform several steps to accomplish this. However, if you store the formatting commands in a style, you only need to apply the style, thus saving the extra time you would otherwise require to apply all this formatting separately.

Styles are a central tool in Microsoft Word. Everything you type into a document has a style attached to it. It can be a style you design or the default style of Word, which is called the Normal style.

Word has four different style types that contain all the formatting necessary to build a document.

STYLE TYPE	DEFINITION
Paragraph	Contains both paragraph and text formatting attributes including indents, tabs, font style, and text size
Character	Formats only characters, not paragraphs
Table	Applied to tables, and handles lines and shading within the tables
List	Presents lists of information using bullets, numbers, and indentation

Introducing the styles tools

You can find the styles in Word on the Home tab in the Styles group.

The Styles group lets you select and change styles.

The Quick Styles Gallery is useful because it gives you quick access to the available styles in the template. You can expand the gallery and navigate through it by using the scroll bar to the right of the styles.

*A. Scroll up. **B**. Scroll down. **C**. More styles.*

You only need to select the text and click a style in the Quick Styles Gallery to apply the style.

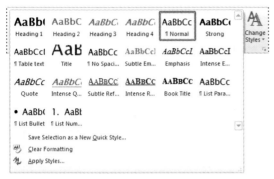

Use the Quick Styles Gallery to select a style.

In this exercise, you will open an existing document located in the Word06lessons folder.

To open the document you need for this lesson:

1   Launch Word.

2   Choose File > Open. Word displays the Open dialog box.

3   Navigate to Word06lessons. Click word0601, and then click Open.

4   Select File > Save As. Word displays the Save As dialog box.

5   In the File Name text box, type **word0601_done** and click Save.

Applying a style

Using a style, you can apply several formatting attributes to text with a single click.

1   In the word0601_done document, place the cursor to the left of History of Amusement Parks, and triple-click to select this text.

2   On the Ribbon, click the Home tab. In the Styles group, click the More Styles icon, which looks like a down arrow with a line above it.

Use the More Styles icon to view the full list of style options.

3   Click Title. Word changes the text to the pre-set Title style.

Understanding heading styles

Heading styles are distinctive because Word allows you to organize a document using headings. Generally, you would use Heading 1 for the document's main heading, Heading 2 for subheadings, and so on.

From a design perspective, a heading should be only one line long, but you can press Shift+Return to create a soft return in the middle of a long heading if you should require it.

In this exercise, you'll apply Heading 1 and Heading 2 styles in the word0601_done document.

1   Place the cursor to the left of First Amusement Parks, and triple-click to select the text.

2   On the Home tab, click the More Styles icon in the bottom-right corner of the Styles group, and select Heading 1 from the Quick Styles Gallery. Word applies the Heading 1 style to the text.

3   Place the cursor to the left of *Bartholomew Fair,* and then triple-click to select the text. In the Quick Styles Gallery, click Heading 2. Word applies the Heading 2 style to the text.

4   Repeat the same steps to apply the following headings to the following text.

- Heading 1
  - *Pleasure Gaining in Popularity,* located at the top of page 2
  - *Amusement Parks in the 21st Century,* located at the top of page 3
- Heading 2
  - *Seasonal Celebrations* on page 1
  - *Pleasure Gardens* on page 1
  - *The Beginning of the Future* on page 2
  - *First Modern Amusement Park* on page 2
  - *Disney Theme Parks* on page 3
  - *Six Flags* on page 3

5   Choose File > Save or simply click on the Save icon in the Quick Access Toolbar.

Switching between style sets

Word has a variety of style sets that can change the look of your document. In this exercise, you'll change the style set that is currently applied to the document.

1   In the Home tab, in the Styles group, click Change Styles.

The Change Styles menu lets you select a different style set, including colors, fonts, and paragraph spacing.

2   Select Style Set. Word displays the Style Set menu.

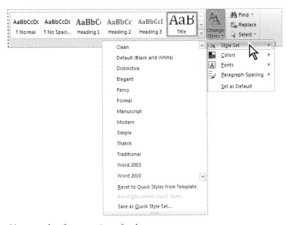

You can select from a variety of style sets.

3   Select Fancy. Notice that Word changes the appearance of the styles that you previously applied. The Heading 1 style is now a banner, and Heading 2 has maroon text. All headlines and text are now italicized. Notice that the styles have also changed in the Quick Styles Gallery.

4   Click File > Save, and then click File > Close.

Identifying the current style

You can determine the style that you are currently using by employing any of the following methods:

- Look for a highlighted style in the Quick Styles Gallery. (Keep in mind that not all styles appear here.)

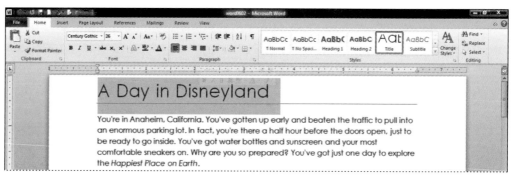

The Quick Styles Gallery highlights the current style.

- Look for the marked style in the Styles task pane. A very long list of all styles appears. Click the dialog box launcher in the Styles group to display the Styles task pane.

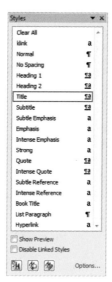

The Styles task pane lists all the styles if you select All Styles in the Style Pane Options dialog box, discussed later in this lesson.

- Look at the Style Inspector (the most reliable method). You can access the Style Inspector by clicking the Style Inspector icon located at the bottom of the Styles task pane.

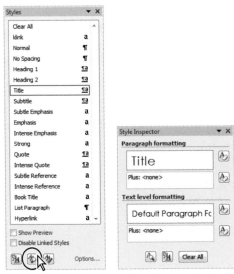

Click the Style Inspector icon to display the Style Inspector.

The Style Inspector displays the current style.

Removing a style

After you apply a style, you might want to return the text to the normal style. To do this, you can use the Clear Formatting command.

In this exercise, you'll open a new document and save it immediately. It is a good practice to frequently save a document while you are working on it.

1 Choose File > Open. Word displays the Open dialog box.

2 Navigate to Word06lessons. Click word0602, and then click Open.

3 Select File > Save As. Word displays the Save As dialog box.

4 In the File Name text box, type **word0602_done**.

5 Click and drag to select *Happiest Place on Earth* at the end of the first paragraph. The text has an orange color, and you'll return it to the normal style.

6 Click the Home tab on the Ribbon. In the Font group, click Clear Formatting.

Click Clear Formatting.

You can also use Ctrl+spacebar to clear formatting.

Creating a new style

You can create your own styles to store formatting information if you cannot find a built-in style that suits your needs. In this exercise, you'll create a style called Strong Green1. After you create it, you'll apply it.

1   In the word0602_done document, click and drag to select the bolded *Main Street* text and the colon that follows it at the top of page 2.

2   Click the down-arrow to the right of the Font Color icon (A) on the mini-toolbar that appears after you make the selection. Word displays the Font Color menu.

3   Select Green Accent 1 Darker 25%, located in the fifth column and the second row of colors from the bottom. Word applies the green color to the selected text.

Click to apply the green color from the menu.

You'll now save the style you just created.

4   Click the More Styles icon in the bottom-right corner of the Styles group. Word displays the Quick Styles Gallery.

5   Select Save Selection as a New Quick Style. A Create New Style from Formatting dialogue box appears asking for more information.

The Quick Styles Gallery menu has an option to save the style to the Quick Styles menu.

6   Type **Strong Green1** in the Name text box, and then click Modify.

In the Create New Style from Formatting dialog box, name a new style.

7   Select Normal in the Style for following paragraph drop-down list.

8 In the Formatting group, click Bold. Be sure that the Add to Quick Style list checkbox in the bottom-left corner of the window is checked, and then click OK.

Format the new style in the Create New Style from Formatting dialog box.

9 Select the following words and click Strong Green1 on the Quick Styles Gallery to apply the style to them all:

On page 2,

- *Adventureland:*
- *New Orleans Square:*
- *Critter Country:*
- *Frontierland:*
- *Mickey's Toontown:*

On page 3,

- *Fantasyland:*
- *Tomorrowland:*
- *Railroad:*

10 Choose File > Save to save your work.

Deleting a style

To delete a style:

1   Press Ctrl+Shift+Alt+S to display the Styles task pane.

2   Scroll to the top of your document. In the Styles task pane, right-click Title. Choose Delete Title from the list. Select Yes when asked to confirm if you would like to delete style Title from the document.

3   Notice the title of your document, *A Day in Disneyland*, is now formatted as Normal text. We now want to reverse this style change.

4   Click the Undo icon (↶) on your Quick Access Toolbar.

Modifying a style

At some point, you might find that an existing style is close to, but not exactly, what you want. Fortunately, you do not have to create a new style; Word lets you modify the existing style. In this exercise, you'll modify a style by changing the text size and font style.

1   Press Ctrl+Shift+Alt+S to display the Styles task pane, if it is not already visible. Be sure that nothing is selected within the document.

2   In the Styles task pane, point to Normal, and Word displays a down-arrow to the right of the style name.

3   Click the down-arrow to display a menu and select Modify.

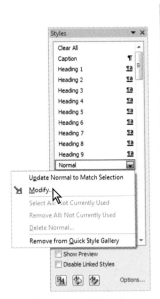

Use the menu to modify a style.

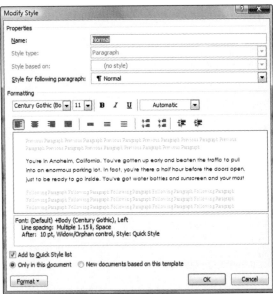

Use the Modify Style dialog box to select new attributes for the style you are modifying.

4 In the Formatting group, choose Comic Sans MS for the font style and 12 for the font size.

5 Click OK.

Notice that in the document only the text that had the Normal styling applied to it has changed to 12-point Comic Sans MS.

Keep the Styles task pane open to use in the next exercise.

Assigning a style shortcut key

A shortcut key makes formatting much easier and faster than using the Quick Styles Gallery. In this exercise, you'll assign Ctrl+S+G to the Strong Green1 style, and then you'll apply the style using the shortcut key.

1 In word0602_done, place the cursor on page 4 below the last line of the document. In the Styles task pane, point to Strong Green1, and Word displays a down-arrow to the right of the style name.

2 Click the down-arrow to display the menu and select Modify. Word displays the Modify Style dialog box.

3 In the bottom-left corner of the dialog box, click Format.

4 Select the Shortcut key.

The Format menu lets you select a variety of options.

5   Press Ctrl+S+G, and confirm that Ctrl+S,G appears in the Press new shortcut key text box. Click Assign on the bottom-left of the dialogue box. Click Close and then click OK.

You can assign shortcut keys for any style in the Customize Keyboard dialog box.

6   On page 4 select the word *Parades* and include the colon. You can locate the text at the beginning of the last paragraph above the *In Conclusion* section.

7   Click Ctrl+S+G, and Word assigns the style Strong Green1 to *Parades*.

8   Choose File > Save to save your work.

Customizing the Quick Styles Gallery

You might want to use a style listed in the Style pane that is not listed in the Quick Styles Gallery. Fortunately, you can easily add and remove styles to and from the gallery. In this exercise, you'll remove a style from the gallery. You will then add a style to the gallery.

To remove a style from the Quick Styles Gallery:

1   Click the down-arrow in the Quick Styles Gallery to scroll down, and locate the No Spacing style.

2 Right-click the No Spacing style, and Word displays a shortcut menu.

Use the shortcut menu to remove a style from the Quick Styles Gallery.

3 Select Remove from Quick Styles Gallery.

Word removes the style from the gallery. If you ever want to add it to the gallery again, it still resides in the Styles task pane.

To add a style to the Quick Styles Gallery:

1 Press Ctrl+Shift+Alt+S to display the Styles task pane, if it is not already visible, and click Options in the lower-right corner of the task pane.

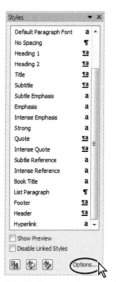

The Options menu lets you add all styles to the task pane.

2 In the Style Pane Options dialogue box, click the down-arrow to the right of the Select styles to show drop-down list. Select All Styles, and click OK.

Word lets you display all styles in your task pane.

3 In the Styles task pane, scroll down to find List Bullet and right-click to display the shortcut menu.

4 Choose the last option, Add to Quick Style Gallery.

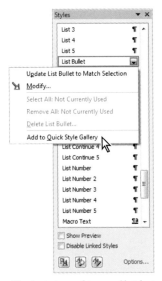

The shortcut menu lets you add styles to the Quick Styles Gallery.

5 Click File > Save, and then click File > Close.

Applying a document theme

A theme in Word is a predesigned set of color schemes and fonts that you can apply quickly to give your document a professionally formatted look. Every theme has three elements:

- Colors (such as for the text and background), graphics, design elements, and hyperlinks
- Different fonts for the heading and body styles
- Effects applied to graphics or design elements, such as 3D, shading, gradation, and drop shadows

Each of the built-in themes controls all three elements.

To open the document you need for this lesson:

1 In Word, choose File > Open. Navigate to Word06lessons; click word0603, and then click Open.

2 Select File > Save As. Word displays the Save As dialog box.

3 In the File Name text box, type **word0603_done** and press Enter.

4 Click the Page Layout tab on the Ribbon. In the Themes group, click Themes to view the options.

5 Select Pushpin. Notice that Word changes the color of the Title style to a darker blue and the accent line below it, along with the other headings, to a brownish orange.

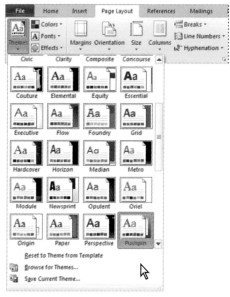

Word offers several themes you can use to customize the appearance of the document.

Customizing a theme

You might like everything about a theme except for one part, such as the font. Fortunately, you can customize a theme and even save it to use again on other documents. In this exercise, you'll modify the theme font. You'll then save the newly created theme so that you can use it again later without having to recreate it.

1   On the Page Layout tab in the Themes group, click Fonts.

2   Select Angles. Word changes the fonts to the Franklin Gothic font set associated with the Angles theme.

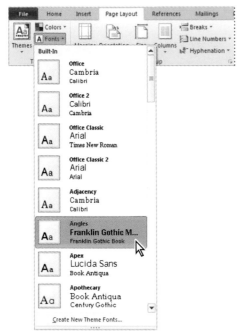

Use the Fonts menu to change the font set associated with the theme.

3   In the Themes group on the Ribbon, click Themes. Word displays the Themes menu.

4   Select Save Current Theme, and Word displays the Save Current Theme dialog box.

5 Type **MyBrownTheme** and click Save.

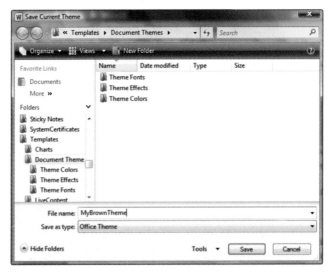

Word saves the theme with the other document themes.

Word saves the theme. You can quickly access this newly created customized theme in the theme drop down list.

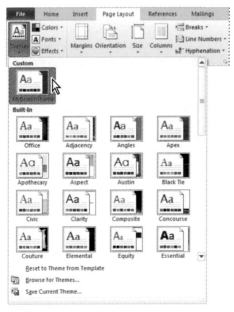

Word displays MyBrownTheme as a custom theme on the Theme menu.

6   Choose File > Save and then File > Close.

Congratulations! You have completed this lesson, where you have discovered how to work with styles and themes to give your document a polished and professional look.

Self study

1   Open word0602_done. Change the style set to Thatch.

2   In word0602_done, change the theme to MyBrownTheme.

3   In word 0602_done, delete the styles Intense Quote and Subtitle Reference from the Quick Styles Gallery.

Review

Questions

1   Name the four style types that Word has defined.

2   What are the shortcut keys you can use to apply a soft return to a long title? What shortcut keys enable you to clear formatting?

3   What are the steps you would use to delete a style?

Answers

1   The four style types are: paragraph, character, table, and list.

2   Press Shift+Enter to apply a soft return. Press Ctrl+spacebar to clear formatting.

3   To delete a style, press Ctrl+Shift+Alt+S to display the Styles task pane. Then right-click the style you want to delete, and select Delete name of style. In the confirmation dialog box that appears, click Yes.

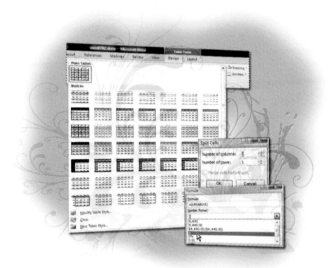

What you'll learn in this lesson:

- Introducing table tools
- Creating a table
- Combining and splitting cells
- Formatting a table
- Adding a formula to a table

Working with Tables

In this lesson, you will discover how to build a table incorporating cells, rows, shading, and other important components of table design.

Starting up

You will work with several files from the Word07lessons folder in this lesson. Make sure that you have loaded the OfficeLessons folder onto your hard drive from *www.DigitalClassroomBooks.com/Office2010*. See "Loading lesson files" on page XXIV.

See Lesson 7 in action!

Use the accompanying video to gain a better understanding of how to use some of the features shown in this lesson. The video tutorial for this lesson can be found at www.DigitalClassroomBooks.com/Office2010.

Introducing the table tools

A table is a way of organizing information. Any time you need information in a grid format, you can use a table. Rows run left to right, and columns run top to bottom in a table. The small boxes in a table are called cells, and they can contain text or graphics. When working with tables, you should be in Print Layout view. To work in Print Layout view, click the View tab, and then click Print Layout in the Document Views group.

When you insert a table, Word displays the table tools for both design and layout. Using these tools, you can design and manage tables. The Design tab lets you apply table styles and borders, and the Layout tab lets you change rows, columns, and cells.

The Table Tools Design tab displays tools to help you design tables.

The tools on the Design tab help you:

- Set table style options
- Select a table style
- Work with table borders and shading

The Table Tools Layout tab displays tools to help you manage tables.

The tools on the Layout tab help you:

- Select table elements, such as columns and rows
- Insert or delete columns and rows
- Work with table borders and shading
- Merge or split cells within the table
- Adjust the size of cells
- Align text within a cell
- Sort and manage data within the table

Creating a table

In Word, you can either draw a table from scratch and then add text, or create the text and transform it into a table. Of the two methods, it is preferable to create the table and then add the text.

In this exercise, you will open a document and save it. You'll then insert a table into the document.

To open the document you need for this lesson:

1   Launch Word. Word displays a blank page.

2   Choose File > Open and navigate to the Word07lessons folder.
Click word0701, and then click Open.

3   Select File > Save As. In the Save As text field, type **word0701_done**, and then click Save.

4   Place your cursor just below the sentence *Nothing Defines a country*. Click the Insert tab, and then click Table.

5   Click and drag across three columns and down six rows. Word creates a table that is the same width as your document's paragraph margins. When you add more columns, each column becomes smaller.

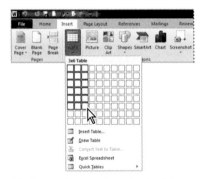

The Insert Table menu lets you drag to select an exact number of columns and rows.

Moving around in a table

When you begin to add text to a table, you can use the keyboard to move from cell to cell. Certain keys perform different functions within the table.

KEY(S)	FUNCTION
Tab	Moves the cursor to the next cell from left to right
Shift+Tab	Moves the cursor backward to the previous cell
Enter	Adds a new paragraph to a cell
Shift+Enter	Breaks up a long line of text in a cell with a soft return
Ctrl+Tab	Indents within a cell

When you press Tab in the last row and column of a table, Word adds another row.

Formatting a table and adding text

Word supplies a variety of formats that you can assign to a table. In this exercise, you'll select and apply a predefined format to the table you created.

1 In word0701_done, click anywhere inside the table. Word displays the Table Tools tab on the Ribbon.

2 Click the Design tab.

The Design tab displays the table styles.

3 Click the More button located to the right of the table styles to view the built-in table styles.

The More button will display more table style options.

4   Select the fourth table from the left in the fifth row, called Medium Shading 2 - Accent 3.

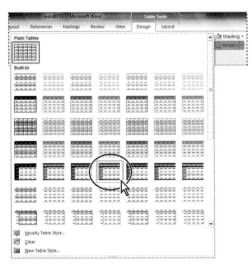

Select from a variety of colors and styles.

5   Click in the top-left corner of the table, type **Country**, and then press the Tab key. Word moves the cursor to the second column.

6   Type **Food**, and press the Tab key. Word moves the cursor to the last column.

7   Type **Culture Hint**.

8   Click Save on the Quick Access Toolbar to save your work.

Selecting cells within a table

Sometimes you'll need to select the text within a single cell, a row or column of cells, or an entire table. Fortunately, Word allows you to easily make selections within a table.

Showing and hiding gridlines

When you are working in a table, sometimes it is easier if you can see the gridlines, especially when you are working in individual cells.

1   In the word0701_done document, click anywhere in the table.

2   In the Table Tools tab, click Layout. In the Table group, click View Gridlines. The View Gridlines button displays the gridlines in a table.

Click View Gridlines.

To hide the gridlines, click View Gridlines again.

Changing the row height or column width

You can change the height of rows and the width of columns to accommodate the information in the table.

When working in a table, be sure that you are in either Print Layout or Web Layout view. You can use the buttons on the status bar in the lower-right corner of the window to switch views.

You'll now change the width of the columns.

1   Click the Print Layout button on the status bar if you are not already in Print Layout view.

Use the status bar to switch views.
A. Print Layout. B. Web Layout.

2   In the table, position the cursor over the right side of the Country column; the cursor changes to a double arrow (↔).

3   Drag the column line to the left about one-half inch, or to one and one-half inches on the ruler, and release the mouse.

When you begin to drag the column line, the ruler appears below the Ribbon.

Resizing a table

If you find that a table's dimensions do not suit your document, you can resize the table. In this exercise, you'll resize the table to be narrower.

1   In Print Layout view, position the cursor over the table. Word displays a handle in the bottom-right corner of the table.

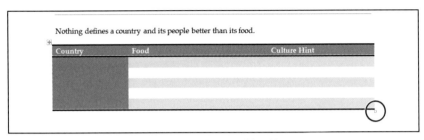

You can resize a table by dragging from the bottom-right corner of the table.

2   Place the cursor over the handle (a double-sided arrow appears) and then drag the corner upward to make the table narrower. As you begin to drag the corner, the cursor changes to a cross. Release the mouse button when the table is the size that you want. Word displays a dashed line to represent the proposed table size.

You can drag the table's bottom-right corner downward to resize the table.

Moving a table

You can move a table to a different location in a document. This exercise shows you the steps to do this.

1   In word0701_done, in Print Layout view, position the cursor within the table. A handle appears in the upper-left corner of the table.

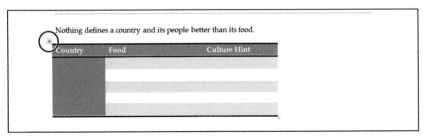

You can select the table by clicking the handle.

2   Click the handle on the table, drag the table down so it lies just below the solid line, and release the mouse button. You may need resize your table so that it sits flush below the line.

To copy a table, click the table handle, and then press Ctrl+C. Place the cursor where you want to copy the table, and press Ctrl+V.

Adding and deleting rows

Word gives you the tools to insert additional rows of information or delete rows that you do not need. When you create a table, you may realize that you did not create enough rows to accommodate the information that you need to include.

In this exercise, you'll insert rows both above and below an existing row.

1 In the word0701_done document, place the cursor anywhere in the second row.

2 On the Table Tools tab, click Layout. In the Rows and Columns group, click Insert Above.

The Insert Above button will insert a new row directly above the selected row.

3 Place the cursor in the bottom row of the table. In the Rows and Columns group, click Insert Below. Word inserts a row at the bottom of the table.

The Insert Below button will insert a new row directly below the selected row.

Be aware that when you delete a row, Word deletes the information contained in the row.

To delete a row:

1 Place the cursor anywhere in the third row.

2 In the Rows and Columns group, click Delete.

You can delete cells, columns, rows, and a table using the Delete menu.

3 Select Delete Rows from the drop-down menu. Word deletes the row.

Adding and deleting columns

Word gives you the tools to insert additional columns of information or delete columns that you do not need. When you create a table, you may realize that you did not create enough columns to suit the information that you need to include.

In this exercise, you'll insert a column to the right of the Food column.

1 In the word0701_done document, place the cursor anywhere in the Food column.

2 On the Table Tools tab, click Layout. In the Rows and Columns group, click Insert Right.

The Insert Right button adds a new column directly to the right of the selected column.

Word inserts a column to the right of the Food column.

3 Place the cursor in the header of the new column and type **Course**.

 Be aware that when you delete a column, Word deletes the information contained in the column.

To delete a column:

1   Place the cursor anywhere in the Culture Hint column.

2   In the Rows and Columns group, click Delete. Select Delete Columns.

Word deletes the Culture Hint column.

Enlarging a table

When you delete a column, the table may appear awkward on the page. When this happens, you can enlarge the table to fit between the page margins.

1   In word0701_done, click anywhere in the table.

2   On the Table Tools tab, click Layout, and then in the Cell Size group, click AutoFit.

Click AutoFit.

3   In the AutoFit menu, select AutoFit Window. Word resizes the table to fit within the boundaries of the page margins.

4   Click File > Save, and then click File > Close.

Word provides other options on the AutoFit menu.

AUTOFIT OPTIONS	
Fixed Column Width	Resizes the column to a specific width.
AutoFit to Contents	Automatically adjusts the width of columns to fit the table data you enter.
AutoFit to Window	Resizes the table so that it fits within a Web browser window or a document page.

Combining and splitting cells

You can combine two or more cells to create one large cell. To open the document you need for this lesson:

1   In Word, choose File > Open.

2   Navigate to the Word07lessons folder. Click word0702, and then click Open.

3   Select File > Save As. Word displays the Save As dialog box.

4 In the Save As text field, type **word0702_done**, and then click Save.

In this lesson, you'll combine the cells in a table row to accommodate the section title. You'll then split a table row into smaller cells.

1 In word0702_done, click and drag to select columns 2 and 3 in row 7. This selection should include the blank cell next to 7 as well as the cell that contains the text, Floor and Tiles.

2 On the Table Tools tab, click Layout.

3 In the Merge group, click Merge Cells.

Merge Cells merges the selected cells into one cell.

Word merges columns 2 and 3 to create one large cell.

4 Click anywhere in row 13. In the Merge group on the Ribbon, click Split Cells.

Split Cells splits the selected cells into multiple new cells.

Word displays the Split Cells dialog box.

The Split Cells dialog box lets you split a large cell into smaller cells.

5 In the Number of columns text field, type **3**. Word splits the cell into three equal parts.

You'll now adjust the cells to match the rest of the table.

6 Hover your mouse over the first line to the right of the number 13 until the cursor changes to a double-sided arrow.

7 Click and drag the line to meet the line to the right of the number in row 12.

8 Hover your mouse over the second line to the right of the number 13 until the cursor again changes to a double-sided arrow.

9   Click and drag the line to meet the line to the right of the word Porcelain in row 12.

10 Click the Save button in the Quick Access Toolbar to save your work.

Splitting a table

You can split one table into two tables. This feature is particularly useful if you realize that the material fits more logically into two separate tables.

In this exercise, you'll split the table in the word0702_done document.

1   Using the word0702_done document, place the cursor anywhere in row 7. This will be the first row of the new table.

2   On the Table Tools tab, click Layout and then in the Merge group, click Split Table to split the table into two.

The Split Table button splits the table into two tables.

3   Choose File > Save.

Aligning text in cells

To make your table text look more uniform, you can align text or numbers with the top, bottom, left, right, or center of the cells.

 By default, Word aligns table entries at the top-left edge of each cell.

1   In the first table in the word0702_done document, place the cursor over the column containing the numbers until the cursor changes to a downward-facing arrow and click to select this row.

2   On the Layout tab in the Alignment group, click the Align Center icon (=) to horizontally and vertically center the text within the selected cells.

The Align Center icon centers the text horizontally and vertically within the selected cell(s).

3 In the second table, place the cursor over the column containing the numbers until the cursor changes to a downward-facing arrow and click to select this row.

4 On the Layout tab in the Alignment group, click the Align Bottom Right icon (⬸) to align the text to the bottom right corner of the selected cells.

The Align Bottom Right icon aligns the text to the bottom right corner of the cell.

Adding shading to cells

You can add shading to cells to call attention to the information contained within the cells. In this exercise, you'll add shading to the title of the two tables.

1 Place your cursor in the cell containing *Miscellaneous Stains*.

2 On the Table Tools tab, click Design.

3 To the right of the table styles, click Shading to display the Shading menu.

Choose the shading for the cell from the Shading menu.

4 Select the gray color located in the second row under the white color, called White, Background 1, Darker 5%. Word shades the cell gray.

5 Repeat the same process for the cell containing the title *Floors and Tiles*.

Formatting a table

You can apply a pre-defined format to a table. In this exercise, you'll apply a format to the second table in the word0702_done document.

1 Click anywhere in the second table, titled *Floors and Tiles*, and then on the Table Tools tab, click Design.

2 In the Table Styles group, click the More arrow on the Styles menu to display the Table Styles menu.

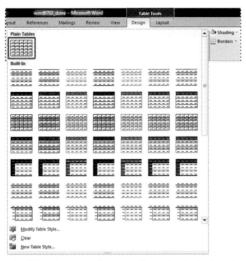

The Table Styles menu offers many colors and styles for the table.

3 Select any table style in the top row. Word applies the table style that you choose to the table your cursor is occupying

4 Choose File > Save and then File > Close.

Adding a formula to a table

You can place a formula in a cell and let Word automatically do the math for you.

To open the document you need for this lesson:

1 In Word, choose File > Open. Navigate to the word07lessons folder and double-click word0703.

2 Select File > Save As. In the Save As text field, type **word0703_done** and click Save.

In this exercise, you'll insert a formula into a table and calculate the total cost of a list of equipment.

1 Place your cursor in the blank, shaded cell located in the bottom row of the table, next to *Total*.

2 On the Table Tools tab, click Layout and then in the Data group, click Formula.

The Formula button adds a formula to a cell to perform a simple calculation.

3 In the Formula dialogue box, leave =SUM(ABOVE) in the Formula drop-down menu because we want the current cell to display the sum of the contents in the above cells. In the Number Format drop-down menu select $#,##0.00;($#,##0.00) to display the calculation in currency. Click OK.

The drop-down menu contains many number formats.

Word adds the column and displays the sum in the number format you chose.

4 In the table, change the top number in the right column to **1160**. Select the sum by clicking to the left of the current total $2,121.00. Keep your mouse cursor over this cell and right click. Choose Update Field and see how Word changes the sum to $1.980.00.

5 Choose File > Save, and then choose File > Close.

Congratulations! You have finished the lesson. In this lesson, you have discovered how to organize and display data in tables using the design and layout tools that Word provides.

Self Study

1 Open the word0703_done document.

2 In the table labeled *On Your Own*:

- Merge all cells in column A
- Delete column D
- Shade row 1 a red color of your choice
- Insert a row under row 4
- Split the cell in column C row 2 into 2 cells
- Split the table after row 2

Review

Questions

1 What is the keyboard shortcut to move the cursor backward to the previous cell in a table?

2 How do you select an entire table?

3 Which AutoFit option resizes the table so that it fits within a Web browser window or a document page?

Answers

1 The keyboard shortcut to move to the previous cell is Shift+Tab.

2 Click the handle in the upper-left corner of the table to select the table.

3 AutoFit to Window resizes the table to fit within a Web browser window or document page.

What you'll learn in this lesson:

- Introducing the graphics tools
- Adding WordArt
- Adding a shape
- Wrapping text around an image
- Working with diagrams

Working with Graphics

In this lesson, you will become familiar with graphic elements and how to use them to add color and interest to your documents. Word can work with many different types of graphics, such as pictures, clip art, and shapes.

Starting up

You will work with several files from the Word08lessons folder in this lesson. Make sure that you have loaded the OfficeLessons folder onto your hard drive from *www.DigitalClassroomBooks.com/Office2010*. See "Loading lesson files" on page XXIV.

See Lesson 8 in action!

Use the accompanying video to gain a better understanding of how to use some of the features shown in this lesson. The video tutorial for this lesson can be found at www.DigitalClassroomBooks.com/Office2010.

Introducing the graphics tools

You can insert pictures, clip art, shapes, SmartArt, charts, and screenshots into a Word document. You'll find the Illustrations group on the Insert tab.

The Illustrations group lets you insert graphic elements, such as clip art.

Depending on which graphic element you choose to insert, Word provides a set of tools associated with the element. For example, if you insert a shape, Word displays the Drawing Tools tab, which offers tools like shape styles and color fills.

In this exercise, you will open an existing document located in the Word08lessons folder.

To open the document you need for this lesson:

1   Launch Word.

2   Choose File > Open and navigate to the Word08lessons folder.

3   Click word0801, and then click Open.

4   Select File > Save As and in the File Name text field, type **word0801_done**. Press Save.

Adding WordArt

WordArt is decorative text that you can add to a document as an eye-catching visual effect. It comes in handy when designing logos for T-shirts and flyers. WordArt is also very helpful in creating greeting cards.

In this exercise, you'll select some existing text and apply WordArt to it.

1   In the word0801_done document, place the cursor to the left of *Happy Birthday Rocky!*, and triple-click to select this text.

2   On the Ribbon, click the Insert tab. In the Text group, click the WordArt icon (*A*).

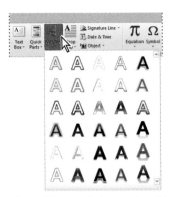

The WordArt menu displays a variety of choices.

3   Select the red letter *A* that is located third from the left in the second-to-last row. This style is called Fill - Red, Accent 2, Warm Matte Bevel.

Word changes the text to the WordArt style you have chosen, and the Drawing Tools tab appears on the Ribbon.

You'll now edit the WordArt by changing the font style, and then you'll add a border and fill.

4   Click the Home tab on the Ribbon, and select Comic Sans MS from the Font Style list in the Font group.

5   Click the Format tab and then click the More icon in the Shape Styles group. The More icon looks like a down-pointing arrow with a line over it.

The Shape Styles menu displays shapes with borders and fills.

6 In the Shape Styles menu, select the style in the third row, second from the left called Light 1 Outline, Colored Fill – Blue, Accent 1.

7 To ensure that the image is centered on the page, select Align located in the Arrange section and choose Align Center.

8 Choose File > Save.

Adding a picture

You can include a picture, such as a .jpg or .png, in your Word document.

1 In the word0801_done document, click below the completed WordArt image and press Shift+Enter twice to leave space between the existing image and the image you are now placing.

2 On the Insert tab, in the Illustrations group, click Picture.

The Picture button allows a picture to be inserted from a file.

3 Navigate to the Word08lessons folder; click word0802, and then click Insert.

Word inserts a picture of a koala in a tree and displays the Picture Tools tab on the Ribbon. Notice that the picture is selected and has handles around its edges.

4 Press Ctrl+E to center the image on the page.

 To delete a picture, click on the picture to select it, and then press the Delete key.

Cropping a picture

You can crop a picture, screen shot, or clip art to reduce its size or change the focus of the image. In this exercise, you'll remove some of the dark background and greenery in the picture so that the focus is on the koala and the tree.

1 In the word0801_done document, click the image of the koala to select it, and then click the Picture Tools tab.

2 In the Size group on the Ribbon, click Crop.

Click Crop in the Size group.

Word displays crop handles on the edges of the picture. As you begin to drag, the cursor changes to a cross (+).

3 Click the middle handle on the right side of the picture and drag until the top handle touches the edge of the tree.

Drag the crop handles to eliminate the unwanted part of the picture.

Word blackens the area it will remove.

4 Click the middle handle on the left side of the picture and drag toward the koala, leaving a small amount of greenery around the koala.

5 Press Enter. Word removes the blackened cropped areas.

Cropping with a special shape

You might want to crop the picture using a special shape to outline it.

1 In the word0801_done document, click the picture of the koala if it is not already selected.

2 In the Size group, click the down arrow on the Crop icon. Word displays the Crop menu.

The Crop menu lets you crop the picture using a special shape.

3   Select Crop to Shape. Word displays the Shape menu.

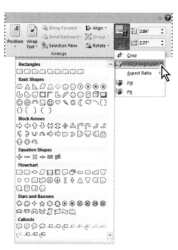

The Shape menu contains a variety of shapes.

4   Select Oval, which is the first shape in the first row of the Basic Shapes section. Word applies the oval shape to the picture.

5   Click File > Save, and then click File > Close.

Adding a screenshot

You can insert a screenshot of a screen in Word or in another application, such as Excel. The Screenshot command in Word can capture an image and place it into a Word document. In the following steps, you'll first open a Word document and then an Excel document.

1   In Word, choose File > Open and navigate to the Word08lessons folder.

2   Click word0803, and then click Open.

3   Select File > Save As. In the File Name text field, type **word0803_done** and press Save.
      Now you'll open the Excel document:

4   Open the Excel program. Choose File > Open.

5   In the Word08lessons folder, click word0804 and then click Open.

6   Click word0803_done on the status bar that runs along the bottom of your screen to select this Word document. Place the cursor below the paragraph ending *for the last three years*, and then press Enter. This is where you will place the screenshot.

7   Click the Insert tab on the Ribbon, and in the Illustrations group, click Screenshot.

Word displays the Screenshot menu that lists the open applications.

The Screenshot menu lets you capture the whole screen or a portion of the screen.

8   Select Screen Clipping. Word displays the dimmed Excel spreadsheet and the cursor changes to a cross (+).

9   Click the upper-left corner of the chart entitled *2008 – 2010 Income Summary*; drag the cursor to select the chart, and then release the mouse.

Word displays the chart in the word0803_done document.

10   Press Ctrl+E to center the chart.

11   Click the word0804 document on the status bar to toggle to the Excel spreadsheet, and then click File > Exit.

Adding a caption

A caption is a title (such as *Figure 1*) or explanation that can identify or explain an image. In this exercise, you'll add a caption to the chart in the word0803_done document.

1 Click the chart and then click the References tab on the Ribbon. In the Captions group, click Insert Caption.

2 In the Caption text field, type a **:** (colon) after *Figure 1*, and then type **The Cookie Place shows a profit**.

3 In the Label drop-down menu, select Figure, if it is not already selected.

The Caption dialog box lets you position the caption.

4 In the Position drop-down menu, select Above selected item, and then click OK. Word applies the caption to the figure.

To delete a caption, select it and click Delete.

You can now save and close this document.

5 Click File > Save, and then click File > Close.

Inserting a clip art image

You can add clip art images to your document. When you search for an image, you can specify the types of media you want to search for: illustrations, photographs, videos, and audio. In this exercise, you'll search for clip art in all media formats. You may need an Internet connection for some parts of this exercise.

1   Choose File > Open and navigate to the Word08lessons folder.

2   Click word0805, and then click Open.

3   Select File > Save As and in the File Name text field, type **word0805_done**. Press Save.

Now, you'll add some clip art to the table in the word0805_done document.

1   In the table, click the cell in the first row under Image, and then click Insert on the Ribbon.

2   In the Illustrations group, click Clip Art. Word displays the Clip Art window to the right of the document.

3   In the Results should be drop-down menu, deselect all checkboxes except the Audio checkbox.

4   In the Search for text field, type **raindrops** and click Go. Word displays the search results.

You can search for illustrations, photographs, video, and audio clips in the Clip Art window.

5 Select Rain on Lake. Because this is a .wav audio file and is larger than a .jpg file, it might take several seconds for the .wav file to appear in the table.

To hear the .wav file once it appears in your document, simply double-click the icon. Your default audio program plays the file.

6 Place the cursor in the Image column of the squirrel eating row.

7 In the Results should be drop-down menu, deselect the Audio checkbox and select the Illustrations and Photographs checkboxes.

8 In the Search for text field, type **squirrel eating** and click Go. Word displays the illustrations and photographs that match the search criteria.

9 Select the photograph on the left. Word inserts the photograph in the table.

Now let's resize the image so that it fits better within the table.

To resize the image:

1 Click the photograph to select it, if it is not already selected, and then click the Picture Tools tab.

2 In the Size group, in the Shape Height text field (🔲), type **1** and press Enter. Word resizes the photograph of the squirrel so that the height is now 1 inch.

Adding a shape

You can add graphic shapes such as lines, arrows, and stars. In this exercise, you'll add a heart to a document and then you'll use the Shape tools to format the heart shape.

1 In word0805_done, click the Insert tab on the Ribbon and then in the Illustrations group, click Shapes.

Click Shapes in the Illustrations group on the Ribbon.

2   In the Basic Shapes group, click the heart. The cursor changes to a cross (+).

Word offers a variety of shapes to insert into a document.

3   Click anywhere under the paragraph entitled *Valentine's Day*, which ends with the words *Victorian England*. **Drag down and to the right to** create a heart shape and release the mouse button.

Word selects the heart and displays the Drawing Tools tab.

4   In the Shape Styles group, click the More icon to the right of the Shape Styles to display the Shape Styles menu.

Click the More icon to reveal additional Shape Styles options.

5 Select Subtle Effect, Turquoise, Accent 3 in the fourth column from the left four rows from the top to apply the shape style to the heart.

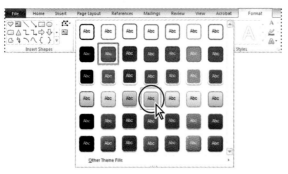

The Shape Styles menu lets you choose both subtle and dramatic styles.

6 With the heart still selected, click Shape Effects in the Shape Styles group.

Click Shape Effects.

7 From the Shape Effects menu, select Bevel, and then select the effect in the top row of the first column, called Circle to add the effect to the heart.

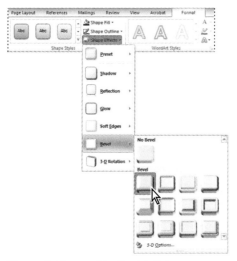

You can select from a variety of beveled effects.

8 Select File > Save to save your work.

Wrapping text around an image

When you insert an image into a Word document, you can control the way that text wraps around the image. Word provides text wrapping options so that you can work with text and graphics to achieve the layout result you want.

WRAPPING STYLE	ICON	DESCRIPTION
In line with text		Text does not wrap around the graphic.
Square		Text flows in a square around the graphic regardless of its shape.
Tight		Text flows around the graphic's outside edge; this style works well with a non-square shape.
Through		Text flows around the graphic.
Top and bottom		Text flows around the top and bottom of the graphic but leaves blank space on the sides.
Behind text		Text flows over the graphic as if the graphic were not there.
In front of text		Text flows behind the graphic.

In this exercise, you'll wrap the text around an image.

1   In word0805_done, click the picture of the dog on page 2. Word places handles around the image and displays the Picture Tools tab on the Ribbon.

2   Click the Format tab, and then click the Wrap Text icon in the Arrange group.

Click the Wrap Text icon to reveal text wrapping options.

3   Select Square. Notice that the text forms a square boundary around the image.

You can display graphics and text in a variety of ways.

Adding a picture effect to a graphic

You can apply many effects to graphics in a document, such as shadow, reflection, glow, soft edges, bevel, and 3D, by using the Picture Effects menu. In this exercise, you'll apply soft edges to a picture of a golden retriever.

1 In word0805_done, select the picture, if it is not already selected. On the Format tab, in the Picture Styles group, click Picture Effects.

Click Picture Effects in the Picture Styles group to reveal the Picture Effects options.

2 Select Soft Edges. Word displays the Soft Edges menu.

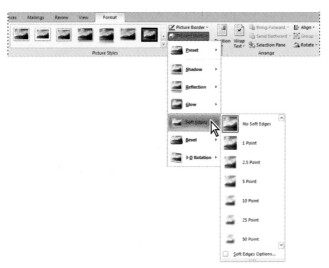

You can apply a degree of softness, or blur, to the edge.

3 Select 2.5 Point and notice how the edges around the picture changed.

4 Select File > Save to save your work.

Working with diagrams

SmartArt is a tool that quickly arranges graphics into a layout in your Word document. For example, you can create diagrams, such as organization charts and process diagrams.

1 In word0805_done, click under the title *Diagrams* on page 2, and then click the Insert tab.

2 Click SmartArt in the Illustrations group.

Click SmartArt.

3 Word displays the Choose a SmartArt Graphic dialog box. From the list on the left, select Hierarchy to display the Hierarchy menu.

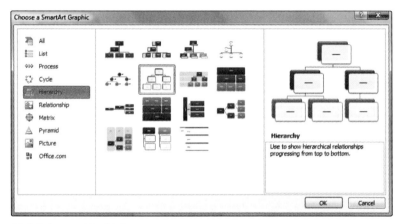

Word displays a variety of choices.

4 Select the second choice from the left in the second row called Hierarchy, and then click OK. Word displays the SmartArt graphic, and the SmartArt tools appear on the Ribbon.

5 In the Type your text here box, type the following names in this order and be sure not to press Enter after each name, just simply press the down arrow or click the next Text field: **Amanda Russell**, **John Mack**, **Candace Bailey**, **Jim Stevens**, **Kim Huff**, **Keith Jones**.

You can type directly into the text fields, if you prefer.

6   On the Smart Tools tab, click Design, and then click Change Colors.

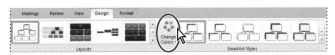

Click Change Colors.

7   In the Colorful group, select the third diagram from the left called Colorful Range – Accent Colors 3 to 4.

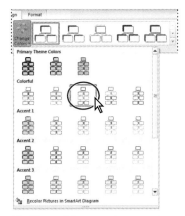

The Change Colors menu gives you options to accent your diagram.
Please circle the third diagram from the left in the Colorful group.

8   Double-click anywhere outside the diagram to finish.

9   Click File > Save, and then click File > Close.

Congratulations! You have completed this lesson, where you have discovered how to work with graphics to add color and interest to your document.

Self study

1   Open word0801_done, and click the WordArt graphic of Happy Birthday Rocky. Select a blue-colored WordArt option to replace the one you created in the lesson.

2   Select the picture of the koala and crop the image with a shape other than an oval.

3   Open the word0805_done document, and add the caption *Man's Best Friend* to the golden retriever photograph.

Review

Questions

1 If you want your text to flow around a graphic that is not square, which wrapping style would work best?

2 Which option in the Illustrations group would you use to create a diagram?

3 When you search for clip art, what are the four media file types that you can look for?

Answers

1 You should choose Tight if you want the text to flow around the graphic's outside edge.

2 You would use the SmartArt option.

3 The four media file types you can look for are illustrations, photographs, audio, and video files.

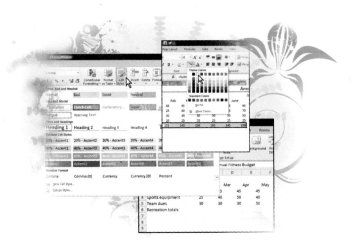

What you'll learn in this lesson:

- Inserting rows and columns into a worksheet
- Merging and formatting cells
- Adjusting cell width and increasing font size
- Copying and pasting to a range of cells

Microsoft Excel 2010 Jumpstart

In this lesson, you will get a general introduction to Microsoft Excel 2010. This lesson is intended to provide a quick introduction, so you can jump right in and get your feet wet. If you aren't ready for a quick overview, feel free to skip this lesson and move to Lesson 2, "Getting Started with Microsoft Excel 2010," and then return to this lesson later.

Starting up

You will work with a file from the Excel01lessons folder in this lesson. Make sure that you have loaded the OfficeLessons folder onto your hard drive from *www.DigitalClassroomBooks.com/Office2010*. See "Loading lesson files" on page XXIV.

See Lesson 1 in action!

Use the accompanying video to gain a better understanding of how to use some of the features shown in this lesson. The video tutorial for this lesson can be found at www.DigitalClassroomBooks.com/Office2010.

The project

In this lesson, you will open an existing worksheet. You will then add data and format the worksheet.

1 Launch Microsoft Excel 2010.

2 Choose File > Open and navigate to the Excel01lessons folder that you copied to your computer from the DVD that came with your book, and then double-click excel01. An Excel document opens to display a worksheet.

The Excel workspace is similar to that of other Microsoft Office applications. The tools are conveniently located on the Ribbon running across the top of the window.

The Ribbon displays different tools depending on the tab that you click.

You can enter data into any cell of a worksheet by typing directly in the cell or using the formula bar. The formula bar appears directly below the Ribbon and displays the contents of the selected cell. The Name box appears to the left of the formula bar and displays the cell address.

A. Name box. *B*. Formula bar.

3   Click File > Save As. Excel displays the Save As dialog box.

Excel lets you name the file in the Save As dialog box.

4   Type **excel01_done**, and then click Save.

Inserting rows and columns into a worksheet

You can add rows and columns to a worksheet to include more data. When you insert a row, you must first select the row below where you want the new row to appear. For example, if you want a new row to appear between rows 1 and 2, you must select row 2 and then insert the row.

When you insert a column, you must select the column to the right of where you want the new column to appear. For example, if you want a column to appear between columns B and C, you must select column C, and then insert the column.

In this exercise, you'll add a row and a column to a worksheet and label them.

1   In the excel01_done document, move the cursor to the left side of row 7, and click to select the row. On the Home tab, in the Cells group, click Insert to insert a row above the selected row.

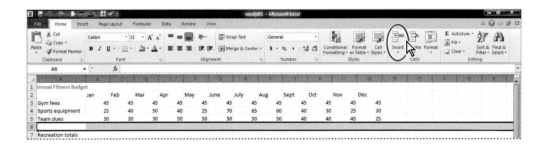

2   In cell A7, type **Transportation**.

3   Move the cursor to the top of column H, and click to select the column. On the Home tab, in the Cells group, click Insert twice. Excel inserts two columns to the left of the selected column.

4   Click cell H2 and then type **Jan-Jun Total**. Click cell P2 and then type **Jul-Dec Total**.

If you want to insert more than one row or column, select the number of rows or columns that you want to insert before you apply the Insert command. For example, if you want to insert two rows, select two existing rows.

5   Choose File > Save to save your work.

Merging and formatting cells

Sometimes you need to create a single large cell. For example, you can merge many cells to make room for a worksheet title to give the worksheet a cleaner appearance.

In this exercise, you'll merge cells and center the text within the resulting cell. Then you'll add a cell style to the title.

1   In the worksheet, click cell A1 and drag to cell P1. In the Home tab in the Alignment group, click Merge and Center.

Excel merges the cells and centers the text Annual Fitness Budget.

2 In the Styles group, click Cell Styles to displays the Cell Styles menu.

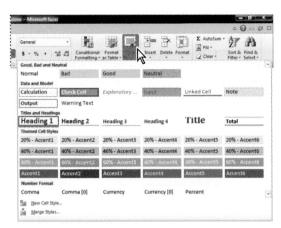

You can quickly select a style for a cell in the Cell Styles menu.

3 Select Heading 1. Excel changes the font size and style to Heading 1 and adds a line under the row.

Adjusting cell width and increasing font size

In this exercise, you'll adjust the width of a row of cells to allow the text to fit more comfortably within the cells.

1 Place the cursor to the right of row H, and move the cursor over the border until the cursor changes to a cross with arrows pointing right and left. Click and drag the border line until the words *Jan-Jun Total* fit comfortably within the cell, and then release the mouse button.

2 Repeat step 1 for row P with the words *Jul-Dec Total*.

3 Click cell H2; press and hold Ctrl, and then click cell P2. Excel selects both cells.

4 In the Font group, click Increase Font Size (A˙) twice to increases the font size to 14 points.

5 Select File > Save.

Copying and pasting to a range of cells

You can easily copy a cell to a range of cells.

1 Click cell B7 and type 25. Place the cursor over the bottom–right corner of the cell, and the cursor changes to a cross (+). Click and drag across the row, all the way through cell G7, and then release the mouse button. Excel copies the number 25 across the range of cells.

2   Click cell J7 and type 30. Place the cursor over the bottom-right corner of the cell, and the cursor changes to a cross (+). Click and drag across the row, all the way through cell O7, and then release the mouse button. Excel copies the number 30 across the range of cells.

3   Click anywhere outside your current selection to de-select.

4   Click File > Save.

Adding a column of numbers

You can add a column of numbers using the AutoSum function. In the following steps, you will use the AutoSum function to add a range of cells.

1   Place the cursor in cell B8, and then click the Home tab.

2   In the Editing group, click the AutoSum button (Σ) and then press Enter. Excel displays the recreation total for *January*.

3   Repeat steps 1 and 2 for cells C8, D8, E8, F8, and G8.

4   Click cell H8; click AutoSum and press Enter. Excel adds the Recreation totals for *January* through *June* and displays the total of these amounts.

Adding a fill

You can make a range of cells stand out from the rest of a worksheet by applying a fill to the range.

1   Click and drag from cell B8 through cell G8, and then release the mouse button.

2   In the Font group, click the arrow next to the Fill Color icon (△) and Excel displays the Fill Color menu.

3   Select the third color in the top row; Tan Background 2.

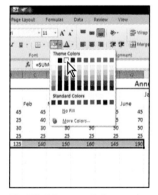

The Fill Color menu displays a variety of choices.

4   Click File > Save, and then click File > Close.

Congratulations! You have started to see some of what Microsoft Excel 2010 has to offer with this quick tour of several significant features. Throughout the book, you will learn about these features in greater depth.

Self study

1   In the excel01_done document. Click cell J8, and perform the AutoSum function for the July column of numbers. Perform the AutoSum function for August through December, and calculate the July through December total.

2   In excel01_done document, select cells J8 through O8 and apply a yellow fill. Select cells B3 through G3 and increase the font size to 12.

Review

Questions

1   What are two ways to add data to a cell?

2   If you want a row to appear above row 4, which row would you select before you apply the Insert command?

3   If you want a column to appear between columns C and D, which column would you select before you apply the Insert command?

Answers

1   You can type directly into the cell or type the data into the formula bar.

2   You would select row 4, and then click Insert for a row to appear above row

3   You would select column D and then click Insert for a column to appear between columns C and D.

What you'll learn in this lesson:

- Introducing Microsoft Excel
- Understanding the components of a worksheet
- Introducing the elements of the Excel user interface
- Using the Help function

Getting Started with Microsoft Excel 2010

In this lesson, you will get a general introduction to Excel. You will look at the user interface and some basic Excel features. Finally, you will learn how to use the Help application for when you run into problems.

Starting up

You will work with a file from the Excel02lessons folder in this lesson. Make sure that you have loaded the OfficeLessons folder onto your hard drive from *www.DigitalClassroomBooks.com/Office2010*. See "Loading lesson files" on page XXIV.

See Lesson 2 in action!

Use the accompanying video to gain a better understanding of how to use some of the features shown in this lesson. The video tutorial for this lesson can be found at www.DigitalClassroomBooks.com/Office2010.

What Is Excel?

Excel is a spreadsheet program where you can enter numbers and data into the rows or columns of an Excel worksheet and then create calculations, graphs, and statistical analysis from the data you've entered. Even if you don't have strong math skills, you'll find that Excel makes computations easy to understand. If you already have a good background with mathematics, you'll be able to do more complex calculations. Excel makes it easy and painless to manipulate numbers and data. Computations are done behind the scenes, and when the data changes, so do the results of formulas.

In addition to numbers, Excel is also useful for organizing data such as lists of names and addresses.

How can you use Excel?

You can use Excel to track data, analyze it, and perform calculations on the data, and then you can present the data in a variety of ways. The following table shows a few ways in which you can use Excel.

USE	EXPLANATION	EXAMPLE
Accounting	You can use the powerful calculation tools to create financial statements	Profit and loss statement
Budgeting	You can create business or personal budgets	An event budget or a retirement budget
Billing and sales	You can manage billing and sales data	Sales invoices
Reporting	You can create a report that summarizes and analyzes your data	Stock market forecast reports
Planning	You can create a plan for any event or activity	A weekly class plan or vacation plans
Tracking	You can keep track of a collection of related data	An inventory list to track equipment
Using calendars	The grid-like workspace makes it easy to create a custom calendar	An academic calendar or fiscal year calendar

Exploring the Excel workspace

When you launch Excel 2010, the application opens to a workspace window with a File menu and several tabs running across the top. The File menu lets you access Backstage view. The tabs are the Ribbon organizers. The tools that you need for entering and manipulating data are contained in the Ribbon. The worksheet contains a formula bar, cells, rows, and columns. Finally, the status bar at the bottom keeps you updated with important information such as the current Excel mode and the layout view you are in.

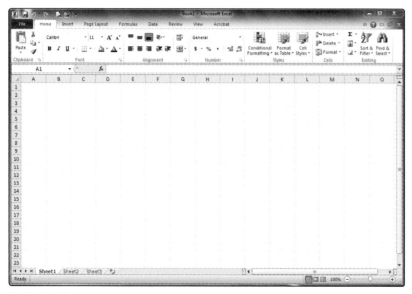

The Excel workspace.

Now let's open a document and practice using the Ribbon commands and hot keys. Hot keys are keyboard shortcuts within Excel that can help you maximize productivity. You can display the key tips for these keyboard shortcuts while you work until you become accustomed to accessing the commands you use most often.

1 Launch Excel.

2 Click File > Open. In the Open dialog box, navigate to OfficeLessons > Excel02lessons > excel0201, and click Open.

3 Press and release the Alt key to display the Ribbon key tips for the Quick Access Toolbar and the tabs.

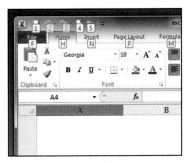

The basic key tips in Excel.

The hot keys for the Quick Access Toolbar are numbers, while the tips for all Ribbon commands are numbers, letters, or letter combinations.

4 If you have Print Preview as a command on the Quick Access Toolbar, press **4** to display the print preview. The number 4 key is the hot key for the Quick Access Toolbar Print Preview command.

5 Click the File tab to close print preview and return to the document.

6 In the first column of the Weekly Meal Planner, click the word Monday and drag to the word Saturday to select the column. Press Alt+H to view the Home tab key tips. Then press 1 to apply a bold font to the days of the week.

Working in Backstage view

You can access Backstage view from the File menu. Some of the file-related options on the menu are standard and others are new to Excel 2010. The following table lists the options on the File menu and describes what each one does.

If you press Alt when you are in the File menu, the File menu key tips are displayed.

OPTION	DESCRIPTION
Save	Saves a file
Save As	Saves a file with the name you specify
Open	Opens an existing file
Close	Closes an open file
Info	Displays a page of specific file information and allows you to protect the document, prepare the document for sharing, and manage versions of the file
Recent	Displays a list of recently opened files so you can open a file more conveniently
New	Displays a page with options to open a new document, such as a blank workbook. You can also create a new document from a template
Print	Displays the print options and a print preview
Share	Displays options that allow you to share the file with others
Help	Displays a window where you can search for help on any Excel topic or obtain contact information for the Microsoft Help Desk
Options	Displays a screen where you can change the default settings in Excel.
Exit	Exits the Excel application

Setting and removing a password requirement

You can use the Backstage view options to set permissions on a file so that anyone opening it needs a password. This is helpful if you are sending out a file containing sensitive data for review and want only certain individuals to have access to it. You can also remove the password requirement when you no longer need it.

To set a password requirement:

1 Click File > Info > Protect Workbook > Encrypt with Password. The Encrypt Document dialog box is displayed.

Enter a password in the dialog box.

2 Type **myword** in the Password box, and click OK.

3 Retype **myword** to confirm the password, and click OK.

A password is now required to open the workbook.

Removing security restrictions

To remove the password requirement:

1   Click File > Save As.

2   In the Save As dialog box, click Tools.

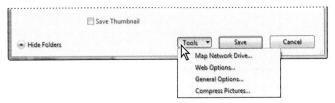

Click Tools to display a menu.

3   On the Tools menu, click General Options.

4   In the Password to Open box in the General Options dialog box, delete the password and click OK.

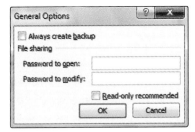

Delete the password previously created.

5   In the Save As dialog box, navigate to OfficeLessons. Click on the Excel02lessons folder, rename the file to **excel0201_working**, and click Save.

6   Choose File > Close.

Worksheet basics: a quick tour of Microsoft Excel

Before you can completely understand the capabilities of Excel, you need to understand the components of the program. Let's begin by working with a basic worksheet.

1 In the Excel program, choose File > Open. Navigate to the Excel02lessons folder and click on excel0202. This is a simple worksheet of names and addresses.

A worksheet is a type of ledger. It consists of a grid made from columns and rows.

A. Rows. B. Tabs. C. Quick Access Toolbar. D. Ribbon. E. Columns. F. Title bar.

Take a look at the Ribbon at the top of the Excel interface. The Ribbon is an important element in Excel 2010 because it contains the buttons and controls for accessing Excel commands. The commands that display on the Ribbon change, depending on which tab you have clicked.

2 Click the Insert tab. The Ribbon changes to display different commands.

The commands are divided into groups, and the group labels are on the bottom of the Ribbon. For example, Tables, Illustrations, Charts, Sparklines, Filter, Links, Text, and Symbols are the groups found on the Insert tab. When you want to insert a chart, for example, you can use the commands in the Charts group to insert the type of chart that you want.

3 Click the File tab to display Backstage view.

4 Click the Home tab.

Exploring worksheets

Now, let's explore the worksheet.

1 Click on the letter A in the upper-left corner of the worksheet. The letters along the top represent columns. Notice that the column title is Last, indicating the last name. Other column names are First, Address, City, State, and Zip.

2 Click on the number 2 to the left of column A. The numbers represent the rows of entries. Notice that clicking the number selects the entire row.

3 Click on *Simpson* in cell A12. This text is contained in a cell. Each piece of data occupies a cell, and each cell can contain any of the following types of data:

- Text
- Numbers
- Formulas

4 The way you identify a cell is by its location. Click *Empire State Building* in column C. Follow the row over to the far left. The number 7 identifies the row. The location of this cell, then, is C7 (column C, row 7).

Let's take a closer look at the Excel user interface.

The Excel user interface

The Excel window consists of various elements. These include standard Windows elements, such as the title bar and status bar. The window also has Office-specific elements, such as the Ribbon and the File tab. There are also Excel-specific elements such as tools and options that you can use to enhance your work.

Customizing the Quick Access Toolbar

The Quick Access Toolbar gives you convenient, one-click access to your favorite tools. Currently, the toolbar in the document displays the Save, Redo, and Undo options.

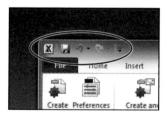

The Quick Access Toolbar provides easy access to commonly used commands.

Let's customize the toolbar to include the Print Preview and Spelling & Grammar buttons. If you have completed Microsoft Word lessons, you will find this to be a familiar process.

To customize the Quick Access Toolbar:

1 If the document excel0202 is not open, click File > Open. In the Open dialog box, navigate to OfficeLessons > Excel02lesson > excel0202, and click Open.

2   Click the Customize Quick Access Toolbar button ( ).

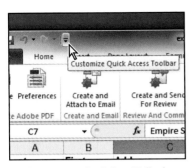

*Use the Customize Quick Access Toolbar button
to add or remove items from the toolbar.*

3   Click the Print Preview and Print option on the drop-down menu, then repeat the
process, except this time click the Spelling option on the menu.

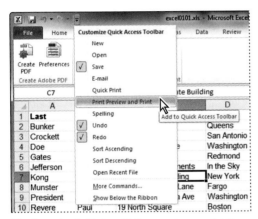

*The Customize Quick Access Toolbar menu lets you select items
to appear on the toolbar.*

The Print Preview and Spelling icons both appear on the toolbar.

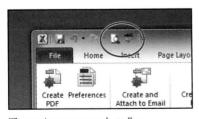

The new icons appear on the toolbar.

4 Click the Print Preview icon you just added to the Quick Access Toolbar. Excel displays a preview of the excel0202 document as it would look printed, along with the printing options.

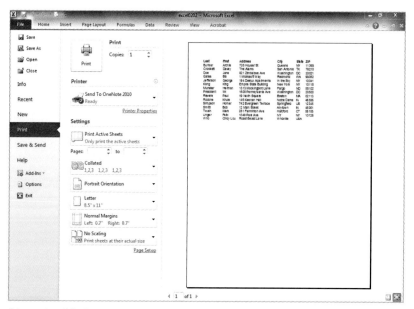

Print preview of the document.

5 Click the Zoom to Page icon (⊙) on the bottom-right corner of the Excel preview window to take a close look at the document.

6 Click the Margins icon (▦) which is located next to the Zoom to Page icon, to display margins. Page margins are the blank spaces between the worksheet data and the edges of the printed page. To change margins, you can drag the margins to the height and width that you want.

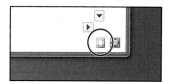

The Margins icon lets you adjust the document's margins.

7 Click the File tab at the top of the screen to close print preview and return to the document.

Removing buttons from the Quick Access Toolbar

To remove a button from the Quick Access Toolbar:

1 Right-click the Spelling & Grammar icon (✋) on the toolbar to display a shortcut menu. A menu is displayed providing options for modifying the Quick Access Toolbar and this icon.

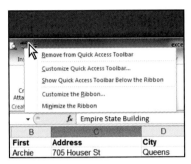

The Shortcut menu to remove toolbar buttons.

2 Click Remove from Quick Access Toolbar to remove the Spelling & Grammar button.

Using the Zoom and Page View options

The Zoom and Page View control options are located in the bottom-right corner of the status bar. This feature allows you to zoom in and out in 10 percent increments with each mouse-click.

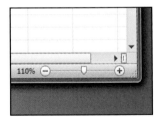

Zoom and Page View options.

1 Using the Zoom control, click the Plus sign button until the zoom reaches 120 percent. Take a closer look to examine the document more carefully. You can always zoom in more to enlarge the view.

2 Click the Page Layout View button (▭) located to the left of the Zoom control.

3 At the top of Page Layout view, click to place your cursor in the text that says Click to add header, and then type **Important Addresses**. Then click outside of the header text box to deselect it.

4 Click the Normal View button (▦).

Naming a worksheet

Labeling the tabs on your worksheet pages is an easy way to identify their content and organize the information they contain. This is especially useful if you have several related worksheets within a workbook.

The excel0202 workbook has three tabs. Let's rename them Guests, Menu, and Shopping List:

1 Right-click the tab labeled Sheet1, which is located at the bottom of the worksheet. A shortcut menu is displayed.

Use the shortcut menu to rename a tab.

2 Click Rename. Excel highlights the tab name, Sheet1.

3 Type **Guests** to rename this sheet.

4 Right-click the Sheet2 tab label.

5 Click Rename in the shortcut menu that appears.

6 Type **Menu** to name this sheet.

7 Right-click the Sheet3 tab label.

8 Click Rename in the shortcut menu that appears.

9 Type **Shopping List**, renaming this sheet, and then click back on the Guests tab.

Naming and saving workbooks

Now that the sheet, or tabs as they appear, are all relabeled, let's name the workbook and save it.

1 Click File > Save As. In the Save As dialog box that appears, use the Navigation pane to select OfficeLessons > Excel02lessons.

2 Type **excel0202_rename** in the File name box. Excel displays the new workbook name in the title bar.

Changing page setup options

Page setup is often the key to making a worksheet more readable. You can adjust the page orientation and margins to control how a worksheet displays when it is printed. For example, your workbook data might be too wide to fit on a standard-sized sheet of paper in portrait (tall) format. You can change the page orientation to landscape (wide) to give the contents of the worksheet more space, or in case you want to add more columns of data later.

1   On the Ribbon, click Page Layout > Orientation > Landscape.

2   Click File > Print to view your page in landscape orientation.

3   Click the File tab to return to your document. Notice that Excel has marked the edge of your page with a dotted line. This represents the right margin of the page.

Shading cells and changing Font Color

To give your worksheet some style, you can add shading and color to the cells and text. You will highlight the first two columns of your worksheet with yellow, shade the top line with blue, and change the top line font color to white.

1   Select the first two columns by clicking column A and then dragging to the right through column B.

2   Click the Home tab and in the Font group, click on the down arrow next to the Fill Color button (). Excel displays a menu of possible fill colors.

3   Click the yellow square under Standard Colors.

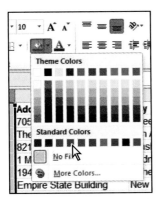

You can change the fill color of the cells.

4 Click Row 1 to select it, and click the down arrow next to the Fill Color button again.

5 From the available fill colors, click Blue Accent 1; the fifth color in the first row under Theme Colors.

6 To be able to see the text in line 1, you will need to change the font color to white to contrast with the dark blue shading. With the first row still selected, in the Home tab, choose the down arrow next to the Font Color button (<u>A</u>).

7 Under Theme Colors, click White.

8 Click Save and then choose File > Close.

Working within a workbook

A workbook can contain many worksheets. By default, Excel supplies three worksheets when you start a new blank workbook. If you need more, you can add them. You can also delete any sheets you do not need.

It's important that you become familiar with the major components of a worksheet and how to move around within it. To practice, you will build a workbook from a template. A template is a preformatted document on which you can base a new document. You'll also add a worksheet to the workbook and name the worksheet.

1 Click File > New > New from existing.

2 Navigate to the Excel02lessons folder and double-click Weekly meal planner.

3 Click the Insert Worksheet tab (🗐) at the bottom of the worksheet. Excel adds a new worksheet entitled Sheet1.

4 Right-click the Sheet1 tab to display the Worksheet menu.

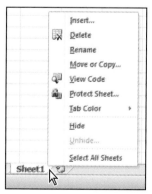

The Worksheet menu.

5 Click Rename, and type **Grocery List** in the selected area. Click anywhere on the worksheet to apply the name change.

6 To save the workbook, click File > Save As. The Save As dialog box appears.

7 Navigate to the Excel02lessons folder, type **excel0203_working** in the File name box, and click Save.

Understanding the worksheet area

To get the most from Excel, you should be familiar with the worksheet area and its components, and comfortable with entering data into a worksheet. Data can be text, such as column labels, or numbers (also called values). You can enter data into any cell in an Excel worksheet by typing directly into the cell. You can also enter data using the formula bar. The formula bar is located at the top of the worksheet and displays the cell address and the contents of the active cell. Excel left-aligns text and right-aligns numbers.

You will be working with text only on this worksheet.

1 In the excel0203_working document, click on the Weekly Meal Planner tab so that this worksheet is active.

2 Click *Sunday* and notice that the formula bar displays the cell location and contents.

The Formula bar.

3 Click in the cell just below *Breakfast* and next to *Sunday*. The cell is outlined in black, indicating that it is active and that you can enter data into it.

4 Type **English breakfast muffins and coffee** and press Tab. This moves you to the cell to the immediate right.

5 Type **Tuna salad sandwiches and iced–coffee** and press Tab.

Instead of entering data directly into each cell, you can type it in the Cell Contents box of the formula bar. The Cell Contents box is located to the right of the (*fx*). As long as a cell is active, you can use the Cell Contents box to enter contents into that cell.

6 Click the Cell Contents box, type **Lasagna and Salad**, and press Return.

7 Click the Name Box, the left-most box in the formula bar, which contains the current cell location. You will enter the cell location of the next cell you want to edit.

8 Type E3 and press Return. Notice that the E3 cell under snack is now selected.
   Type **Apple**.

9 Click File > Save, then File > Close.

Convert Excel documents from prior versions to Excel 2010

While in Backstage view, you can easily convert an Excel document saved in a previous version to an Excel 2010 document. Let's practice with an Excel file from the Excel02lessons folder.

To convert an old Excel document:

1   Choose File > Open. Navigate to Excel02lesson, and double-click to open the file named excel0204.xls. Notice that it opens up in Compatibility Mode.

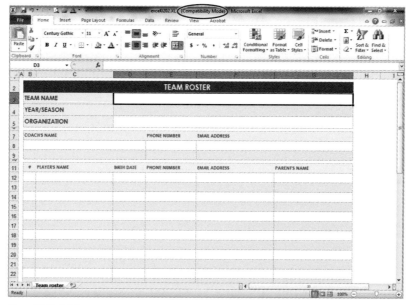

Compatibility Mode.

2   Click File > Info > Convert. Excel displays the Microsoft Excel dialog box.

3   Click OK, then click Yes when asked to reopen the workbook. Notice that Compatibility Mode is no longer visible on the title bar.

4   Choose File > Save As. In the Save As dialogue box rename the file to **excel0204_converted**, and then click Save.

5   Choose File > Close to close the workbook.

Getting help

If you ever get stuck, you can get help at any time when you are in the Excel program.

1   Click File > Help to display the Help options.

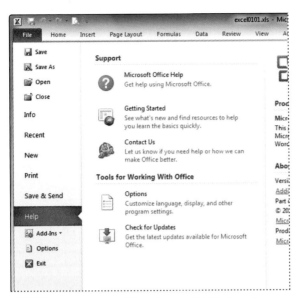

Click Help at any time to search for assistance, within Excel or online at
www.office.microsoft.com.

2   Click Getting Started. The Getting Started with Excel 2010 window appears. Help offers
several Getting Started options on the this webpage.

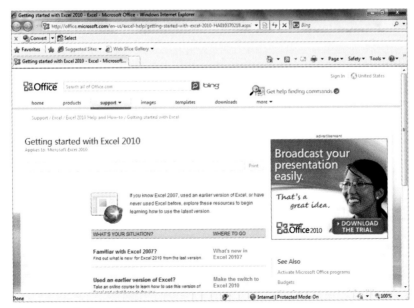

The options on the Getting Started page.

3 Scroll down to Never used Excel before.

4 Click Basic tasks in Excel 2010. Help displays the Basic tasks in Excel 2010 page.

5 Scroll down to see the Help topics, and click a topic that interests you.

6 When you are done, click the X in the upper-right corner to close the browser window.

Now that you are familiar with some of the basic features in Excel, you can move on to working with worksheets.

Self study

1 Open excel0202. Add the Open button to the Quick Access Toolbar.

2 While in the document, increase the zoom level to 150 percent, and then decrease it to 120 percent.

3 Change the shading of the top line to any light color that you like, and change the font color to any dark color that you like.

4 Open any document in Excel. Practice using the hot keys:

- Activate the Insert tab and take a look at the different commands and their hot keys.

- Activate the Page Layout tab and use the Margins hot key to see what happens.

- Activate the View tab and use the Zoom hot key to zoom in.

5 Using the Options menu in Backstage view, add the Insert Cells button to the Quick Access Toolbar.

Review

Questions

1 What are the Ribbon groups on the Page Layout tab?

2 How do you access Backstage view in Excel?

3 In excel0202, what is the cell location of the town where Cindy Lou Who lives?

4 What are two ways to enter data into a cell?

5 What does the Tab key do when you are navigating through an Excel worksheet?

Answers

1 The Ribbon groups on the Page Layout tab are Themes, Page Setup, Scale to Fit, Sheet Options, and Arrange.

2 Click the File tab on the Ribbon to display Backstage view.

3 D16 is the cell location of Whoville, Cindy Lou Who's hometown.

4 You can add data into a cell by typing into the cell or by entering the data in the Cell Contents box of the formula bar.

5 The Tab key moves the cursor to the next cell to the right.

What you'll learn in this lesson:

- Generating a new workbook from an existing one
- Selecting, deleting, and modifying cells
- Copying and pasting data
- Merging cells
- Formatting cells for numbers

Editing Cells

In this lesson, you will learn how to edit information in cells, and transfer data between workbooks and between cells. You will also learn how to merge cells and format them for numbers.

Starting up

You will work with several files from the Excel03lessons folder in this lesson. Make sure that you have loaded the OfficeLessons folder onto your hard drive from *www.DigitalClassroomBooks.com/Office2010*. See "Loading lesson files" on page XXIV.

See Lesson 3 in action!

Use the accompanying video to gain a better understanding of how to use some of the features shown in this lesson. The video tutorial for this lesson can be found at www.DigitalClassroomBooks.com/Office2010.

Generating a new workbook from an existing one

You can generate a new workbook from one that already exists by using the New from Existing option on the Available Templates page. This comes in handy if you need to base a new workbook on the format of one you have already completed. When you use this feature, Excel makes a copy of the file you want to use as your template. When it creates the copy, Excel appends the number 1 to the end of the filename to avoid overwriting the original file.

Let's create a vacation itinerary from a document that was once a weekly meal planner. Using the existing document format saves time, by eliminating the need to create everything from a blank document.

1   Launch Excel.

2   Click File > New > New from existing.

The New tab displays many options to start a new workbook such as; blank workbook, recent template, sample template, or New from existing.

3   In the New from existing dialogue box, navigate to OfficeLessons > Excel03lessons > excel0301, and then click Create New. Notice how Excel names the file excel03011.

Selecting cells

When you select a cell, you can apply changes to it. If you want to apply changes to multiple cells at once, you need to select them all first. You can select one or multiple cells by using of the following cell combinations:

IF YOU WANT TO SELECT...	THEN
A range of cells	Click the first cell in the range. Drag across the cells and release the mouse button.
All cells in a worksheet	Click the Select Worksheet button ( ) located between the row and column headers.
Non-consecutive cells	Press and hold Ctrl while clicking cells.
Non-consecutive columns and rows	Press and hold Ctrl while clicking column or row headers.
Multiple columns	Click and drag across column or row headers.

Let's select a column:

1   In excel03011, position the mouse pointer over the E column header. The mouse pointer changes to a small down arrow.

2   Click the column header. Excel highlights the E column.

Now that you have selected a column, you can make changes to it. In the next example, you will delete the column.

Deleting data or cells

Beginning with the weekly meal planner, you're now going to adjust the rows and columns to make the document more suitable for the new workbook you are creating. When deleting data, you have to decide whether you want to delete just the data contained within the cell or the entire cell.

If you only want to delete the contents of the cell, just press the Delete key. This leaves the cell but removes the contents.

Deleting an entire column

1   If it isn't still selected from the previous exercise, click the column header for column E.

2   Click Home. In the Cells group, click the down arrow next to the word Delete to display the Delete Cells menu. Click to select the Delete Cells option.

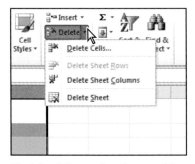

The Delete Cell menu allows the user to delete cells, rows, or columns from the sheet or table.

You can also right-click a cell in the column, and click Delete to display the Delete dialog box. In the dialog box, click Entire Column and then click OK.

When you delete a cell, column, or row by right-clicking it, Excel displays a menu.

The Delete dialogue box provides multiple options for deleting cells.

To delete selected rows:

1   Click the row 8 header and drag down through to row 15.

2   Click Home. In the Cells group, select Delete.

You can always click the Undo button (⤺) on the Quick Access Toolbar if you delete something by mistake.

In your current spreadsheet, you should only have four columns and seven rows with text.

Using the Clear command

In the Editing group, the Clear button (⌀) has a unique function in Excel. For example, you may need to remove an entry while retaining the cell format. This is when you would want to use the Clear command. When you click the Clear button, Excel displays a drop-down menu offering six options that perform a clearing operation.

OPTION	DESCRIPTION
Clear All	Removes both the contents and formatting assigned to the current cell selection.
Clear Formats	Removes just the formatting assigned to the current cell selection without removing the contents.
Clear Contents	Removes just the contents in the current cell selection without removing the formatting assigned to it. This has the same effect as pressing the Delete key.
Clear Comments	Removes just the comments assigned to the cells in the selection without changing the contents or the formatting.
Clear Hyperlinks	Removes hyperlinks from the cells in the selection without removing the formatting.
Remove Hyperlinks	Removes both the hyperlinks and their formatting.

Entering data

Before you enter data into a cell, you must select the cell. If you enter data into a cell that is already populated, then the old data is lost. To finalize the data entry, you can either press Enter or click outside the cell. To clear an entry made without losing previous data, press ESC before navigating away from that cell. If data was already changed, you can select the undo button to revert back to previous data.

To enter data:

1   In excel03011, select Row 1 by clicking the row header.

2   Type **London Vacation Itinerary** in place of Weekly Meal Planner and press Enter.

The space is too small for the data that you entered. To fix this, you can merge the cells to match the formatting of cell A1.

3   Click to select cell A1, press and hold Shift, and then click and drag to the end of column D.

4   Click Home. In the Alignment group, select Merge and Center, and then press Enter.

5   Click to select cell A3 and type **Day 1**.

6   Make the following additional changes to column A:

   • Select cell A5 and type **Day 2**.

   • Select cell A7 and type **Day 3**.

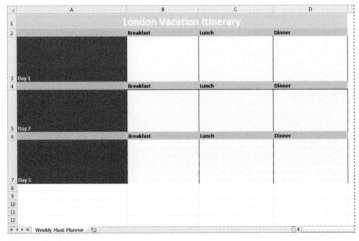

The completed changes.

Copying and pasting within Excel

You can copy a range of cells and paste it into another range of cells within the worksheet.

1   Click cell B2, and type **Morning**.

2   Press Tab, the cursor is now positioned in cell C2, and type **Afternoon**.

3   Press Tab, the cursor is now positioned in cell D2, and type **Evening**.

4   Click cell B2.

5   In the Home tab, click Copy (⬚) in the Clipboard group.

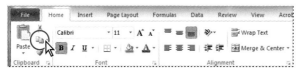

The Copy button copies the selection and places it on the clipboard.

6   Click cell B4, and click Paste (⬚). Click cell B6, and click Paste.

You have now replaced all the cells that contained Breakfast with Morning by using the Paste command. You could have also used the keyboard shortcut Ctrl+V.

7   Repeat the procedure to copy and paste *Afternoon* replacing *Lunch*. You can use Ctrl+C to copy and Ctrl+V to paste, if you prefer.

8   Repeat the procedure again to copy and paste *Evening* replacing *Dinner*.

Copying from Word and pasting into Excel

The Clipboard is a standard Windows feature that you can use to help with pasting selections. When you use the Copy or Cut command, the selection moves to the Clipboard.

In Excel as in Word, you can collect multiple selections in the Clipboard, and then paste them into a document. The Clipboard serves as a holding area for up to 24 selections in Microsoft Office documents.

To view the Clipboard, click the dialog box launcher in the bottom-right corner of the Clipboard group on the Home tab.

The Clipboard dialogue box launcher shows the Office Clipboard Task Pane.

The Clipboard task pane contains the last several items that you copied.

Clipboard task pane.

To copy from a Word document and paste the selection into an Excel worksheet:

1 Launch Word.

2 In Word, click File > Open. The Open dialog box appears.

3 Navigate to OfficeLessons > Excel03lessons and select excel0302.

4 Select the morning activity for Day 1 and click Home > Copy, in the Clipboard group.

5 Make the Excel document active by clicking the Excel document on the status bar: excel03011.

6 Click the dialog box launcher in the Clipboard group to display the Clipboard and its contents, if it is not already visible.

7 Click cell B3.

8 In the Clipboard task pane, click the Tower of London activity that you just copied to it. Excel pastes the selection into cell B3. The selection needs to be contained in the one cell, so you will wrap the text within the cell.

9 In the Home tab and in the Alignment group, select Wrap Text.

10 Repeat the copy-and-paste procedure using text from the Word document for the following:

- Day 1 Afternoon and Evening
- Day 2 Morning, Afternoon and Evening
- Day 3 Morning, Afternoon and Evening

11 Click File > Save. The Save As dialogue box will appear. Navigate to Excel03lessons folder and click Save.

12 Click File > Close.

13 In the Word document. Click file > Exit to close Word.

Paste Options

You may have noticed that when you paste a selection into a cell, a drop-down menu appears in the lower-right corner of the selected cell.

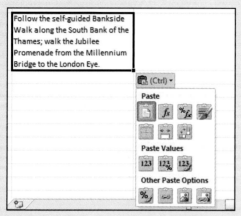

Paste Options menu.

The paste options that Excel displays in this menu only apply for the active selection:

- The Paste option pastes text, values, formulas, and cell formatting into the cell.

- The Keep Source Formatting option copies the formatting from the original cells and pastes it into the destination cell along with the data.

Formatting cells for numbers

The Number group on the Home tab displays the Number Format drop-down menu that offers options to format numbers. The format of a cell defines how Excel treats and displays the data stored inside the cell. In this exercise, you'll practice formatting numbers.

To open the document you need for this lesson:

1   Choose File > Open. Excel displays the Open dialog box.

2   Navigate to the ex03lesson folder.

3   Click excel0303 and then click Open.

4   Select File > Save As. Excel displays the Save As dialog box.

5   In the Save As text box, type **excel0303_done** and then click Save.

6   Click cell B2 and drag to cell B3; in the Number group, in the Number Format drop-down menu, select Currency.

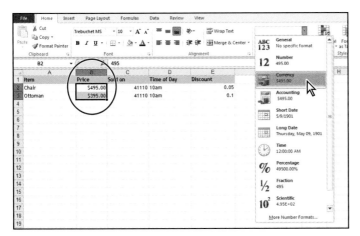

You can select a variety of number formats.

Excel adds decimal places and a currency symbol to each number.

7   Click cell C2 and drag to cell C3; in the Number group, click the Launch Dialog Box button located on the lower-right side of the Number group to open the Format Cells dialog box.

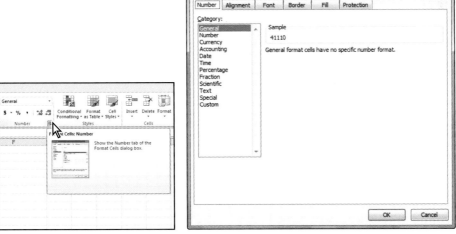

The Launch Dialog Box button displays the Format Cells dialog box.

8 In the Category list, click Date. Excel displays the date formats you can choose.

9 Select the fourth choice on the list, 3/14/01, and then click OK.

10 Highlight cells D2 and D3 and select Percentage from the Number Format drop-down menu. Excel converts the numbers to percent and adds a percent sign. The following table lists the number formats and explains each one.

FORMAT	DESCRIPTION
General	Use this format for cells with general numbers. Excel does not change the format of the number.
Number	Use this format to display numbers. Excel lets you choose the amount of decimal places and whether to use a separator for values over 999, such as 1,000. You can also control the way Excel displays negative numbers, such as displaying negative numbers in red.
Currency	Use this category to specify a currency symbol.
Accounting	Use this category to specify a currency symbol and align currency symbols and decimal points.
Date	Use this category to display the contents of a cell as a date.
Time	Use this category to display the contents of a cell as time.
Percentage	Use this category to multiply the cell contents by 100 and display the result with a percentage symbol.
Fraction	Use this category to display the number as a fraction.
Scientific	Use this category when you want to display the contents of a cell in scientific notation.
Text	Use this category when you want to enter a text description containing numbers or special characters. Excel treats the numbers as text.

11 Click File > Save, and then click File > Exit.

Self study

Open excel03011 and make the following changes:

1 In the Day 1 Morning cell or B3, replace the contents by typing **Meet friends for breakfast at the hotel**.

2 Click Undo on the Quick Access Toolbar to return the previous contents to the cell.

3 Select the Day 2 Afternoon cell.

4 Copy the cell by selecting it and clicking Home > Clipboard group > Copy.

5 Open the Clipboard task pane to see the selection on the Clipboard.

6 Select the Day 3 Afternoon cell or C7.

7 Click the selection in the Clipboard to paste it into the Day 3 Afternoon cell.

Review

Questions

1 When you use the New from Existing command to create a new workbook, how does Excel avoid writing over the original file?

2 How do you select a range of cells?

3 Which of the Clear commands has the same effect as the Delete key?

4 What happens if you select a populated cell and enter data into it?

Answers

1 When you use the New from Existing command to create a new workbook, Excel appends the number 1 to the end of the filename. This creates a new file without overwriting the existing one.

2 To select a range of cells, click the first cell in the range, drag across the cells, and release the mouse button.

3 Clear Contents has the same effect. Like the Delete key, it removes just the contents in the current cell selection without removing the formatting assigned to the cell.

4 You lose the original data that was in the cell.

What you'll learn in this lesson:

- Selecting and changing font style, size, color, and characteristics

- Aligning text

- Adding borders and shading to a range

- Adding rows and columns and changing column widths and row heights

Formatting Cell Ranges

In this lesson, you will learn how to change the appearance of text, columns, and rows in your spreadsheets. This is useful when you want to present information to others, or simply to make the text more readable.

Starting up

You will work with several files from the Excel04lessons folder in this lesson. Make sure that you have loaded the OfficeLessons folder onto your hard drive from *www.DigitalClassroomBooks.com/Office2010*. See "Loading lesson files" on page XXIV.

See Lesson 4 in action!

Use the accompanying video to gain a better understanding of how to use some of the features shown in this lesson. The video tutorial for this lesson can be found at www.DigitalClassroomBooks.com/Office2010.

Working with fonts

You can change many characteristics of the fonts in your worksheet to give it some style. For example, you might want to increase the font size of the title to make it stand out. Changing the title's color to green and font weight to bold, for example, can give the worksheet a more professional look.

1   Launch Excel.

2   Choose File > Open. In the Open dialog box, navigate to the Excel04lessons folder located in the OfficeLessons folder that you copied to your computer from the DVD that came with this book, and then double-click excel0401 to open the file.

An Excel document opens to an unformatted worksheet.

3   Choose File > Save As, type **excel0401_done** and press Save.

Changing Fonts

Let's start by formatting a document. In the following steps, you'll change the font style, size, color, and characteristics.

1   Click cell A1 to select the title of the document.

2   On the Ribbon, click Home, and then click the dialog box launcher in the Font group.

The Font dialogue box launcher displays the Font tab of the Format Cells dialogue box.

3   In the Format Cells dialog box, make the following selections:

- From the Font menu, select Arial.

- From the list of Font styles, select Bold.

- From list of Font sizes, select 18.

- From the color drop-down menu, select White.

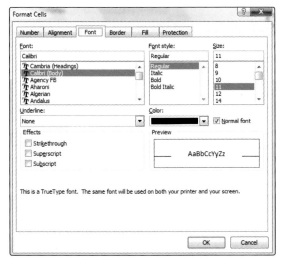

Format Cells dialog box.

4   Click OK. Excel changes the formatting of the title to reflect your selections.

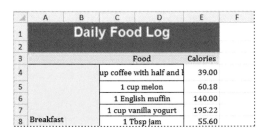

The completed formatting changes.

Aligning cell data

You can control how cell data aligns within your worksheet. Excel automatically aligns data to sit at the bottom of the cell, with text to the left and number data to the right. To improve the appearance of your worksheet, you can change the horizontal and vertical alignment. With the excel0401_done document still open, let's change the text alignment in some of the worksheet cells:

1 Click within the cell that contains *Breakfast*, and if it is not already active, click Home.

2 Click the dialog box launcher in the Alignment group.

Dialog box launcher in the Alignment group displays the Alignment tab of the Format Cells dialogue box.

3 In the Format Cells dialog box that appears, make the following selections in the Alignment tab:

- From the Horizontal drop-down menu, select Center.

- From the Vertical drop-down menu, select Center.

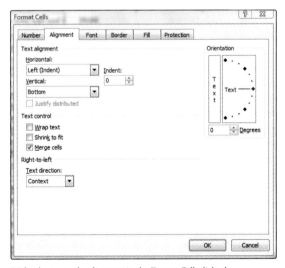

Make changes to the alignment in the Format Cells dialog box.

4 Click OK.

The word *Breakfast* appears in the middle of the cell.

Formatting text

The mini-toolbar appears when you select text. In this exercise, you will use it to format the text in the Breakfast cell. You will then copy the formatting to other cells using the format painter.

1   Double-click inside the Breakfast cell to make the cell active, and double-click the word *Breakfast*.

2   Move your cursor over the faded mini-toolbar that appears above the selected word.

The mini-toolbar allows quick Font selections.

 If the toolbar disappears, right-click to display it again.

3   Select Arial from the Font drop-down menu and click Bold (**B**).

4   Click the Font Color drop-down menu (A), and select the first blue font under Theme Colors.

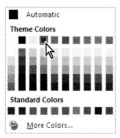

The Font drop-down menu provides many color choices for the selected text.

5   Click Increase Font Size (A˙) until the size of the font reaches 16.

6   Click outside the Breakfast cell and back inside Breakfast cell to deselect the single word and select the entire cell.

7   On the Ribbon, click Home. In the Font group, click the down-arrow to the right of the Fill Color (◈).

8 On the drop-down menu, select the first gray font under Theme Colors.

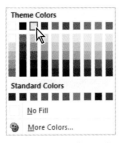

Select the first gray font in the top row under Theme Colors.

Using the format painter

Now, let's copy the formatting of the Breakfast cell to the Lunch, Dinner, and Snack cells using the format painter.

1 Click inside the Breakfast cell.

2 In the Clipboard group, double-click Format Painter (◀). Excel selects the Breakfast cell and adds a paintbrush to the cursor.

 If you click the Format Painter icon only once, it only applies the formatting change once.

3 Click inside the Lunch, Dinner, and Snack cells. These cells now have the same format as the Breakfast cell. Click the Format Painter icon to deactivate the tool.

4 Choose File > Save to save your work.

Adding borders and shading

A range in Excel is a block of cells. In the following steps, you will select and merge cells to make them one unit. Then you will add borders and shading.

1 Click cell H2 and drag to select cells I2 and J2.

2 On the Ribbon, click Home. In the Alignment group, click Merge & Center (⊞). The cells merge into one unit and the text is centered.

3 Repeat the procedure for cells H3, I3, and J3.

Now, you'll add the borders and shading.

4 Click inside cell H2 and drag to cell H3 to select both cell ranges.

5 Click Home. In the Font group, click the down-arrow to the right of Border (⊞).

6   On the Border drop-down menu, select All Borders. This places a border on all lines in the selected ranges.

The Borders drop-down menu displays the many border options

7   To add the shading, click the H2 cell and drag to cell H3, if it is not already highlighted. Then, click the Fill Color drop-down menu in the Font group. Select the first gray shade under Theme Colors.

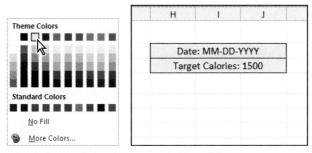

Select the first gray shade in the top row under Theme Colors.

Adding columns and rows

You can add columns and rows to your worksheet if you need to insert information. In the following steps, you'll add a column for Fat between the Food and Calories columns.

1   Click the E column header. This should select the entire column.

2   On the Ribbon, click Home. In the Cells group, click on the down arrow next to or below Insert and select Insert Sheet Columns.

3   Click inside cell E3 and type **Fat**.

4   Click the H column header, and then select Home. In the Cells group, select the down arrow next to or below Delete and select Delete Sheet Columns. Excel deletes column H.

Resizing columns and rows

You can resize the worksheet's columns and rows to make them look more appealing. In the following steps, you'll resize the Food column so the foods listed fit within the column space.

1   Position the cursor over the border of the header between columns D and E.

2   Click and drag the border until all the foods fit within the column.

You can also click Home > Cells group > Format > Autofit Column Width to resize a selected column to fit existing text.

Assigning Number Formats

You can use number formatting to control the appearance of numerical data in your worksheet. Excel offers formatting choices that you can apply to single cells, ranges, columns, rows, or an entire worksheet.

1   Click in the cell under Calories and drag to the end of the column to select it.

2   In the Ribbon, make sure you are on the Home tab, and then click the Number Format drop-down menu in the Number group.

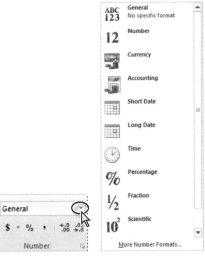

Number group allows you to choose how the values in a cell are displayed.

3 Select Number from the drop-down menu. Notice that Excel adds decimal places to the numbers.

4 Place the cursor in cell H5, select Currency from the drop-down menu, type **12**, then press Enter. Excel adds a dollar sign to the number.

5 Now, place the cursor in cell H6, select Time from the drop-down menu, type **12**, then press Enter. Excel formats the number for time.

6 Press the Save button on the Quick Access Toolbar to save your work.

Finding the sum of a column

You can use AutoSum to quickly sum a range of numbers in a column or row.

1 Click the first empty cell below the Calories column, or cell E24.

2 Select Home > Editing group > AutoSum.

The AutoSum command displays the sum of the selected cells directly after the selected cells.

A formula appears in the cell that you selected, and Excel selects the column above it.

3 Click AutoSum again. Excel displays the total of the Calories column.

Now you will decrease the number of decimal places in the total sum.

4 With the total still selected, select Home > Number group > Decrease Decimal.

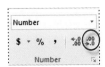

The Decrease Decimal command shows fewer decimal places.

5 Click Decrease Decimal again, so that the total shows a whole number.

6 Select File > Save and then select File > Close.

Congratulations! You have completed the lesson.

Self study

1 In the excel0401_done document, make the following changes:

- In the title Daily Food Log, select Verdana for the font style.

- Choose a light gray font for the color of the title.

- Add italics to the title so it is in bold italics.

2 Select the headings Food and Calories, and use the mini-toolbar to change the font style to Verdana.

3 Remove the column entitled Fat.

Review

Questions

1 What is the purpose of the AutoSum command?

2 What command would you use to copy the format of a cell range to another cell range?

3 If you want the contents of the data in a column to fit between the borders, which command would you use?

Answers

1 AutoSum quickly performs addition on a range of numbers in a column or row.

2 The Format Painter command copies the format of a cell range to another cell range.

3 You would select Home > Cells group > Format > Autofit Column Width to resize a selected column to fit existing text.

What you'll learn in this lesson:

- Understanding Excel formulas
- Function types
- Building an AutoSum formula
- Defining and using range names in a formula

Building Formulas and Functions

In this lesson, you will discover how to build basic formulas and functions in Excel spreadsheets.

Starting up

You will work with several files from the Excel05lessons folder in this lesson. Make sure that you have loaded the OfficeLessons folder onto your hard drive from *www.DigitalClassroomBooks.com/Office2010*. See "Loading lesson files" on page XXIV.

See Lesson 5 in action!

Use the accompanying video to gain a better understanding of how to use some of the features shown in this lesson. The video tutorial for this lesson can be found at www.DigitalClassroomBooks.com/Office2010.

Understanding Excel formulas

Formulas play a critical role in Excel, allowing you to perform calculations on the data in your worksheet. You can build simple to complex formulas by using the tools that Excel provides.

Formula

A formula is a mathematical equation used to calculate a value. In Excel, a formula must begin with an equal sign (=). The equal sign tells Excel to interpret the data in the cell as a formula. For example, if you type **=2+6** in a cell, Excel displays a result (8).

Operator

An operator is a sign or symbol specifying the type of calculation to perform, such as a plus sign (+). In the formula =B1+B2, the operator is the plus sign which adds the values in cells B1 and B2.

Operand

Every Excel formula includes at least one operand, which is the data that Excel uses in the calculation. The simplest type of operand is a number; however, most Excel formulas include references to worksheet data, such as a cell address (B1).

Arithmetic formula

An arithmetic formula combines a numeric operand (a number or a function that returns a numerical value as a result) with an operator to perform a calculation. As you can see in the following table, there are seven arithmetic operators you can use to construct arithmetic formulas.

Examples of arithmetic formulas:

OPERATOR	NAME	EXAMPLE	RESULT
+	Addition	= 10 + 5	15
-	Subtraction	= 10 – 5	5
-	Negation	= -10	-10
*	Multiplication	= 10 * 5	50
/	Division	= 10 / 5	2
%	Percentage	= 10%	0.1
^	Exponentiation	= 10 ^ 5	100000

Comparison formula

A comparison formula combines a numeric operand, such as a whole number, with special operators to compare one operand with another. A comparison formula returns a logical result of 0 or 1. This means that if the comparison is true, the formula returns a value of 1, and if the comparison is false, the formula returns a value of 0.

There are six operators you can use to construct comparison formulas, as shown in the following table.

OPERATOR	NAME	EXAMPLE	RESULT
=	Equal to	= 10 = 5	0
<	Less than	= 10 < 5	0
< =	Less than or equal to	= 10 <= 5	0
>	Greater than	= 10 > 5	1
> =	Greater than or equal to	= 10 >= 5	1
< >	Not equal to	= 10 < > 5	1

Operator precedence

The order in which Excel performs the calculations is important. Excel evaluates a formula according to a predefined order of precedence, which is determined by the formula operators. For the formula =3+5^2, Excel performs the exponentiation before the addition because of the operator precedence, resulting in 28. The following table shows how Excel orders operations.

OPERATION	PRECEDENCE
Parentheses ( )	1st
Negation (-)	2nd
Percentage (%)	3rd
Exponentiation (^)	4th
Multiplication (*) and division (/)	5th
Addition (+) and subtraction (-)	6th
Comparison < = >	7th

Building a formula

You can add a formula to a worksheet cell by starting the formula with an equal sign (=) and then typing the operands and operators. When you add a formula to a cell, Excel displays the formula result in the cell, not the actual formula.

In this exercise, you will open a document and save it. You'll then build a formula.

To open the document you need for this lesson:

1　Launch Excel. Excel displays a blank page.

2　Choose File > Open and navigate to the Excel05lessons folder.

3　Click excel0501 and then click Open.

4　Select File > Save As.

5　In the Save As text field, type **excel0501_done** and then click Save.

6 Click inside cell B5, located to the right of the words *SALES TOTAL*, and then type an equal sign (=). Excel displays the equal sign in the formula bar.

When you type a formula into a cell, it also appears in the formula bar.

You can type the formula directly into the formula bar or into a particular cell.

7 In the worksheet, click cell B2. Excel inserts the cell address into the formula.

8 Type a plus sign (+) to begin adding the data from B2 with other cell contents.

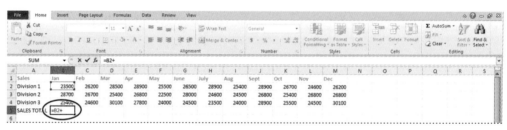

Type the formula in the cell.

9 In the active cell, we will continue to create the formula; click cell B3 and type another plus sign (+) and then click cell B4. The formula bar should now appear as follows: =B2+B3+B4.

10 Press Enter and Excel displays the total of the cells in column B, which represents the sales total for January.

11 Click File > Save, and then click File > Close.

If you need to change a formula, you can click the formula result. In this example, you would click cell B5. Excel redisplays the formula in the formula bar. After you make edits, press Enter.

Understanding Excel functions

To build powerful formulas, you may need to include one or more Excel functions as operands.

Function

A function is a predefined formula. An example is the SUM function that calculates the total of a list of numbers. You can use a function on its own preceded by an equal sign or as part of a larger formula.

Function structure

Every function has two components: a name that always appears in uppercase and arguments that appear within parentheses. Arguments are the inputs the function uses to perform the calculations. An example is SUM(A1,B2,C3), which adds the values of the cells A1, B2, and C3.

Function types

Excel offers a variety of function types, such as math and trig; however, statistical and financial functions are most common; these are shown in the following tables.

FUNCTION	DESCRIPTION
Common Statistical Functions	
AVERAGE	Returns the average of its arguments
COUNT	Counts the numbers in the argument list
MAX	Returns the maximum value of the arguments
MEDIAN	Returns the median value of the arguments
MIN	Returns the minimum value of the arguments
MODE	Returns the most common value of the arguments
STDEV	Returns the standard deviation based on a sample
STDEVP	Returns the standard deviation based on an entire population
Common Arguments for Financial Functions	
rate	The fixed rate of interest over the term of a loan or investment
nper	The number of payments or deposit periods over the term of a loan or investment
pmt	The periodic payment or deposit
pv	The present value of a loan (the principal) or the initial deposit in an investment
fv	The future value of a loan or investment
type	The type of payment or deposit: 0 (the default) for end-of-period payments or deposits; 1 for beginning-of-period payments or deposits
Common Financial Functions	
FV(rate,nper,pmt,pv,type)	Returns the future value of an investment or loan
IPMT(rate,per,nper,pv,fv,type)	Returns the interest payment for a specified period of a loan
NPER(rate,pmt,pv,fv,type)	Returns the number of periods for an investment or loan
PMT(rate,nper,pv,fv,type)	Returns the periodic payment for a loan or investment
PPMT(rate,per,nper,pv,fv,type)	Returns the principal payment for a specified period of a loan
PV(rate,nper,pmt,fv,type)	Returns the present value of an investment
RATE(nper,pmt,pv,fv,type,guess)	Returns the periodic interest rate for a loan or investment

Adding a function to a formula

Excel supplies a variety of built-in functions that you can use when building a formula. In this exercise, you'll calculate annual loan payments using the interest rate (rate), the total number of payments (nper), and the present value (pv) as arguments. You'll be using knowledge that you learned in Lesson 3, "Editing Cells" in this section when you calculate the yearly payment.

To open the document you need for this lesson:

1 Choose File > Open and navigate to the Excel05lessons folder.

2 Click excel0502 and then click Open.

3 Select File > Save As.

4 In the Save As text field, type **excel0502_done**, and then click Save.

5 Click in cell B5, located to the right of *Yearly Payment*, and type the equal sign (=).

6 Click the Formulas tab on the Ribbon, and then click Insert Function (*fx*) found in the Function Library group.

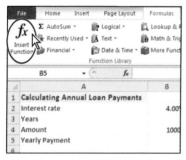 

You can choose a function from a variety of categories.

7 In the Insert Functions dialog box that opens, select Financial from the Or select a category drop-down menu. In the Select a function section, scroll down to select PMT, and then click OK. Excel displays the Function Arguments dialog box.

In the Insert Functions dialog box that opens, select Financial from the Or select a category drop-down menu.

8 Click in the Rate text field, and type **B2** or click on the cell B2. Excel displays the value of cell B2 (.04) to the right of the text field.

9 Click in the Nper text field, and type **B3** or click on the cell B3. Excel displays the value of cell B3 (5) to the right of the text field.

10 Click in the Pv text field, and type **B4** or click on the cell B4. Excels displays the value of cell B4 (10000) to the right of the text field.

11 Click OK, and Excel displays the formula in cell B5. The annual payment is $2,246.27. Excel displays the data as currency because this is a financial function. Lesson 3 "Editing Cells," explains how to format cells for different results. Notice that the result appears in parentheses to indicate a negative value. In loan calculations, money that you pay is always a negative amount. You can now save and close this document.

12 Click File > Save, and then click File > Close.

If you want to calculate the monthly payment, you must convert the rate and term values by dividing the annual interest rate by 12 and multiplying the term by 12. The function PMT(B2/12, B3*12, B4) calculates the monthly payment.

Adding a row or column of numbers

You can add worksheet numbers by building a formula that uses the SUM function. The SUM function is useful in adding individual cells. You can also specify a reference to a column or row in the function's argument to add a column or row of numbers.

To open the document you need for this lesson:

1 Choose File > Open and navigate to the Excel05lessons folder.

2 Click excel0503 and then click Open.

3 Select File > Save As.

4 In the Save As text field, type **excel0503_done** and then click Save.

5 Click in cell C21, type **=SUM(** within the cell, and Excel displays a small banner that shows the function's arguments.

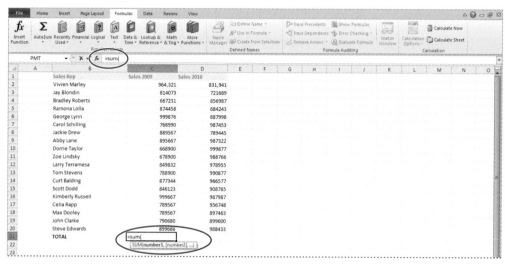

Excel displays the function's arguments in a banner.

Excel displays required arguments in bold type.

6 Click in cell C2 and drag to cell C20 and release. Excel adds a reference for the range to the formula.

7 Type the end parenthesis, **)**, to show you are done adding the data range for this function and press Enter. Excel adds the column of numbers and displays the result in cell C21.

8 Click File > Save, and then click File > Close.

Building an AutoSum formula

You can use the AutoSum formula to add a range of cells. A range can be a single cell, or many cells. You can use AutoSum to add cells in a contiguous (cells joined together) range of cells, or a non-contiguous (cells not joined together) range.

To open the document you need for this lesson:

1 Choose File > Open and navigate to the Excel05lessons folder.

2 Click excel0504 and then click Open.

3 Select File > Save As.

4 In the Save As text field, type **excel0504_done** and then click Save.

5   Click cell M5, and then click AutoSum located in the Function Library group on the Formulas tab.

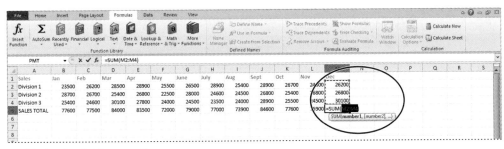

Excel displays the cell addresses to add.

Notice that the formula automatically chooses the cells directly above the current cell to perform the calculation.

The cell you select to display the result should be directly below or to the right of the range you want to add. While adding, if AutoSum encounters a blank row or a cell with text in it, AutoSum stops calculating and displays the result.

6   Press Enter. Excel displays the result in cell M5.

You can also press Alt+= for the AutoSum shortcut.

AutoSum can also perform other functions automatically, such as finding the average. In this exercise, you'll calculate the annual sales average using AutoSum.

1   Click cell N5, and then click the down arrow on the AutoSum button to display the AutoSum drop-down menu.

The AutoSum menu lets you perform many different functions.

2 Select Average, and then press Enter. Excel displays the average sales for the year.

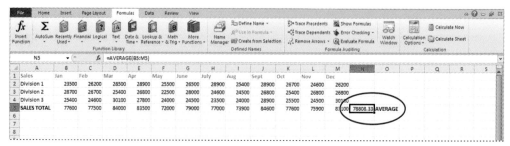

Excel calculates the average of the numbers to the left of the results cell.

3 Click File > Save, and then click File > Close.

Copying a formula

You can copy a formula to a different part of a worksheet. When you copy a formula, Excel adjusts the range references to the new location. In this exercise, you'll copy a formula to an entire column to calculate the average for each student.

To open the document you need for this lesson:

1 Choose File > Open and navigate to the Excel05lessons folder.

2 Click excel0505 and then click Open.

3 Select File > Save As.

4 In the Save As text field, type **excel0505_done** and then click Save.

5 Click in cell E3, and position the cursor over the bottom-right corner of the cell. The cursor changes to a cross (+).

6 Click and drag through cell E20 and release the mouse button. Excel calculates the average for the year for all students and displays the results in column E.

Now, you'll find the best grade for each term. The best grade for Fall is 95 as shown in cell B21. Let's copy the formula to display the best grades for Winter and Spring.

7 Click in cell B21, and then move the cursor over the bottom-right corner of the cell. The cursor changes to a cross (+).

8 Click and drag through cell D21. Excel displays the maximum grades for Winter and Spring.

9 Click File > Save, and then click File > Close.

Defining and using range names in formulas

You can make your formulas easier to build and read by using range names as operands. For example, it is clearer to display a formula as AVERAGE(Expenses) than AVERAGE(B2:B10). Before you can use a range name in a formula, you have to define the name.

To open the document you need for this lesson:

1   Choose File > Open and navigate to the Excel05lessons folder.

2   Click excel0506 and then click Open.

3   Select File > Save As.

4   In the Save As text field, type **excel0506_done** and then click Save.

To define a range name:

1   Click in cell D3, and then click the Formulas tab. In the Defined Names group, click Define Name.

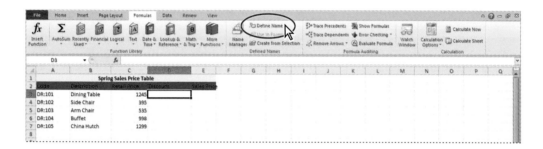

 The first character of the name must be a letter or an underscore (_). The name cannot include spaces or cell references and must be less than 255 characters.

2   In the New Name dialog box, type **Discount_rate** in the Name text field; type **15%** in the Refers to: text field, and then click OK.

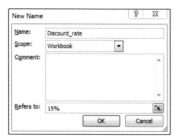

Enter a name in the New Name dialog box.

To use a name to build a formula:

1 Click in cell D3, and then type a equal sign (=).

2 Click in cell C3 to select the retail price for the first item, and then type an asterisk (*).

3 Click Use in Formula in the Defined Names group. Excel displays a list of the defined names. Select Discount_rate and press Enter.

4 In cell D3, click the bottom-right corner of the cell, and drag through cell D7.

Excel displays the discount for each item in column D.

5 Click File > Save, and then click File > Close.

Congratulations! In this lesson you have discovered how to build and use formulas and functions using the tools that Excel provides.

Self study

1 Open the excel0502_done document. Calculate the annual loan payment using a 2.2% interest rate.

2 Open the excel0503_done document. Calculate the sum of the sales for 2010.

3 Open the excel0504_done document. Calculate the sales average for Division 1 and Division 2.

Review

Questions

1 What is the name for a sign or symbol that specifies the type of calculation to perform, such as a plus sign?

2 What are the two possible results for a comparison formula?

3 What are the two components for every function?

4 What character must begin each formula?

Answers

1 A sign or symbol that specifies the type of calculation to perform is called an operator.

2 A comparison formula can return a result of 0 for false or 1 for true.

3 The two components for every function are a name that must appear in uppercase and arguments that appear in parentheses.

4 An equal sign must be the first character in every formula.

What you'll learn in this lesson:

- Exploring chart elements
- Understanding chart types
- Creating a chart
- Adjusting and moving a chart
- Adding chart titles

Displaying Data with Charts

In this lesson, you will discover how to create and format charts in Excel spreadsheets.

Starting up

You will work with several files from the Excel06lessons folder in this lesson. Make sure that you have loaded the OfficeLessons folder onto your hard drive from *www.DigitalClassroomBooks.com/Office2010*. See "Loading lesson files" on page XXIV.

See Lesson 6 in action!

Use the accompanying video to gain a better understanding of how to use some of the features shown in this lesson. The video tutorial for this lesson can be found at www.DigitalClassroomBooks.com/Office2010.

Exploring chart elements

You can quickly convert your worksheet data into easy-to-read charts. A chart is a graphic representation of data. As data in a worksheet changes, the chart changes to reflect this.

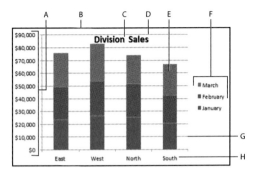

A. Vertical (value) axis. **B.** *Chart area.* **C.** *Chart title.* **D.** *Plot area.*
E. *Data marker.* **F.** *Legend.* **G.** *Gridlines.* **H.** *Horizontal (category) axis.*

Chart area

The chart area consists of everything inside the chart window, including all the chart elements listed below.

Chart title

The chart title identifies the subject of the chart.

Vertical (value) axis

The vertical axis (also known as the value or y-axis) shows the data values in the chart, such as hours worked or units sold.

Gridlines

Gridlines are horizontal and vertical extensions of the tick marks on each axis, and make the chart easier to read.

Horizontal (category) axis

The horizontal axis (also known as the category or x-axis) shows the categories in the chart, such as months of the year or branch offices.

Legend

The legend is a key that identifies patterns, colors, or symbols associated with the data markers in a chart data series.

Plot area

This is the area in the chart where the data is plotted, and includes the axes and data markers.

Data marker

A data marker is a symbol on the chart that represents a single value in the worksheet, such as a bar in a bar chart or a wedge in a pie chart. A group of related data markers (such as all the green columns in the example on the previous page) constitute a single data series.

Understanding chart types

Excel offers several different chart types so that you can select one that corresponds best to the data you want to present. Excel also makes it easy to change the chart from one type to another once it is complete. The following table lists the 11 chart types that Excel offers.

CHART TYPE	DESCRIPTION
Area	Shows the relative importance of values over time. An area chart emphasizes the magnitude of change over time more than a line chart does.
Bar	Emphasizes the comparison between items at a fixed period of time. Values are marked on the horizontal grid, and so the data markers appear as horizontal bars.
Bubble	A type of XY chart that uses three values instead of two. In the third data series, Excel displays the plot points as bubbles; the larger the bubble, the larger the value.
Column	Shows variations in data over a period of time, or compares individual items. Categories appear horizontally and values appear vertically.
Doughnut	Shows how individual parts relate to a whole. A doughnut chart can display multiple data series, with each ring representing a different series.
Line	Shows how a data series changes over time, emphasizing trends rather than amount of change.
Pie	Shows the relationship of parts to a whole. Only one data series is used.
Radar	Shows changes in multiple data series relative to a center point as well as to each other.
Stock	Shows the fluctuation of values over a certain time period, such as stock prices or temperature fluctuations.
Surface	Plots trends in values across two dimensions in a continuous curve, and applies color to indicate where data series are in the same range. This is useful for comparing two data series to find the best combinations between them.
XY	Shows the relationship between numeric values in multiple data series that may not be apparent from looking at the data. In an XY chart, both axes show values.

Creating a chart

You can quickly convert spreadsheet data into an easy-to-read chart.

In this exercise, you will open a document and save it. You'll then create a chart using existing data.

To open the document you need for this lesson:

1   Launch Excel. Excel displays a blank page.

2   Choose File > Open and navigate to the Excel06lessons folder.

3   Click excel0601, and then click Open.

4   Select File > Save As and in the Save As text box, type **excel0601_done**, and then click Save.

5   Click cell A3, drag to cell D3, and then drag down to include rows A8 to D8 and release.

When you select the data for a chart, you can include headings and labels, but do not include totals and subtotals.

6   Click the Insert tab on the Ribbon, and then click Column in the Charts group to display the Column Charts menu.

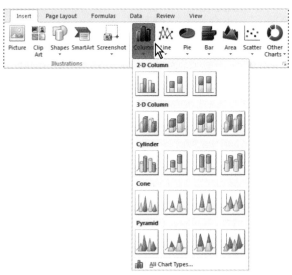

You can choose between 2D and 3D column charts.

7   In the Cylinder group, click the first chart on the left named Clustered Cylinder. Excel displays a chart on the worksheet and the Chart Tools tab on the Ribbon.

Adjusting and moving the chart

Excel allows you to adjust the chart on a worksheet. In this exercise, you'll adjust the size of the chart and then move it to a different location.

1   On the worksheet, move the cursor over the top-left corner of the chart until the cursor looks like a cross with arrows on the ends.

2   Click and drag until the upper-left corner of the chart sits in cell B2, and then release the mouse button.

3   Move the cursor over the bottom-left corner of the chart until the cursor looks like a double-sided arrow. Click and drag down and to the left until the corner of the chart sits in the center of cell A22.

Adding chart titles

In addition to adding a title to your chart, you can also add titles to the horizontal and vertical axes. In this exercise, you'll do all three.

1   In the excel0601_done document, click the top edge of the chart. Excel displays the Chart Tools on the Ribbon.

2   Click the Layout tab, and in the Labels group, click Chart Title to display the Chat Title menu.

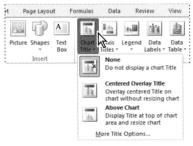

The Chart Title menu offers options for where to display the title.

3   Select Above Chart. Excel adds a text box above the chart and slightly resizes the chart.

4   Type **American Sport Attendance**. Notice that what you type displays in the formula bar. Press Enter, and Excel displays the title in the text box.

5   Choose File > Save to save your work.

Adding a horizontal axis title

1   In the Labels group on the Ribbon, click Axis Titles to display the Axis Titles menu.

2   Click Primary Horizontal Axis Title. Excel displays the Primary Horizontal Axis Title menu.

3   Select Title Below Axis. Excel displays a text box below the horizontal axis.

You can display the title below the title axis or choose not to display a title.

4   Type **Sport** and press Enter. Excel displays the title below the horizontal axis.

Adding a vertical axis title

1   In the Labels group on the Ribbon, click Axis Titles.

2   Click Primary Vertical Axis Title. Excel displays the Primary Vertical Axis Title menu.

3   Select Vertical Title. Excel displays a text box to the left of the vertical axis.

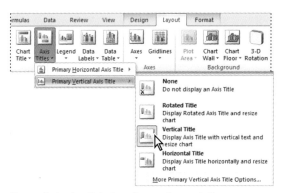

You can display the title horizontally, rotated, or vertically.

4   Type **Attendance**, and press Enter. Excel displays the title vertically.

Positioning a chart legend

The chart legend is a box that appears within the chart area and identifies the colors associated with each data series in the chart. You can move the legend from its default location (at the right of the plot area).

1   In the excel0601_done document, click the chart. On the Layout tab in the Labels group, click Legend to display the Legend menu.

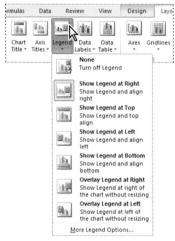

You can display the legend where it fits best on your chart.

2   Select Show Legend at Top. Excel moves the legend to the top of the chart area and adjusts the chart to fit.

3   Choose File > Save to save your work.

Displaying gridlines

Gridlines make a chart easier to read and analyze. Horizontal gridlines are useful with area, bubble, and column charts, while vertical gridlines are helpful with bar and line charts. In this exercise, you'll display the primary vertical gridlines in the chart.

1   In the excel0601_done document, click the chart and then in the Axes group on the Layout tab, click Gridlines.

2 Click Primary Vertical Gridlines. Excel displays the Primary Vertical Gridlines menu.

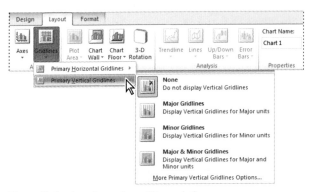

You can display the major or minor gridlines, or both.

3 Select Major Gridlines. Excel displays the major gridlines associated with the different categories.

Displaying a data table

You can make it easier to interpret a chart by adding a data table, which displays the source data for the chart. You can display the data table either with or without a legend. In this exercise, you'll include a legend.

1 In the excel0601_done document, click the chart, and in the Labels group on the Layout tab, click Data Table to display the Data Table menu.

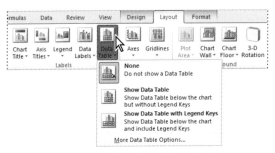

Excel lets you insert a data table with or without a legend.

2 Select Show Data Table with Legend Keys. Excel displays the data table and a legend.

3 Choose File > Save to save your work.

Changing the chart layout and style

Chart layout elements include the title, data labels, legend, gridlines, and data table. You can use Chart Tools to change the appearance and layout of the chart and its elements.

1   In the excel0601_done document, click the chart, and then click the Design tab.

2   In the Chart Layout group, click the More arrow located to the right of the chart layouts. (It looks like a down arrow with a line above it.) Excel displays the Chart Layouts menu.

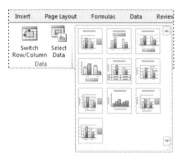

Excel offers 10 chart layouts.

3   Select Layout 1, which is located in the upper-left corner of the menu.

4   In the Chart Styles group, click the More arrow on the lower-right corner of the chart styles to display the Chart Styles menu.

Excel offers styles with various colors.

5   Select Style 35 to apply the style to the chart.

6   Click File > Save, and then click File > Close.

Formatting chart elements

You can customize the appearance of a chart by formatting the elements in the plot area.

To open the document you need for this lesson:

1 Choose File > Open and navigate to the Excel06lessons folder.

2 Click excel0602 and then click Open.

3 Select File > Save As and in the Save As text box, type **excel0602_done**. Click Save.

4 Click on any one of the percentages on the pie chart to select all five. Then on the Format tab under Chart Tools, click Text Outline in the WordArt Styles group to display the Text Outline menu.

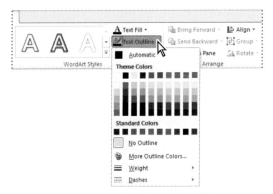

Text Outline allows users to choose from a variety of colors.

5 Select white, the first color on the left in the first row.

6 Move the cursor over the legend until the cursor changes to a star with arrows pointing outward, and then click. Excel selects the legend.

7 Press Ctrl+B to apply a bold font.

The legend is now bold.

Customizing a chart background

You can customize the background of a chart. For example, you can add a solid background, a textured fill, or a background picture. Be sure, however, that your background does not distract from the information in the chart. In this exercise, you'll add a color fill.

1   In the excel0602_done document, click the chart. In the Format tab, in the Shape Styles group, click Shape Fill to display the Shape fill menu.

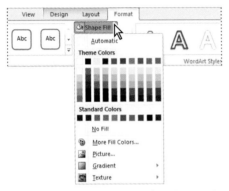

You can choose from a variety of colors for the background.

2   Select the fifth color over from the left in the second row, Blue Accent 1 Lighter 80%.

3   Choose File > Save to save your work.

Changing a chart type

If you are unhappy with the chart type you've chosen, you can change it to one that displays the data more effectively. In this exercise, you'll change the chart type to a bar chart.

1   In the excel0602_done document, click the chart and in the Design tab in the Type group, click Change Chart Type to open the Change Chart Type dialog box.

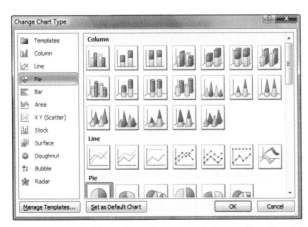

You can experiment with a variety of chart types in the Change Chart Type dialog box.

2 Select Bar from the list on the left side of the dialog box; select the first bar chart in the Bar group, and then click OK. Excel displays the data in a bar chart.

Because the legend does not serve a purpose in this type of chart, you'll hide the legend.

3 Click the Layout tab on the Ribbon, and in the Labels group, click Legend to display the Legend menu.

4 Select None. Excel hides the legend.

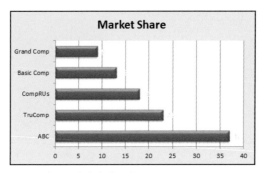

You can relocate or hide the legend.

5 Click File > Save, and then click File > Close.

Editing a chart element

Excel makes it easy to edit the elements in a chart. In this exercise, you'll edit the legend in a line chart.

To open the document you need for this lesson:

1 Choose File > Open and navigate to the Excel06lessons folder.

2 Click excel0603 and then click Open.

3 Select File > Save As. Excel displays the Save As dialog box.

4 In the Save As text box, type **excel0603_done** and then click OK.

5 In the worksheet, click the chart and then click the Design tab.

6   In the Data group, click Select Data to open the Select Data Source dialog box.

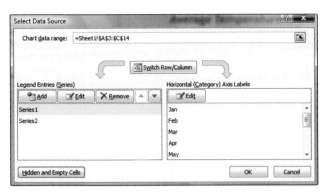

You can edit the legend entries in the Select Data Source dialog box.

7   In the left window, click Series 1, and then click Edit directly above it. Excel displays the Edit Series dialog box.

The Edit Series dialog box lets you enter a name for the series.

8   In the Series Name text field, type **Low**, and click OK. Excel changes Series 1 to Low in the left window.

9   In the left window, click Series 2, and then click Edit. Excel displays the Edit Series dialog box.

10   In the Series Name text field, type **High**, and click OK. Excel changes Series 2 to High in the left window.

11   Click OK. Excel changes the legend in the chart to read Low and High.

12   Choose File > Save to save your work.

Applying a style to a chart element

You can use Excel styles to make your charts look attractive and consistent. Each style applies its own background, outlines, and special effects. You simply select a specific chart element, apply a style to it, and you're done.

1   In the excel0603_done document, click the top line of the grid in the plot area. Excel selects the plot area.

2   Click the Format tab, and then click the More arrow in the bottom-right corner of the shape styles. Excel displays the Shape Styles menu.

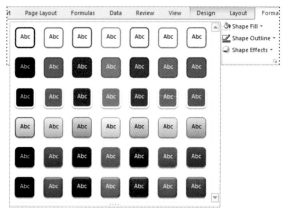

You can choose from many styles and colors in the Shape Styles menu.

3   Select the second style in the fourth row called Subtle Effect – Blue, Accent 1. Excel applies the style to the plot area.

4   Click the cursor on the outer corner of the chart so that the entire graph area is selected. In the Format tab, click the More arrow in the bottom-right corner of the shape styles. Excel displays the Shape Styles menu.

5   Select the farthest style to the right in the fourth row called Subtle Effect – Orange, Accent 6. Excel applies the chart background.

6   Click File > Save, and then click File > Close.

Adding Sparkline graphics to a worksheet

Sparkline graphics are simple cell-sized graphics that show data trends. As you can see in the following table, Excel offers three types of Sparklines.

SPARKLINE TYPE	DESCRIPTION
Line	Displays a simple line chart within a cell
Column	Displays a simple column chart within a cell
Win/Loss	Displays a simple win/loss chart within a cell

For this exercise, you'll reopen the excel0601_done document.

To open the document you need for this lesson:

1   Choose File > Open and navigate to the Excel06lessons folder.

2   Click excel0601_done and then click Open.

3   Click cell B5, drag to cell D5, and then release the mouse button. You may need to drag the graph down to view rows 5 through 7.

4   Click the Insert tab on the Ribbon, and in the Sparklines group, click Line. Excel displays the Create Sparklines dialog box showing the selected data range in the Data Range text box.

The Create Sparklines dialog box lets you indicate where you want the graphic to appear.

5   On the worksheet, click cell E5 and in the dialog box, click OK. Excel displays the graphic representing the data trend in baseball attendance.

6   Repeat steps 4 to 6, selecting cells B6 to D6 for the data and cell E6 to display the graphic. This time, Excel shows an upward trend for basketball attendance.

7   Click File > Save, and then click File > Close.

To edit the Sparkline graphic, edit the data to which the Sparkline refers.

Congratulations! You have completed this lesson. In this lesson you have discovered how to create and format charts using the tools that Excel provides.

Self study

1 Open the excel0601_done document. Create a Sparkline graphic for ice hockey attendance.

2 Display a data table for the American Sport Attendance chart.

3 Display major primary vertical gridlines.

Review

Questions

1 What is the name of the area of a chart that contains the gridlines?

2 What chart type emphasizes variations over a period of time, where categories appear horizontally and values appear vertically?

3 When you select the data for a chart, what should you not include?

Answers

1 The area of a chart that contains the gridlines is called the plot area.

2 A column chart is the type that emphasizes variations over a period of time, where categories appear horizontally and values appear vertically.

3 When you select the data for a chart, you should not include totals and subtotals.

What you'll learn in this lesson:

- Understanding data lists
- Setting data validation rules
- Converting a range to a table
- Creating a data table
- Summarizing data with subtotals

Analyzing Excel Data

In this lesson, you'll discover how to use Excel to analyze data. When you analyze data, you apply tools to organize, study, and reach conclusions about a collection of information.

Starting up

You will work with several files from the Excel07lessons folder in this lesson. Make sure that you have loaded the OfficeLessons folder onto your hard drive from *www.DigitalClassroomBooks.com/Office2010*. See "Loading lesson files" on page XXIV.

See Lesson 7 in action!

Use the accompanying video to gain a better understanding of how to use some of the features shown in this lesson. The video tutorial for this lesson can be found at www.DigitalClassroomBooks.com/Office2010.

Understanding data lists

With Excel, you can maintain a large collection of related data in a data list, also known as a database, which is a table of worksheet data that uses only column headings. Each row, referred to as a record, contains information about the category displayed in the column heading. The top row of the worksheet holds the categories that you want to track, such as a name or street address.

 Each column heading must be unique.

Sorting a range

A range is a collection of two or more cells that you can work with as a group. You can then fill the range with values and sort the range data, based on the values in one or more columns. Sorting makes the range easier to read and analyze. You can sort the data in ascending or descending order. Ascending order arranges the values alphabetically from A to Z or numerically from 0 to 9; descending order arranges the values alphabetically from Z to A or numerically from 9 to 0.

Sorting data on a single field

In this exercise, you'll sort data on a single field, the year of the movie, in ascending order.

To open the file you need for this lesson:

1   Choose File > Open. Excel displays the Open dialog box.

2   Navigate to the Excel07lessons folder and double-click excel0701 to open the file.

3   Select File > Save As. Excel displays the Save As dialog box.

4   In the Save As text box, type **excel0701_done** and then click Save.

5   In the worksheet, click cell C2; click the Data tab, and in the Sort & Filter group, click Sort (⊞). Excel displays the Sort dialog box.

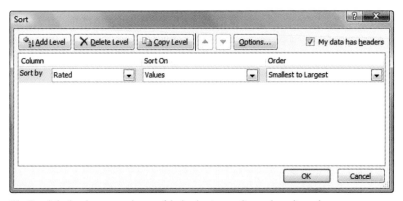

The Sort dialog box lets you sort by any of the headers in ascending or descending order.

6 Click the Sort by drop-down arrow, and select Year.

7 Click the Order drop-down arrow, and select Smallest to Largest; then click OK. Excel sorts the list from the earliest to the most recent movie.

If you only want to sort the data in a single column, you can click any cell inside the column you want to sort, and then in the Sort & Filter group, click either the Sort A to Z (⅔↓) or Sort Z to A icon (⅔↓).

Sorting data on multiple fields

Sometimes you need to sort on more than one field. In the best movies of all time worksheet, you'll sort by the director's name and then the name of the movie.

1 In the excel0701_done worksheet, click the Most Popular tab located in the bottom-left corner of the worksheet; click cell D2, and then in the Sort & Filter group, click Sort. Excel displays the Sort dialog box.

2 Click the Sort by drop-down arrow, and then select Director.

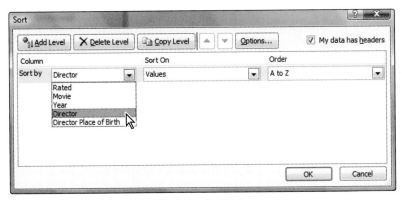

The Sort by drop-down list displays the headings in the worksheet.

3   Click Add Level. Excel adds another level, or category.

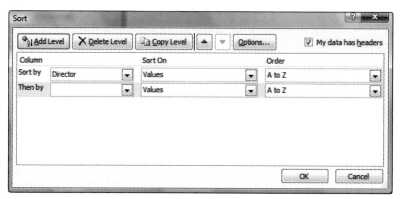

You can add another category to the sort.

4   In the Then by drop-down list, select Movie, and then click OK. Excel lists the directors' names in alphabetical order because you told Excel to sort the directors' names first. Steven Spielberg has multiple movies on the list, so his movies are in alphabetical order because you sorted the additional category, Movie.

If the data you want to sort is across a row rather than down a column, click Options in the Sort dialog box; click Sort left to right, and then click OK.

Filtering a range

When you want to view only portions of the data, you can use a filter. Unlike a sort, which sorts the entire worksheet, a filter selects records to display based on certain criteria.

1   Click the Best tab in the bottom-left corner of the worksheet; click cell B2, and in the Sort & Filter group, click Filter. Excel displays a drop-down arrow at the top of each column that contains data.

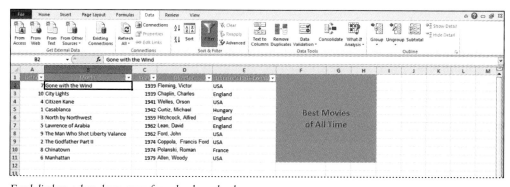

Excel displays a drop-down arrow for each column head.

2   Click the arrow on the lower-right corner of cell E1; deselect England, France, and Hungary, and then click OK.

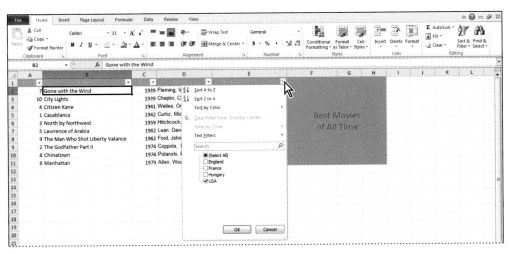

Deselect the categories you want to hide.

Excel displays only the movies with directors from the United States and a filter icon (⟱) in place of the arrow in the column you filtered.

To remove the filter, click the Filter icon and select Clear Filter From. Excel displays all records in the column.

3   Choose File > Save, and then choose File > Close.

Setting data validation rules

You can apply validation criteria to data entry cells so that they accept only certain values. You can also display a message to users when they enter data into the cell. This can prevent them from making incorrect entries in the worksheet.

To open the file you need for this lesson:

1   Choose File > Open and navigate to the Excel07lessons folder.

2   Click excel0702 and then click Open.

3   Select File > Save As. Excel displays the Save As dialog box.

4   In the Save As text box, type **excel0702_done** and then click Save.

5   In the worksheet, click the cell to the right of Account Number or cell D5. On the Data tab on the Ribbon, in the Data Tools group, click Data Validation (🔲). The Data Validation dialog box appears.

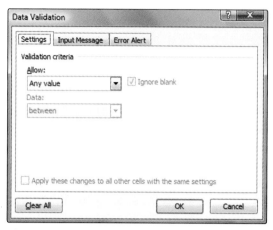

The Data Validation dialog box lets you set allowed values.

6   On the Settings tab, click the down arrow to the right of the Allow drop-down list and select Whole number.

7   In the data drop-down list, select between; in the Minimum text box, type **0**, and in the Maximum text box, type **999999**.

8   Click the Input Message tab, and click the Show input message when cell is selected check box, if it is not already checked.

9   In the Title text box, type Account Number; in the Input message text box, type **The entry must be a whole number between 0 and 999999**, and then click OK.

Notice that the message appears below the Account Number text box when you select the cell.

10   Make sure cell D5 is still selected and type **.25** and press Enter. You will notice an error message telling the user that the restricted values are set and the value you entered is invalid.

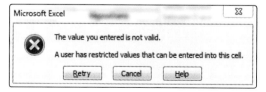

The error message appears warning you that the value is not valid.

11 Choose File > Save, and then choose File > Close.

The following table lists the data validation settings you can choose from.

SETTING	DESCRIPTION
Any value	Removes any previous restrictions and cancels data validation
Whole number	Restricts the entry to a whole number that falls within a certain range or adheres to parameters that you specify
Decimal	Restricts the entry to a decimal number that falls within a certain range or adheres to parameters that you specify
List	Restricts the entry to a list that you choose
Date	Restricts the entry to a date that falls within a certain range or on or before a particular date
Time	Restricts the entry to a time that falls within a certain range or on or before a particular time of the day
Text length	Restricts a text entry so that its length in characters is neither below nor above a certain number, or falls within a range that you specify
Custom	Restricts the entry to the parameters specified by a particular formula entered in another cell of the worksheet

Converting a range to a table

You can apply the Excel table tools to any range by converting a range to a table. You can then add, edit, and sort data in that table.

To open the file you need for this lesson:

1 Choose File > Open and navigate to the Excel07lessons folder.

2 Click excel0703 and then click Open.

3 Select File > Save As. Excel displays the Save As dialog box.

4 In the Save As text box, type **excel0703_done** and then click Save.

5 Click cell B3; click the Home tab, and then in the Styles group, click Format as Table (⊞). Excel displays the Format as Table gallery.

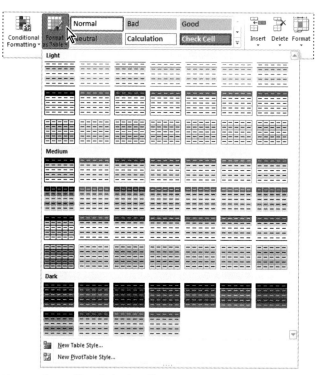

You can select a table style for the table.

6 Select the fourth design from the left in the first row of the Medium group. Excel converts the range to a table and applies the table style you chose, and the Table Tools tab appears on the Ribbon.

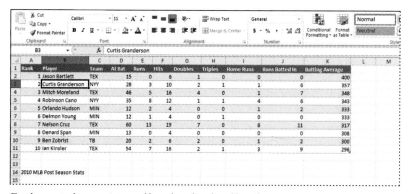

Excel converts the range into a table and applies the table style.

To convert a table back into a range, select any cell within the table; click the Design tab, and then click Convert to Range in the Tools group. Excel displays a confirmation dialog box. Click Yes.

7   Choose File > Save, and then choose File > Close.

Creating a data table

A data table is a range of cells used for testing and analyzing outcomes; it can show you how changing certain values within a formula can affect the outcome of the formula. Excel has two types of data tables: A one-variable data table gauges the effect of changing one input cell within the table. A two-variable data table gauges the effect of changing two input cells within the table. You should not confuse a data table with regular Excel tables that you learned about in the section, "Converting a range to a table." A data table is a special range that Excel uses to calculate multiple solutions to one formula.

In this exercise, you'll type several values for the interest rate and then determine how the result fluctuates based on which value you apply to the formula.

To open the file you need for this lesson:

1   Choose File > Open and navigate to the Excel07lessons folder.

2   Click excel0704 and then click Open.

3   Select File > Save As. Excel displays the Save As dialog box.

4   In the Save As text box, type **excel0704_done** and then click Save.

5   Click cell A8, type **2%**, and then press Enter. Excel displays the value as a percentage.

6   Click each cell beginning with A9 and ending with A13 and type the following values: **2.5%, 3%, 3.5%, 4%,** and **4.5%**.

7   Select cells A7 and B7 and drag down to row 13.

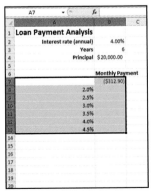

Select the formula and the values.

8   Click the Data tab, and in the Data Tools group, click What-If Analysis (⚡). The What-If Analysis drop-down menu appears.

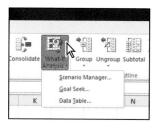

The What-If Analysis menu offers three options.

9   Select Data Table. Excel displays the Data Table dialog box.

Click the cell where the formula resides to display it in the Data Table dialog box.

10   Click the Column input cell text box; click cell B2, and then click OK.

Excel displays the monthly payment for each interest rate.

11   Choose File > Save, and then choose File > Close.

Summarizing data with subtotals

If you need a quick summary of data, Excel offers a tool called automatic subtotals, which are formulas that Excel automatically adds to a worksheet.

To open the file you need for this lesson:

1   Choose File > Open and navigate to the Excel07lessons folder.

2   Click excel0705 and then click Open.

3   Select File > Save As. Excel displays the Save As dialog box.

4   In the Save As text box, type **excel0705_done** and then click Save.

5   Click cell C2; click the Data tab, and then click Subtotal () located in the Outline group. The Subtotal dialog box appears.

You can select where to add the subtotal and the function to perform in the Subtotal dialog box.

6   Click OK. Excel displays the total for each state and the grand total.

7   Click the Save button on the Quick Access Toolbar, but do not close this document because you will use this in the next exercise.

Exporting Excel data to Word

After creating an Excel worksheet, you might want to include the Excel data in a Word report. Excel lets you export Excel data to a Word document. You can perform a simple replication of data, or you can export Excel tools with the data, so you can make changes after you have exported it.

Exporting data

You can export Excel data to a Word document. If you then want to make changes, you can use the Word tools to edit and format the data. In this exercise, you'll use the Copy and Paste commands.

1   Launch Microsoft Word. Word displays a blank page.

2   Select File > Save As. Word displays the Save As dialog box.

3   Navigate to the Excel07lessons folder.

4   In the Save As text box, type **excel0705_exported**, and then click Save.

5   In the Excel based excel0705_done worksheet, click the data in cells A1, B1, and C1 and drag down to row 21.

6 Press Ctrl+C, and then click the Word based named excel0705_exported on the status bar at the bottom of the window.

7 In the excel0705_exported document, press Ctrl+V. Word displays the Excel data in Word format. You can format and edit the data using Word tools.

Exporting data and tools

You can also export a worksheet to Word and then use the Excel tools to make changes if needed. In this exercise, you'll use the Paste Special command.

1 In the excel0705_done worksheet, click the data in cells A22, B22, and C22; drag down to row 41, and then press Ctrl+C.

2 Switch to the excel0705_exported document; place the cursor below the data that you pasted in the previous exercise.

3 Click the Home tab on the Ribbon. In the Clipboard group, click the down-arrow under the Paste icon. Word displays the Paste menu.

The Paste menu displays options such as Paste Special.

4 Select Paste Special. Word displays the Paste Special dialog box.

5 Select Microsoft Excel Worksheet Object; click the Paste link radio button, and then click OK. Word displays the data. Double-click the imported data, and Excel tools become available to use for editing and formatting.

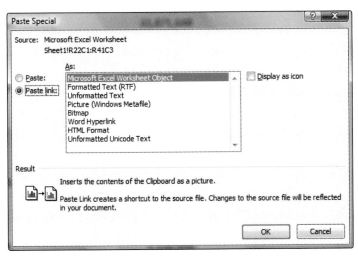

The Paste Special dialog box displays options to paste in various formats.

6 In the Excel program, choose File > Save, and then choose File > Close. In the Word program, choose File > Save, and then choose File > Exit.

Creating a PivotTable

A PivotTable is a versatile method of summarizing data. You tell Excel the fields to display and how to display them.

To open the file you need for this lesson:

1 Choose File > Open and navigate to the Excel07lessons folder.

2 Click excel0706 and then click Open.

3 Select File > Save As. Excel displays the Save As dialog box.

4 In the Save As text box, type **excel0706_done** and then click Save.

Before you begin creating a PivotTable you will always want to:

- Remove any blank rows or columns
- Be sure that each column has a heading
- Be sure that the cells have the proper formatting for their data types

5 Click cell A1 and drag over to cell F1, and then down to row 20.

6   Click the Insert tab and in the Tables group, click PivotTable (⬚).

Excel displays the selected range in the Create PivotTable dialog box. Be sure that you click the New Worksheet radio button if it is not already selected.

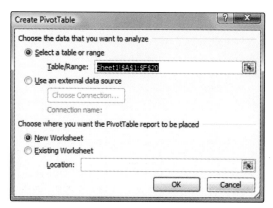

Choose the data that you want to analyze in the Create PivotTable dialog box.

7   Click OK. Excel displays a new worksheet and a blank PivotTable, and the PivotTable Tools tabs appear on the Ribbon .

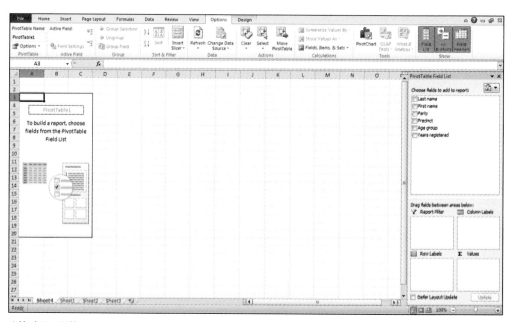

A blank PivotTable.

8 In the PivotTable Field List located in the upper-right corner, click Precinct and drag it down to the Row Labels quadrant, and repeat the procedure for Party. Excel displays the PivotTable on the left. Notice that the PivotTable has listed the parties in each precinct.

9 Click and drag Party from the PivotTable Field List to the Values quadrant. Excel displays the count for each party in each precinct as well as the grand total.

10 Click and drag Age group from the PivotTable Field List to the Row Labels quadrant. Excel breaks the parties into age groups.

11 Choose File > Save to save your work.

Creating a PivotChart

A PivotChart is a visual representation of a PivotTable. In this exercise, you'll rearrange the PivotTable data, and then create a PivotChart to represent that data.

1 In the excel0706_done worksheet, click Precinct in the Row Labels quadrant and drag it up to the PivotTable Field List. Then click Age group and drag it to the PivotTable Field List. The PivotTable now shows a list of the parties and a count of each.

2 On the PivotTable Tools tab, click Options, and then in the Tools group, click PivotChart (📊). The Insert Chart dialog box appears.

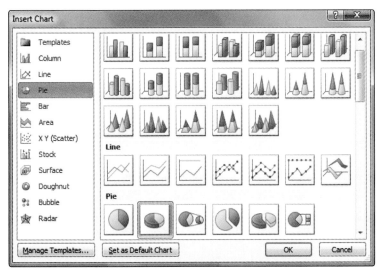

The Insert Chart dialog box offers a variety of choices for a PivotChart.

3 Select Pie from the column on the left; select the second chart from the left in the Pie group called Pie in 3-D, and then click OK.

Excel displays a pie chart depicting the data in the PivotTable, and the PivotChart Tools appear on the Ribbon.

4 Click the Design tab, and click the More arrow in the bottom-right corner of the Chart Styles group. Excel displays the Chart Styles gallery .

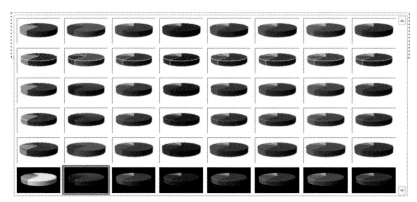

The Chart Styles gallery displays choices for the PivotChart.

5 Select the second chart from the left in the bottom row.

Now, you'll change the chart layout.

6 In the Chart Layouts group, click the More arrow in the bottom-right corner of the Chart Layouts group. Excel displays the Chart Layouts gallery.

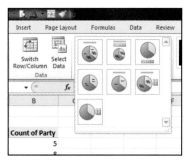

The Chart Layouts group lets you change the layout of the chart.

7 Click the first layout on the left in the top row.

8 Choose File > Save, and then choose File > Exit.

Self study

1   Open the excel0701_done worksheet, and sort the best movies of all time by their rating from last to first.

2   In the excel0701_done worksheet, include all years in the sort except 1939.

3   Open the excel0706_done worksheet, and change the chart layout to Layout 6, the third from the left in the second row.

Review

Questions

1   What is another name for a data list?

2   In a data list, what is a row called?

3   When you sort data, what is the purpose of the Add Level command?

4   Which data validation setting would you choose if you wanted to remove previous restrictions and cancel data validation?

Answers

1   A data list is also known as a database.

2   A row in a data list is called a record.

3   The Add Level command lets you sort data by an additional category.

4   You would choose the Any value setting.

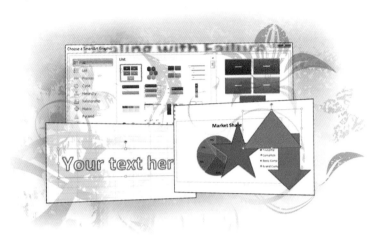

What you'll learn in this lesson:

- Manipulating graphics
- Moving graphic objects to a new layer
- Importing and adjusting graphics
- Formatting clip art and imported pictures

Adding Graphic Objects

In this lesson, you'll discover how to add, manage, and manipulate graphics in an Excel worksheet. You will work with shapes, text boxes, WordArt, and SmartArt to enhance a worksheet.

Starting up

You will work with several files from the Excel08lessons folder in this lesson. Make sure that you have loaded the OfficeLessons folder onto your hard drive from *www.DigitalClassroomBooks.com/Office2010*. See "Loading lesson files" on page XXIV.

See Lesson 8 in action!

Use the accompanying video to gain a better understanding of how to use some of the features shown in this lesson. The video tutorial for this lesson can be found at www.DigitalClassroomBooks.com/Office2010.

Manipulating graphics

You can use graphic objects to enhance regular spreadsheet data. Excel supports graphics that you create yourself, such as shapes, and those that you import using the Clip Art and Picture commands. Once you create or import a graphic, you can then transform it within Excel.

The following table describes the tools you can use to insert and format graphics in Excel.

TOOL	DESCRIPTION
Picture	Use the Picture tool to insert a picture from a file
Clip Art	Use the Clip Art tool to insert drawings, movies, sounds, or stock photography
Shapes	Use the Shapes tool to insert ready-made shapes
SmartArt	Use the SmartArt tool to insert diagrams
WordArt	Use the WordArt tool to add stylized text

When you add a graphic to an Excel spreadsheet, Excel displays the image with handles around it so that you can resize, shape, and rotate the graphic.

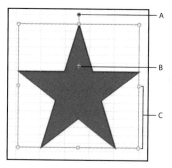

A. Rotating handle. *B*. Shaping handle.
C. Sizing handle.

To select a graphic, you simply click it; to select multiple graphics, you hold down the Shift or Ctrl key as you select each graphic. You can then manipulate all graphics that you selected as a group.

You can manipulate graphics in many ways in Excel, as shown in the following table.

ACTION	METHOD
Size	Position the cursor on the sizing handle, and the cursor becomes a double-headed arrow. Drag to increase or decrease the size and shape. Hold down the Shift key to retain the image's original proportions as you make it larger or smaller.
Rotate	Position the cursor on the rotation handle, and the cursor becomes a curved arrow. Click and drag the rotation handle to rotate the image clockwise or counter-clockwise around the rotation handle.
Shape	Position the cursor on the shaping handle, and the cursor becomes an arrowhead. Drag the cursor to reshape the side or section of the image. Note that reshaping a 3D graphic can alter its perspective.
Move	Position the cursor on the graphic, and the cursor becomes a cross with arrows. Drag the graphic to its new location in the worksheet.
Snap to grid	For a drawn graphic, such as a predefined shape, text box, clip art, or WordArt, click the Drawing Tools tab. In the Arrange group, click Align (📄), and then select Snap to Grid.
	For an imported picture or digital photo, click the Picture Tools tab. In the Arrange group, click Align, and then select Snap to Grid.
	For SmartArt, click Format on the SmartArt Tools tab. In the Arrange group, click Align, and then select Snap to Grid.
Nudge	Click a graphic and press an arrow key (up, down, left, or right). Excel moves the image a small amount in the direction of the key you pressed.
Delete	Click a graphic and press the Delete key.

Moving graphic objects to a new layer

When you add a graphic to a worksheet, the graphic lies on an invisible layer over the worksheet cells; as a result, the graphic hides some of the cells. Similarly, if you add another graphic, the new graphic lies on a new layer, and covers the first one.

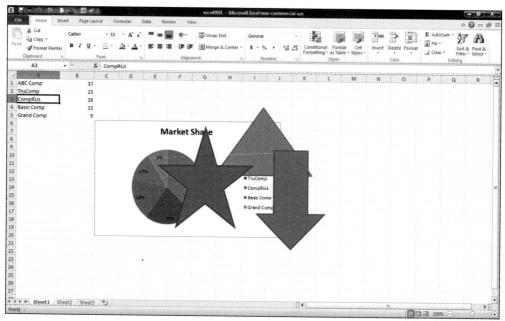

Each graphic lies on a separate layer.

To open the file you need for this lesson:

1 Launch Microsoft Excel 2010.

2 Choose File > Open and navigate to the Excel08lessons folder.

3 Double-click excel0801 to open the file.

4 Select File > Save As. Excel displays the Save As dialog box.

5 In the Save As text box, type **excel0801_done** and then click Save.

6 Click on the star, and then click the Format tab. In the Arrange group, click Selection Pane (🖳). Excel displays the Selection and Visibility pane.

The Selection and Visibility
pane lists the graphic layers.

7 In the Selection and Visibility pane, click Isosceles Triangle 2, and then click the up-arrow twice (this arrow is located at the bottom of the pane in the Re-order group). Excel moves Isosceles Triangle 2 to the top of the list. Notice that the triangle in worksheet also moves to the top layer and is completely visible.

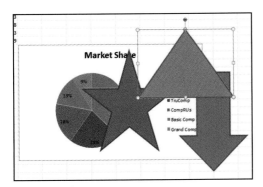

Click an icon to display a menu.

8 With the triangle still selected, click the down-arrow in the Re-order group. Excel moves the triangle back one layer. Notice that part of the triangle is now obstructed.

9 In the Selection and Visibility pane, click the icon to the right of Isosceles Triangle 2 (👁) to remove the triangle from view. Click the icon again and Excel displays the triangle.

You can also use the Picture or Drawing Tools tab on the Ribbon to move graphics forward and backward in a worksheet. To view this tab, you must have a picture or drawing selected.

TOOL	ACTION
Bring Forward	Brings the image one layer higher
Bring to Front	Brings the image to the top layer
Send Backward	Sends the image one layer lower
Send to Back	Sends the image to the bottom layer

Aligning graphics

You can click the Format tab and use the Align menu in the Arrange group to align graphic objects even though they exist on separate layers.

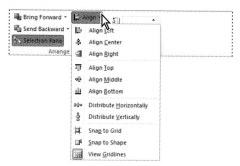

The Align menu offers a variety of methods to align objects.

1 In the excel0801_done worksheet, click the icon to the right of the Chart 1 graphic to hide it.

2 Click the star and drag it to the left so it no longer touches the other objects.

3 Click the arrow and drag it to the right so it no longer touches the other objects.

4 Click the star; press the Shift key, and then click the triangle and the arrow. Selection boxes appear around each graphic.

5   In the Format tab, in the Arrange group, select Align and then choose Align Bottom. Excel bottom-aligns all three graphics.

6   Again, in the Arrange group, select Align but this time choose Distribute Horizontally. Excel distributes the objects to be evenly-spaced along a horizontal plane.

Grouping graphics

Sometimes you need to work with more than one graphic, such as when you want to rotate multiple shapes by the same amount. Excel lets you group the graphics and then perform the rotation so that you do it in one operation.

1   If all three graphics are not still selected, click the star; press the Shift key, and then click the triangle and the arrow. Selection boxes appear around each graphic, and Excel displays the Drawing Tools on the Ribbon.

2   Click the Format tab, and in the Arrange group, click Group (⊞) and select Group from the menu. Excel places a single set of sizing handles around the graphic group.

3   In the Arrange group, click Rotate (▲). The Rotate menu appears.

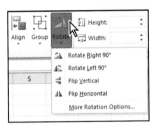

Use the Rotate menu to rotate graphics horizontally, vertically, left, or right.

4   Select Rotate Right 90°, and then select Flip Vertical. Excel rotates all the graphics in one motion.

5   Click Group and select Ungroup. Notice that each graphic now has individual sizing handles and no longer behaves as a single entity.

6   Select File > Save, and then select File > Close.

Importing and adjusting graphics

In Excel, you can import clip art from a library, as well as pictures saved in various file formats.

Importing clip art

1   Click File > New. Excel displays the Available Templates page.

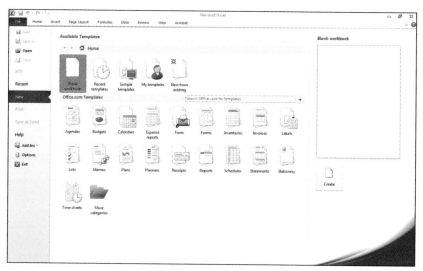

Excel displays available templates to use for your worksheet.

2   Click Blank workbook and then click Create. Excel displays a blank worksheet.

3   Click File > Save As and navigate to the Excel08lessons folder.

4   In the Save As text box, type **excel0802_done** and then click Save.

5   Click the Insert tab on the Ribbon, and then click Clip Art (⊞) in the Illustrations group. The Clip Art pane to the right of the worksheet appears.

6 In the Search for text box, type **monthly sales**, and then click Go. Excel displays the clip art image or images that match the search criteria in the Clip Art pane.

You can search for a clip art image in the Clip Art pane.

7 In the worksheet, click cell A3, and then click the image you want in the Clip Art pane. Excel imports the image to the worksheet.

Importing picture files

If you want to include an image such as a digital photo or a scanned image that is saved in a graphic file format, you can use the Picture icon in the Illustrations group on the Ribbon.

1 Click cell H3, click the Insert tab on the Ribbon, and then click Picture (▨) in the Illustrations group. The Insert Picture dialog box appears.

2 Navigate to the Excel08lessons folder.

3 Select excel0803, and then click Insert.

Excel inserts the image to the right of the Monthly Sales clip art image.

Formatting clip art and imported pictures

When you import a graphic into a worksheet, Excel displays the Picture Tools tab.

The Picture Tools tab displays the tools you can use to format images.

Adjusting images

The Adjust group in the Format tab offers the following tools to format images.

TOOL	DESCRIPTION
Correction	Use the Correction tool to increase or decrease the picture's sharpness, brightness, or contrast.
Color	Use the Color tool to select a new color for the image.
Artistic Effects	Use the Artistic Effects tool to apply a special effect to the image.
Compress Pictures	Use the Compress Pictures tool to compress all images or selected graphics in the worksheet to reduce the file size.
Change Picture	Use the Change Picture tool to open the Insert Picture dialog box where you can select an image in a new graphics file to replace the existing picture.
Reset Picture	Use the Reset Picture tool to remove all formatting changes that have been made to a picture and return it to its original format.

1   Click the Monthly Sales image on the excel0802_done worksheet; in the Adjust group on the Ribbon, click Corrections. The Corrections menu appears with the current settings highlighted.

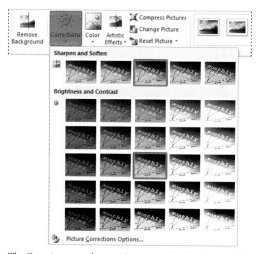

The Corrections menu lets you sharpen or soften the image and adjust its brightness or contrast.

2   In the Brightness and Contrast group, click the image to the right of the current selection (in the third row, the fourth image from the left). Notice that Excel adjusts the brightness.

3   Click Color, and the Color menu appears with the current settings highlighted.

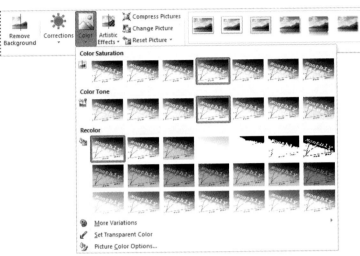

The Color menu lets you adjust the color saturation and tone. It also lets you recolor the image.

4   In the Recolor group, click the farthest image to the right in the second row. Notice that Excel adjusts the color to orange.

5   In the worksheet, click the spreadsheet image and then click Artistic Effects. Excel displays the Artistic Effects menu.

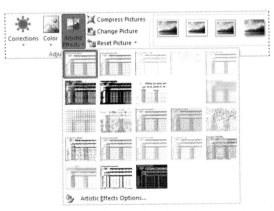

The Artistic Effects menu lets you add an effect to the image, such as blur.

6   Select the middle image in the bottom row. Excel changes the effect to Photocopy.

7 Click the More arrow located to the right of Picture Styles. Excel displays the Picture Styles menu.

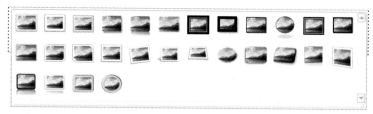

Use the Picture Styles menu to add a style to a picture.

8 Select the image for Center Shadow Rectangle. Excel changes the picture style.

9 In the Adjust group, click Change Picture (). The Insert Picture dialog box appears.

10 Select excel0804 and click Insert. Excel inserts the new picture with the settings of the previous picture.

11 Select File > Save, then File > Close.

Working with shapes

The Shapes gallery stores a wide variety of predefined shapes, such as basic shapes and block arrows. In this exercise, you'll create a shape and edit it.

To open the file you need for this lesson:

1 Choose File > Open and navigate to the Excel08lesson folder.

2 Click excel0805 and then click Open.

3 Select File > Save As. Excel displays the Save As dialog box.

4 In the Save As text box, type **excel0805_done** and then click Save.

5   On the Insert tab, in the Illustrations group, click Shapes. Excel displays the Shapes menu.

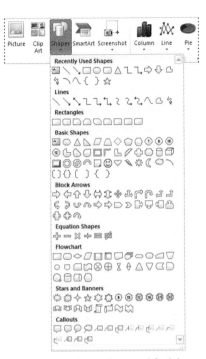

The Shapes menu lets you draw a predefined shape.

When you draw a rectangle or an oval, you can draw a square or a circle by holding down the Shift key as you drag the mouse.

6   Click the parallelogram located in the Basic shapes group (this is the fifth shape from the left in the top row).

7   Click the upper-left corner of cell C3, drag to the upper-right corner of cell D3, and then drag down to the bottom of row 7. Release the mouse button.

Excel automatically adds a blue fill to the shape. You will now change the shape using the drawing tools.

8 In the Insert Shapes group, click Edit Shape. Excel displays the Edit Shape menu.

The Edit Shape menu lets you change the shape or edit the points on the shape.

9 Select Edit Points. Excel changes the border color to red. Place the cursor on the lower-right corner of the parallelogram, click and drag to the right until you reach the right side of column E.

10 On the Edit Shape menu, select Change Shape and choose the rectangle. Excel now changes the parallelogram to a rectangle.

11 In the Insert Shapes group, click Text Box. Click anywhere in the rectangle and Excel displays a blinking cursor within the shape.

12 Type **Text box**. Excel displays the text in white.

13 Click the More arrow to the right of the Shape Styles group. Excel displays the Shape Styles menu.

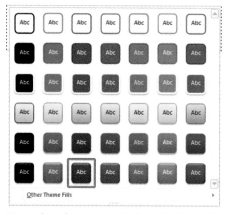

You can choose from a variety of styles on the Shape Styles menu.

14 Select the third style over from the left in the bottom row called Intense Effect – Red, Accent 2.

15 Select File > Save, and then select File > Close.

Working with text boxes

A text box is a rectangular shape that allows you to insert text within it. In a worksheet, you can use a text box to call attention to a graphic or explain a chart. In this exercise, you'll add a text box to further explain a chart.

To open the file you need for this lesson:

1   Choose File > Open and navigate to the Excel08lessons folder.

2   Click excel0806 and then click Open.

3   Select File > Save As. Excel displays the Save As dialog box.

4   In the Save As text box, type **excel0806_done** and then click Save.

Adding a text box

A text box behaves like other graphic objects in that you can move and format it, although it is unlike other graphics because you can add text and format the text within it.

1   On the Insert tab, in the Text group, click Text Box (⚈).

2   Click the top-left corner of cell A10; drag over to the right edge of cell A10 and down to the bottom of row 20, and then release the mouse button. Excel displays the Home tab on the Ribbon.

3   Double click cell A21, then click and drag to select all the text. Press Ctrl+X to cut the selected text.

4   Click in the upper-left corner of the text box created, and press Ctrl+V. Excel pastes the paragraph into the text box.

Resizing and formatting a text box

After adding a text box, you can format the text by changing the font style, font size, and many other characteristics of the text box.

To change the formatting of the text within a text box, use the Font and Alignment groups on the Home tab.

Use the Font and Alignment tools to format text within a text box.

In this section, you'll change the font to Arial, the size to 12 pixels, and the font style to bold. You'll then resize a text box, and add a border and fill.

1 Double-click the border of the text box. On the Home tab, click the down-arrow to the right side of the Font group and select Arial.

2 Click the down-arrow to the right side of the font size and select 12. Click the Bold (**B**) and Italic (*I*) icons.

3 In the Alignment group, click the Center icon (≡).

4 Click and drag the sizing handle in the bottom-middle of the text box until you reach the line below row 26.

5 Select the Format tab and in the Shape Styles group, click the third style called Colored Outline - Red, Accent 2. Excel displays a red border around the text box.

6 Click the Shape Fill icon (◇). The Shape Fill menu appears.

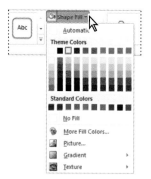

Select a fill for the text box from the Shape Fill menu.

7 Select the third color from the left in the top row, directly under Theme Colors. Excel applies a gray fill to the text box.

Inserting WordArt

WordArt is text that behaves as a graphic. You will find the WordArt command on the Insert tab in the Text group on the Ribbon. Be sure that the text box is not selected before you begin this exercise.

1   Click on any cell outside of the text box, and then click the Insert tab on the Ribbon. In the Text group, click WordArt (*A*). The WordArt gallery appears.

The WordArt gallery displays many different WordArt styles.

2   Click the second style from the left in the top row, Fill – None, Outline – Accent 2. Excel displays your choice in a text box.

3   Click the border of the text box and drag the WordArt below the chart.

The WordArt text box looks like a graphic.

4   Click three times to the left of the Y in Your text here. Excel selects the text.

5   Type **Test drive a car today!**

6   Select File > Save, and then select File > Close.

Inserting SmartArt graphics

SmartArt graphics let you build lists and diagrams easily. You can construct organizational charts and flow diagrams and many other structures with the SmartArt tools.

To open the file you need for this lesson:

1 Choose File > Open and navigate to the Excel08lessons folder.

2 Click excel0807 and then click Open.

3 Select File > Save As. Excel displays the Save As dialog box.

4 In the Save As text box, type **excel0807_done** and then click Save.

5 Click Insert on the Ribbon, and in the Illustrations group, click SmartArt (📊). The Choose a SmartArt Graphic dialog box appears.

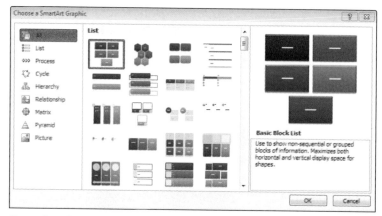

You can choose from many formats for your SmartArt graphic.

6 In the dialog box, select Cycle from the list on the left; on the right side, select Block Cycle (the third diagram from the left in the top row) and then click OK.

Excel displays the SmartArt tools on the Ribbon, and the diagram with the cursor blinking.

7 Type **Make a mistake**, and click the word Text on the next line.

Pressing Tab or Enter does not advance the cursor to the next text box.

8   Repeat this process for the next four lines and enter the following text:

- **Feel bad for a minute**
- **Pick yourself up**
- **Dust yourself off**
- **Start over again**

9   Click the SmartArt Tools Design tab on the Ribbon, and in the Create Graphic group, click Text Pane (▤). The text pane disappears.

10 Click Change Colors (⁝⁝) to the left of the SmartArt Styles group. The Change Colors gallery appears.

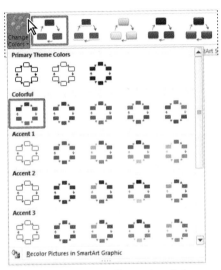

The Change Colors gallery offers a variety of colors.

11 Select the first choice on the left under Colorful.

Adding a screenshot

You can use the Screenshot tool in the Illustrations group to capture an entire window or a portion of a window. You can then insert the screen image into a worksheet. In this exercise, you'll open a document, capture a part of the document, and insert it into an Excel worksheet.

To open the file you need for this lesson:

1 Open Microsoft Word and choose File > Open navigate to the Excel08lessons folder.

2 Click excel0808, and then click Open. Scroll down so that all the text on the page is visible.

3 Switch back to Excel by clicking on the Excel button found on the status bar which is along the bottom of your monitor. In the excel0807_done worksheet, on the Insert tab in the Illustrations group, click Screenshot. The Screenshot menu appears.

Use the Screenshot tool to capture a window or part of a window.

 Excel displays a thumbnail image of each program that is open.

4 Select Screen Clipping. Excel displays the program window and the cursor becomes a cross (+).

5 Click in the upper-left corner of the Word document; drag to include all the text, and then release the mouse button. Excel copies your selection from the Word document and pastes it on the Excel worksheet.

6 Click the screenshot. The cursor changes to a cross with arrows on each end. Drag the image down below the diagram. Excel displays the Picture Tools tab on the Ribbon.

7 On the Ribbon, click Picture Border found in the Picture Styles group. Excel displays the Picture Border menu.

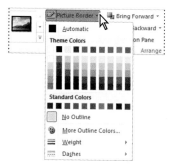

Use the Picture Border menu to select a color and weight for the border.

8 Select the fourth color from the left in the top row under Theme Colors.

You can now close the Word document without saving.

Adding a theme

You can use a theme to change the appearance of your worksheet. A theme consists of three elements: the color scheme, fonts, and effects. In this exercise, you'll apply a theme to a worksheet.

1 In the excel0807_done worksheet, click the Page Layout tab. In the Theme group, click Themes. Excel displays the predefined themes.

2 Select Essential, which is located in the fifth row, fourth from the left. The theme changes.

3 Select File > Save, and then select File > Exit.

Congratulations! You have completed the lesson. In this lesson, you have learned about Excel graphics and how to create and import graphic objects into an Excel worksheet.

Self study

1 Open excel0805_done; use the resize handles to make the rectangle larger and wider.

2 Use the Shapes tool to create a star. Add a yellow fill to the shape.

3 Select the text box and the star, and align their bottom edges. Now group them.

Review

Questions

1 Which graphics tool would you use to create a diagram quickly and easily?

2 Which keys would you use to move an image a small amount to the right, left, up, or down?

3 Which tool would you use to return the graphic to its original format?

Answers

1 You would use the SmartArt tool to create a quick-and-easy diagram.

2 You would use the arrow keys to nudge the graphic.

3 You would use the Reset tool to remove all changes and return the graphic to its original format.

What you'll learn in this lesson:

- Saving and converting a presentation to PowerPoint 2010
- Applying a theme and changing theme colors
- Changing the slide layout and aligning text
- Adding pictures and text to a slide and adding a style to the pictures

Microsoft PowerPoint 2010 Jumpstart

In this lesson, you will get a general introduction to Microsoft PowerPoint 2010. This lesson is intended to provide a quick introduction so you can jump right in and get your feet wet.

Starting up

You will work with several files from the PPT01lessons folder in this lesson. Make sure that you have loaded the OfficeLessons folder onto your hard drive from *www.DigitalClassroomBooks.com/Office2010*. See "Loading lesson files" on page XXIV.

See Lesson 1 in action!

Use the accompanying video to gain a better understanding of how to use some of the features shown in this lesson. The video tutorial for this lesson can be found at www.DigitalClassroomBooks.com/Office2010.

The project

In this lesson, you will create a presentation using a template. Using the most popular features of PowerPoint 2010, you will build an informational presentation about calming upset clients.

To begin the project:

1 Launch Microsoft PowerPoint 2010.

2 Choose File > Open. Navigate to the PPT01lessons folder that you copied to your computer from the DVD that came with your book, and then double-click pp0101_done to open the file. A PowerPoint document opens to the cover page of a presentation. In this exercise, you will recreate this document. Choose File > Close to close the document.

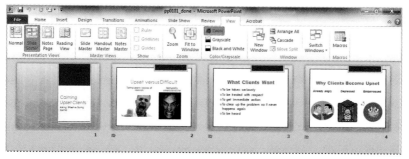

The completed presentation.

The PowerPoint workspace is similar to other Microsoft Office applications. The tools are conveniently located on the Ribbon running across the top of the window.

The Ribbon displays different tools depending on the tab that you click.

Creating a presentation from an existing file

You'll start by opening a template and adding elements to it.

1 Choose File > Open. PowerPoint displays the Open dialog box.

2 Navigate to the OfficeLessons folder and open the PPT01lessons folder. Click pp0101, and then click Open.

The template appears on your screen.

3 Click inside the Click to add title box and type **Calming Upset Clients**.

4 Click inside the Click to add subtitle box. Where the cursor starts blinking, type **Staying Effective during Conflict**.

Saving and converting a presentation from prior versions

Saving a file right after you create it is good practice. It makes it easy to save modifications as you build the document and helps PowerPoint recover your file if your computer or software stops working correctly.

The template you are using for this presentation was saved in a version of PowerPoint prior to 2007. You can quickly and easily convert a PowerPoint presentation saved in a previous version of PowerPoint to the newer .pptx file format.

Notice that in the title bar, after the title of the open presentation, PowerPoint displays the words *Compatibility Mode*. In Compatibility Mode, not all features of PowerPoint 2010 are available to you.

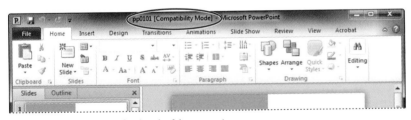

Compatibility Mode appears after the title of the presentation.

1 Click File > Info > Convert. PowerPoint displays the Save As dialog box.

2 In the File name box, type **pp0101_working** and click Save. Compatibility Mode no longer appears on the title bar. PowerPoint saves the file as a .pptx file, which is compatible with PowerPoint version 2007 and greater.

Applying a theme and changing colors

PowerPoint includes several themes to help you design your presentation. When you choose a theme, PowerPoint applies the same look and feel to all the slides. Then, you can change the colors of the theme to enhance the look. You can also apply the theme to only selected slides.

In this exercise, you'll select and apply a theme and change its colors.

1 With pp0101_working open, on the Ribbon, click Design. In the Themes group, click the down arrow on the right to display the All Themes drop-down menu, and select Austin.

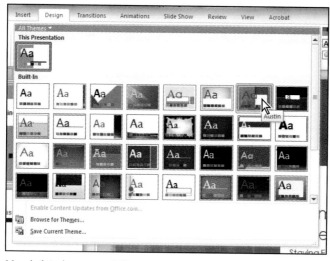

Many built-in themes are available to you.

The colors of the presentation change to a brighter green with a black accent.

Now you'll apply blue and red to replace the green and black.

2 Continue to work on the Ribbon in the Design tab. In the Themes group, click the Colors drop-down menu (■). PowerPoint displays the Colors menu.

3 On the Colors menu, select Concourse.

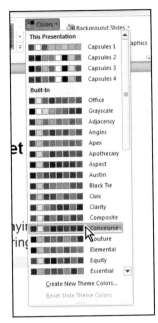

Select Concourse on the Colors menu to replace the theme colors with new colors.

Changing the slide layout and aligning text

PowerPoint includes many predesigned slide layouts such as a title with two content sections or a picture with a caption.

In this exercise, you'll change a slide layout and center the title.

1 In the Slides view, which is the area of the slides along the left side of the screen, right-click slide. A shortcut menu appears.

The shortcut menu displays options for the slide.

2 From the shortcut menu, select Layout > Comparison. The slide layout changes to the comparison layout.

You will now align the title text to center it. When aligning text, you have many options. You can align text horizontally left, center, or right. You can also justify the text by aligning it both left and right, leaving space between words to accommodate the justification of the text. PowerPoint also allows you to change the direction of the text.

3 Click to the left of the word *Upset* in the title text box, and on the Ribbon, click Home. In the Paragraph group, click Center (≡) to center the slide title.

If you apply a new slide layout and are not happy with the result, you can return the slide to its default state by clicking the Reset button (⛶) on the Home tab.

Adding pictures and text to the slide

You will now add two pictures to the Upset versus Difficult slide. Slide layouts display icons that allow you to add an object such as a table, chart, or graphic to the slide.

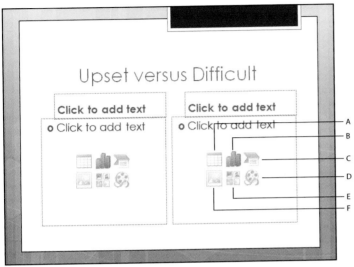

Click the appropriate icon to add an object like a picture to the slide. **A**. *Insert table.* **B**. *Insert chart.*
C. *Insert small art graphic.* **D**. *Insert media clip.* **E**. *Insert clip art.* **F**. *Insert picture from file.*

1   Within slide 2, click Insert Picture from File in the left box. The Insert Picture dialog box appears.

2   Navigate to PPT01lessons in your OfficeLessons folder, click pp0102.jpg, and then click Insert. PowerPoint inserts the picture into the box.

3   Above the picture, click inside the Click to add text box and type **Temporary lapse of reason**. Press Ctrl+E to center the text within the text box.

4   Within slide 2, click Insert Picture from File in the right box. The Insert Picture dialog box appears.

5   Navigate to the PPT01lessons folder in your OfficeLessons folder, and then double-click pp0103.jpg. PowerPoint inserts the picture into the box.

6   Above the picture, click in the Click to add text box and type **Naturally unreasonable**. Press Ctrl+E to center the text within the text box.

Adding a style to a picture

A picture style is a way of framing a picture. Picture styles include simple frames, soft edge rectangles, shadows, and beveled edges.

In this exercise, you'll add a shadow to the pictures on slide 2.

1 Select the picture under Temporary lapse of reason. When you select a picture, the Picture Tools tab is highlighted. Click on the Format tab just underneath the Picture Tools tab to confirm that the Format options are visible on the Ribbon.

The Picture Tools allow you to adjust, enhance, arrange, and size pictures.

2 In the Picture Styles group, click on the More button to view all visual styles for the picture. Select Drop Shadow Rectangle from the menu.

Select Drop Shadow Rectangle to apply a drop shadow to a picture.

3 Select the picture under Naturally unreasonable, and select Drop Shadow Rectangle to apply a drop shadow to the other picture on the slide. Select File > Save to save your work.

Applying slide transitions

You can add transition effects, such as fades, dissolves, and wipes, to control how one slide advances to another. You can also control the speed of the transition.

When applying slide transitions, you should use them sparingly and be consistent by choosing one transition or similar transitions for all slides. You want your audience to focus on the presentation, not the transitions.

You can apply different slide transitions as you move from one slide to another. PowerPoint gives you many transition options. In this exercise, you'll apply a transition to the slide. To begin, you need to be in Slide Sorter view.

1   On the Ribbon, click View, and then in the Presentation Views group, click Slide Sorter.

*Slide Sorter view allows you to view the slides
so that you can move them if needed.*

2   Select slide 2, Upset versus Difficult, and then on the Ribbon, select Transitions > Fade.

You can choose a subtle or exciting transition option or a transition with dynamic content.

3   Click the symbol located under the bottom-left side of the slide to preview
the transition.

Click the symbol to preview the transition.

4   Double-click the slide to return to Slide view.

On the Home tab in the Font group, you can adjust the font to make the title stand out.
You will apply a shadow to the title.

5 In the slide, click and drag to select the slide title, and then in the Font group, click Text Shadow.

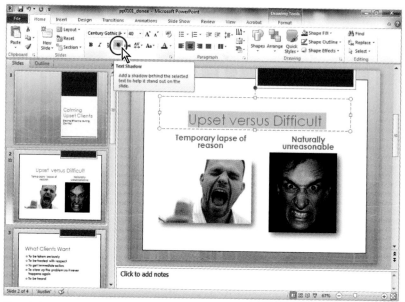

Text Shadow places a shadow around the text.

Adding effects and animating text

You can emphasize text in many ways in your presentation, such as by applying a bold effect to a font, adding a shadow, and animating the text. In this exercise, you'll apply a shadow, change the font, assign a bold effect, and animate the text to fly in one bullet point at a time. Then you will set a duration to the animation and preview the slide to see the results of your work.

1 In Slide view, click slide 3, What Clients Want. Place the cursor before the word *What* in the title and click three times to select *What Clients Want*.

2 On the Ribbon, select Home. In the Font group, click Text Shadow.

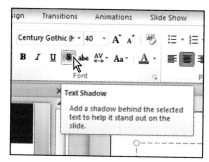

Click the Text Shadow button to make the letters cast a shadow.

You'll now change the title font to Arial Black because a heavy font casts a more effective shadow, and then you will select the bullet points on the slide and add a bold effect.

3 In the Font group, click the Font drop-down arrow and select Arial Black. Press Ctrl+E to center the title.

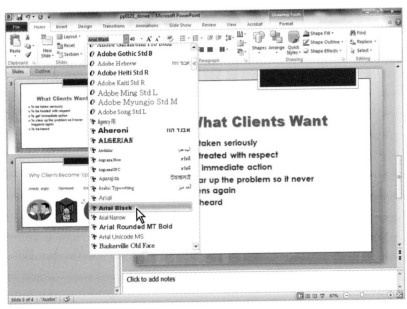

Arial Black is a strong font that casts a bold shadow.

4 Place the cursor before the word *To* in the first bullet. Click and drag down to the word *heard* in the last bullet.

5 In the Font group, click the Bold icon (**B**), and then click the drop-down arrow in the Font size drop-down menu and select 28.

6 Click the bullet to the left of the text *To be taken seriously* to select the bullet point. On the Ribbon, select Animations > Float In.

You can apply animations for entrance, exit, or emphasis.

7 In the Timing group, set the Duration to 02:00.

8 On the Ribbon in the Preview group, click Preview to view the effect of the animation. You can also select the Play Animations icon (☆) located next to the slide number in the slide preview panel on the left hand side of your screen.

Applying animation to pictures and text boxes

As you have discovered in the previous exercise, you can use animation on plain text phrases. In this exercise, you'll apply animation to text boxes and pictures.

1   Select slide 4, Why Clients Become Upset, and hover the cursor around the words *Already angry* until the cursor appears as a cross with arrows on the ends, and then click to select the text box.

2   On the Ribbon, click Animations > Appear.

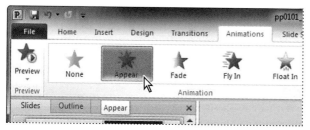

Click Appear.

Notice that the number 1 appears to the left of the text box to indicate that this animation happens first. All subsequent numbers also indicate the order of appearance on the slide.

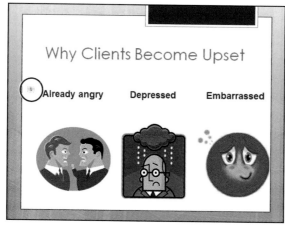

The numbers indicate in which order the elements of the slide appear.

3 Click the picture under *Already angry*, and then select Animation > Bounce. You might have to scroll through the list or click the More button to see the Bounce option.

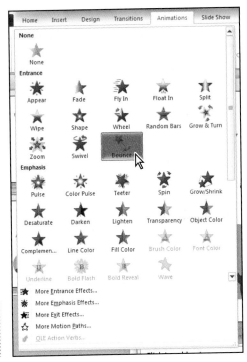

Click the drop-down arrow to display the Animations menu.

4 Repeat steps 1 to 3 for the word *Depressed* and its picture, and then for *Embarrassed* and its picture.

Be sure to create the animations in the order that you want them to appear.

5 Select Animations > Preview to view the result of your work.

6 Select File > Save to save your work, and then select File > Close to close it.

Congratulations! You have started to see some of what PowerPoint 2010 has to offer with this quick tour of several significant features.

Self study

1 To examine the different themes available to you in PowerPoint, navigate to the PPT01lessons folder and double-click to open the pp0101_working file. Select the Design tab. Click the down-arrow to the right of the Themes group to display the All Themes drop-down menu, and select Agency, then Austen, and finally Equity.

2 Using the View tab on the Ribbon, change the view to the Slide Sorter view and then back to Normal.

3 Click Normal and select slide 3 in Slides view. Change the layout of the slide to Title Only to see what happens, and then click Undo.

4 Select slide 2, Upset versus Difficult, and change the slide transition to Uncover.

Review

Questions

1 List three examples of subtle slide transitions that you can apply to a slide.

2 Which of the following fonts would be most effective for a shadow effect and why? Arial, Book Antiqua, Arial Black, Verdana

3 How would you preview an animation?

Answers

1 You can apply cut, fade, push, wipe, split, reveal, random bars, shape, uncover, cover, or flash.

2 Arial Black is the most effective because a heavy font casts a bolder shadow.

3 On the Ribbon, click Animations. In the Preview group, click Preview to view the effect of the animation.

What you'll learn in this lesson:

- PowerPoint 2010 Basics
- Navigating the user interface
- Customizing the Quick Access Toolbar
- Adding slides and entering related notes

Getting Started with Microsoft PowerPoint 2010

In this lesson, you will discover more about PowerPoint and what you can do with it. You will become familiar with the basic capabilities of PowerPoint 2010 and gain an understanding of the user interface. You will practice putting together a presentation.

Starting up

You will work with several files from the PPT02lessons folder in this lesson. Make sure that you have loaded the OfficeLessons folder onto your hard drive from *www.DigitalClassroomBooks.com/Office2010*. See "Loading lesson files" on page XXIV.

See Lesson 2 in action!

Use the accompanying video to gain a better understanding of how to use some of the features shown in this lesson. The video tutorial for this lesson can be found at www.DigitalClassroomBooks.com/Office2010.

Understanding Microsoft PowerPoint

PowerPoint helps you share your ideas on screen, helping you communicate when you give presentations either in-person or on-line. Whether you are delivering training, demonstrating ideas, explaining concepts and procedures, or giving any other kind of presentation, PowerPoint helps you tie together your ideas and concepts with images, text, multimedia, and sound. You can also include effects and create transition between slides to introduce sections or different concepts.

Your presentation can include charts and diagrams from Excel and documents from Word. You can even include compelling multimedia.

Presentation basics

You'll start by looking at the basics of the PowerPoint application and then begin constructing a presentation. You can build a presentation from a blank slate or from a pre-designed template or you can use a theme. A theme is similar to a template which gives your presentation a certain look. The difference is that themes can be changed very easily.

A template has a preformatted layout that stores styles, fonts, background color, and design, along with many other items, which makes it more difficult to modify.

As you start to design presentations, remember to think about the audience and the type of impact you want to have on them. Are you trying to inspire them, inform them, or maybe solve their problems? This will dictate the type of content you'll want to include. Always keep your audience in mind, because successful presentations are those that reach and connect with your audience.

Creating a new presentation

1 Choose Start > Programs > Microsoft Office > Microsoft PowerPoint 2010. A blank title page opens, ready for you to add text, graphics, or other content.

2 Place your cursor before Click to add title. Notice that the cursor lies in the center of the text box. This is where you will add text for the title of this presentation. In this text box, type **Nature's Own Pet Food**.

3   Now, place your cursor in the Click to add subtitle text box and then type **Natural Food for Dogs and Cats**.

To the left, notice a small version of the slide under the Slide tab and adjacent to this the Outline tab. PowerPoint displays small icons for each slide in the Slides view. You can use this view to navigate between slides by double-clicking on them, or use this to arrange the sequence of your slides.

The Slides view.

4   Click the Outline tab in the viewing area. You can see that PowerPoint keeps track of each slide in outline format as you build your presentation. You can use this to view and organize the thoughts and topics in your presentation.

5   Click Slides to return to the Slides view.

6   Choose File > Save As. The Save As dialog box appears. Navigate to the OfficeLessons folder. Click the PPT02lessons folder and type **pp0201** in the File name box, and then click Save. You will continue to use this file for practice, so keep it open.

Powerpoint's user interface

PowerPoint's interface includes standard Windows elements, such as the title bar and status bar. The window also contains Office-specific elements such as the Ribbon and the File tab and PowerPoint-specific elements such as tools and options that you can use to enhance your work.

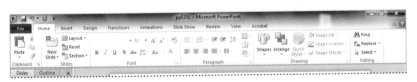

The PowerPoint Tools are located on the Ribbon.

Customizing the Quick Access Toolbar

The Quick Access Toolbar is a convenient place to store and access the commands you use most often. The Quick Access Toolbar is located on the top left of the PowerPoint window. By default, the toolbar displays the Save, Undo and Redo tool icons. You can add icons as you find useful. In this exercise, you'll add a command that will come in handy throughout the lesson, making it easy to add new slides to your PowerPoint presentation files.

1   On the Quick Access Toolbar, click the Customize Quick Access Toolbar located on the right end of the toolbar to display the Customize Quick Access Toolbar menu. PowerPoint displays the Customize Quick Access Toolbar menu.

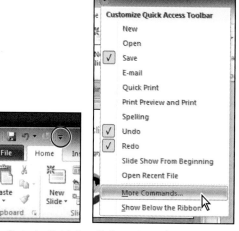

Use the Customize Quick Access Toolbar option to place commands at your fingertips.

2   In the Customize Quick Access Toolbar menu, click *More Commands*, and then click
New Slide > Add > OK.

*You can add commands to the Quick Access Toolbar that are not initially displayed by
choosing More Commands.*

3   Click File > Save to save the file.

*The colors you choose set the tone and demeanor for your presentation. Use appropriate colors for
your audience and industry. While pink might be a good choice for a presentation you'll give at a
cupcake store convention, it might not be well received by a group of bankers.*

Applying a theme

The Ribbon that runs across the top of the PowerPoint window has many of the commands you need to prepare a presentation. The Design tab holds the commands that help with presentation design such as themes, fonts, colors, and backgrounds.

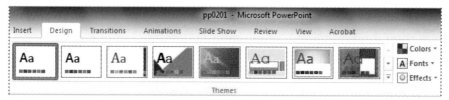

The Themes group on the Design tab allows you to apply themes to your presentation.

In the Themes group of the Design tab, you can find built-in themes to apply to your presentation to create consistent slides using the same colors, design, and font. In this exercise, you'll apply a theme to the presentation.

1 With the pp0201 presentation still open from a previous exercise, click the Design tab.

2 Click the drop-down menu to the right of the Themes group. From the display of themes, click Solstice.

Select Solstice from the Built-in Themes menu.

When you apply the Solstice theme, the title of the presentation changes to include embossed black text and a decorative bar.

Keep the slides simple with lots of white space. Your message can get lost in too many words. Use pictures to tell your story. A picture does say a thousand words, so let the picture talk.

Adding a slide and related notes

When adding a new slide to a presentation, you can select the type of slide based on the theme or template you select. Some slides are for the introduction or transition between sections, while others may be for the main portion of a presentation. In this exercise, you will add a new slide that contains speaker's notes.

1 Continuing to work with the file pp0201, on the Ribbon, click Home. In the Slides group, click the New Slide drop-down arrow.

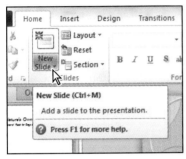

Click the drop-down arrow to display a list of styles.

2 On the New Slide menu, select Title and Content.

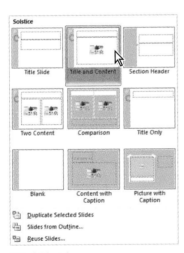

List of slide styles

3 Click inside the Click to add title text box, and type **Our Pet Nutrition Philosophy** to create the title.

4 Click inside the Click to add text box, and type the following bullet points:

- **Use only high quality ingredients**
- **Use nutrient-rich, unaltered ingredients**
- **Use highly-controlled cooking methods**
- **Use no artificial preservatives, colors, or additives**

Using the Notes pane

Now you'll open a Word document and copy notes for the speaker to place them in the presentation. The Notes pane helps guide a presenter when delivering a presentation. It is located below the slides so you can write notes to remind the presenter of concepts or ideas that should be discussed while displaying the slide. You can include particular words to explain the slide or specific statistics or data that support the slide. The Notes pane provides information that can be made visible to the presenter but hidden from the audience during a presentation.

Don't try to put all your information into each slide. Rather, use the slides to complement what the presenter is discussing. A slide listing bullets of everything the speaker is discussing cause the audience to focus on the slides rather than the speaker. With this approach, the notes become even more important, because the primary information will be coming from the presenter, with the slides serving as visuals to reinforce the message.

Use the Notes pane to add information for the presenter to share with the audience during the presentation.

1   Minimize the PowerPoint window by clicking the Minimize button in the upper right corner of the window.

Click the Minimize button.

2   Select Start > Programs > Microsoft Office > Microsoft Word 2010.

3   Select File > Open. In the Open dialog box, navigate to OfficeLessons > PPT02lessons, and then double click pp0202.docx.

4   In pp0202, click and drag to select the bullet points, and then press Ctrl+C or right-click with your mouse and choose Copy to copy the bulleted text.

5   To switch back to the pp0201presentation, press Alt+Tab which lets you switch between open programs. Release the Tab key once the PowerPoint window displaying the pp0201 presentation is selected. In the pp0201 presentation, click inside the Notes pane at the bottom of the screen, then press Ctrl+V to paste.

6   Place the cursor at the top border of the Notes pane. When the cursor changes to a vertical arrow (⬍), click and drag the cursor upwards to make the Notes pane larger.

You can drag the border between the Notes pane and the slide to decrease the Notes pane view and make the slides more visible.

Notice that the text is copied from Microsoft Word without the bullets. If you want to add bullets to text in the Notes panel, select the text, and then choose Paragraph > Bullets (≔).

7   Click Save in the quick access toolbar to save your work.

Adding a shaped text box

In this exercise, you'll add a shaped text box along with a picture into a presentation.

1   On the Ribbon, click Home. In the Drawing group, click Rounded Rectangle.

You can find many shapes in the Drawing group.

 Smaller monitors might not display all shapes. You would then click Shapes and then select the rounded rectangle.

2   Click on the slide 2 just under the word *additives* and then drag until the rounded rectangle is the width of the bulleted list, and the bottom of the rectangle is approximately one-half inch from the bottom of the slide.

3   With the rounded rectangle still selected on the slide, click the Shape Fill drop-down arrow in the Drawing group. On the Shape Fill menu, select No Fill. The color inside the rectangle disappears.

4   On the Shape Fill menu, select Picture.

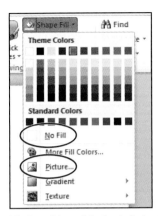

The Insert Picture dialog box is displayed.

5   Navigate to PPT02lessons and double click pp0202b. PowerPoint inserts the selected photograph into the rounded rectangle.

6   In the Drawing group, click the Shape Outline drop-down arrow, and select No Outline from the Shape Outline menu. The outline disappears.

You may want to resize the shape to display the photograph a bit clearer. You can do this by clicking and dragging the corners of the shape.

Adding a text box

You can add a text box and blank slide that varies from the design theme or template so that some slides have variations of the theme. You can control text formatting including color and size. In this exercise, you'll add a blank slide and text box.

1   With slide 2 selected, on the Quick Access Toolbar, click the New Slide drop-down arrow and then select Blank.

2   On the Ribbon, click Insert > Text Box from the Text group.

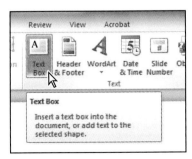

Select Text Box from the Text group to add a new text box to the page.

3 Move the cursor over the new slide, then click and hold down on the mouse where you want the upper-left corner of the new text box to start and drag to the right, releasing when the box is as wide as you want it.

4 Press Alt+Tab to switch back to the pp0202 Word document. Click within the text three times to select all the text under *Copy to text box Slide 3*. Right click the mouse to display the context menu, and select Copy.

5 Press Alt+Tab to switch back to the pp0201 presentation and with your cursor still blinking inside the text box you created, then press Ctrl +V to paste the text.

If you want to move the text frame to a different location on the page, position your cursor over the outside edge of the text frame, then click and drag to move the entire text frame to another location. You can also click and drag any of the round points at the corners of the text frame to adjust the size of the frame.

6 Click once to insert the cursor before the opening quotation mark. Click and drag to select all the text through the closing quotation mark. You'll now change the attributes for this text, so keep this text selected.

7 On the Ribbon, select Home.

You can customize the attributes for text in your presentation using the Font group found within the Home tab of the Ribbon.

Make the following selections from the Font group:

- Century Gothic for font style
- 36 for font size
- Bold
- Orange for color

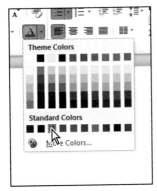

You can choose from a variety of colors for your font.

8 With the text still selected, in the Paragraph group, click Center to place the text in the center of the text frame horizontally.

Select Center from the Paragraph group to position the text in the center of the frame.

Adding a picture

Photographs and pictures can make your presentation more appealing. After inserting a picture, you can adjust its size and position in the presentation.

In this exercise, you'll add a new slide and then add a photograph to the slide.

1   On the Ribbon, select Home. In the Slides group, click the New Slide drop-down arrow.

2   From the Slides menu, select Title and Content.

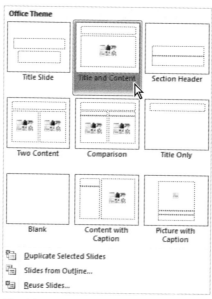

The Slides menu offers a variety of slide styles to suit your content.

3   In the Click to add title text box, type **A Healthy Pet is a Happy Pet** and press Ctrl+E to center the title.

4   In the slide, click the Insert Picture from File. icon

Click the icon to insert a picture.

5 Navigate to OfficeLessons > PPT02lesson. Double click pp0203.jpg.

PowerPoint inserts the picture and displays the Picture Tools tab on the Ribbon.

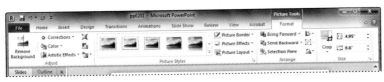

Use Picture Tools to format the image.

6 In the Picture Styles group, click Drop Shadow Rectangle.

Drop Shadow Rectangle is one of many styles available when placing pictures.

7 Click File > Save As. The Save As dialog box is displayed. In the File name box, type **pp0201_complete**.

You have completed a short presentation for the Nature's Own Pet Food Company. As you can see, your presentations can be exciting and powerful. PowerPoint allows you to add elements like graphics, text boxes, and themes to enhance your presentation.

Getting help

You can always get help when you are working on a PowerPoint presentation. You can click the Help button (?) located in the upper-right corner of the window. You can also get help from the File menu.

The File menu offers three help options.

If you need help on getting started with PowerPoint 2010, PowerPoint offers the Getting Started help option. You can also contact Microsoft for help by email, chat or phone.

To use the search option for help on PowerPoint:

1 Click File > Help. The Microsoft Support options are displayed.

2 Under Support, click the Microsoft Office Help button. The PowerPoint Help window is displayed.

PowerPoint searches for help within the program and on-line.

3 Type **animate** in the Search box to find how to animate text and graphics in PowerPoint.

4 Press Enter or click the Search icon ($\mathcal{P}$). PowerPoint displays the search results for the topic.

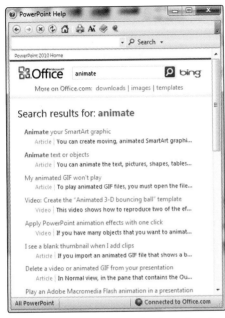

You can choose from many topics within the search results.

5 Select Animate text or objects. An article on how to animate text or object is displayed.

Self study

1 Launch PowerPoint 2010, and click File > New. Experiment with the different templates that are available. Click the Theme folder and look at the different Theme options. When you hover over a theme with the cursor, the slide takes on the look of the theme.

2 Add the Font Color icon to your Quick Access Toolbar.

3 Open pp0201_complete and practice adding different types of slides to the presentation such as Content with Caption, Picture with Caption, or a Section Header.

Review

Questions

1 What is the purpose of the Notes pane in PowerPoint?

2 What is a template?

3 What are some of the help options available in PowerPoint?

Answers

1 The Notes pane helps guide the presenter when giving a presentation. It is located below the slides and you can write notes to yourself to remind the presenter to include a concept or idea.

2 A template has a preformatted layout that stores styles, fonts, background color, and design.

3 Use the Microsoft Office help button to search for topics that answer your question or use the Getting Started with PowerPoint 2010 if you are a newer user. You can also contact Microsoft by email, chat or phone.

What you'll learn in this lesson:

- Creating a table and entering text
- Working with table styles and shading
- Merging cells
- Creating a chart

Working with Tables and Charts

In this lesson, you will discover how tables and charts can display data to help illustrate an idea. A table is effective for organizing data using the column-and-row format. A chart can turn numeric data into a visual element that your audience can quickly interpret and understand.

Starting up

You will work with several files from the PPT03lessonss folder in this lesson. Make sure that you have loaded the OfficeLessons folder onto your hard drive from *www.DigitalClassroomBooks.com/Office2010*. See "Loading lesson files" on page XXIV.

See Lesson 3 in action!

Use the accompanying video to gain a better understanding of how to use some of the features shown in this lesson. The video tutorial for this lesson can be found at www.DigitalClassroomBooks.com/Office2010.

Table basics

You'll start by looking at the basics of building a table and then you'll begin to construct a table within a presentation. There are some terms you should know before you build a table.

NAME	DESCRIPTION
Header row	The name of the labels along the top row that explain what is contained in each column
Cells	The boxes where rows and columns intersect that contain a data item
Row labels	The labels in the first column that describe what information is in each row
Borders	The lines in the table that define where the rows and columns are
Gridlines	The gray lines that show where the columns and rows will be if you apply a border

	Quarter 1	Quarter 2	Quarter 3	Quarter 4
East	5	8	5	6
West	3	4	4	9
North	3	8	9	6
South	8	7	7	9

*A. Row label. **B**. Border. **C**. Cells. **D**. Gridline. **E**. Header row.*

Tables are a good choice for side-by-side comparisons of measurable data, while charts allow you to present data visually for impact.

Creating a table

In this exercise, you'll create a table and enter text.

1 Choose Start > Programs > Microsoft Office > Microsoft PowerPoint 2010. A blank title page opens. You'll open an existing PowerPoint file for this exercise.

2 Choose File > Open. PowerPoint displays the Open dialog box.

3 Navigate to the OfficeLessons folder. Double-click the PPT03lessons folder, select the file pp0301, and then click Open. A PowerPoint presentation opens entitled Destined to Travel.

4 Choose File > Save As, type **pp0301_complete** in the Name text field and press Save.

To the left of the PowerPoint workspace, notice that PowerPoint displays a small version of the slides in the presentation under the Slides tab. You can use this view to navigate between slides or to arrange the sequence of your slides. When you double-click a slide in Slide view, it displays in full view in the PowerPoint workspace.

Slide view displays a miniature version of the presentation.

5 Click slide 2, Day Trips from Rome, to display the slide in full view, and then click the Insert Table icon (▦) in the middle of the slide.

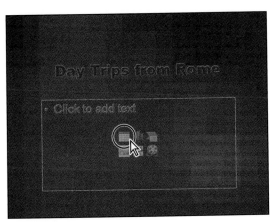

Click the Insert Table icon to begin creating a table.

6 In the Number of columns list box, select 3, and in the Number of rows list box, select 5. Click OK.

Select the number of rows and columns you want in the Insert Table dialog box.

PowerPoint inserts a table in the presentation and displays the Table Tools tab on the Ribbon.

Use the table tools for table design and layout.

Adding text to a table

In this exercise, you'll add text to the table you just created. First, you will open a Word document, select the table, and copy the contents from the table. Then you'll paste the information into the table in the presentation. You will then format the text by increasing the font size.

1 Select Start > Programs > Microsoft Office > Microsoft Word 2010.

2 Select File > Open. In the Open dialogue box, navigate to OfficeLesson > PPT03lessons, and then double click pp0302. A Word document opens entitled PowerPoint Lesson 3.

3 In pp0302, select the table under Day Trips from Rome by clicking the small box with the cross in the upper-left corner of the table.

4 Right-click anywhere in the table to display the shortcut menu, select Copy, and press Alt+Tab to return to the PowerPoint presentation.

5   Click the Table Tools tab, and then click the Layout tab.

6   In the Table group, click Select > Select Table.

Use the Ribbon to select the table.

7   Place the cursor in the first cell of the table and press Ctrl+V. PowerPoint pastes the contents of the table you copied into this table.

Now you'll increase the font size to 18 points to make the text more visible.

8   On the Ribbon, select Home and in the Font group, click the Increase Size icon (A˙) three times until the text size reaches 18 points.

9   Click File > Save. After you save a document with the correct name, you just have to click the Save icon (🖫) on the Quick Access Toolbar, press Ctrl+S, or File > Save to save any changes.

Use the Ribbon to select the table.

Selecting table elements

You can always click and drag to make selections, but you can also select most table elements with just a click.

ELEMENT	HOW TO SELECT
Cells	Place the cursor in the first cell and drag through the cells you want to select.
Rows	Place the cursor to the left of the row you want to select until you see the right-pointing arrow, and then click. PowerPoint selects the row.
Columns	Place the cursor above the column you want to select until you see the downward-pointing arrow, and then click. PowerPoint selects the column.
Table	Select the Table Tools Layout tab, and then in the Table group, click Select.

You can also select rows and columns by clicking the Table Tools Layout tab and clicking Select Column or Select Row.

Adding rows and columns

Once you have created a table, it is easy to add rows and columns. When you want to insert rows and columns, you must first select part of the table. For example, if you want to insert two columns, you select two columns in the table, and then select Insert Left or Insert Right, depending on where you want to insert the columns. You can perform the same procedure for rows to insert multiple rows at one time.

In this exercise, you'll add two rows of information to the table. On the Ribbon, when you click the Table Tools Layout tab, the Rows and Columns group displays all the tools you need to add rows above or below the selected row or rows.

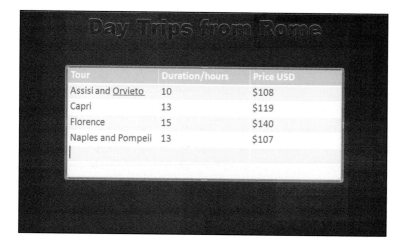

1 To the left of the PowerPoint table, hover your mouse over the outside border to the left of the word Florence until the cursor changes to a right-pointing arrow. Drag downward to select the two rows beginning with Florence and with Naples and Pompeii. PowerPoint highlights the bottom two rows of the table.

2 On the Ribbon, click the Table Tools Layout tab and select Insert Below in the Rows and Columns group.

Two rows appear at the bottom of the table.

3 In the Tour column under Naples and Pompeii, type **Ancient Ostia Small Group**. Finish the row by typing **4** for duration and **$53** for price.

4 In the Tour column under Ancient Ostia Small Group, type **Ancient Ostia Half Day**. Finish the row by typing **4** for duration and **$65** for price.

Aligning text within columns and rows

The Table Tools Layout tab in the Alignment group has the tools you need to align text within the columns and rows of the table. In this exercise, you'll select the table and align the text within it horizontally and vertically within the cells. You'll then enlarge the column to fit the text.

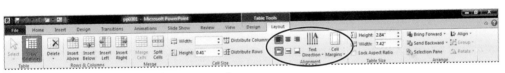

PowerPoint offers horizontal and vertical alignment commands.

1 In the pp0301 _complete.pptx file, select the table on the *Day Trips from Rome* slide by hovering, and clicking anywhere near the border of the table once the cursor changed to display two arrows. You can tell that the entire table is selected if the border around the table appears thick and there is not one visible insertion point.

2 On the Ribbon, click the Table Tools Layout tab. In the Alignment group, click Center, and then click Center Vertically. The text within the table centers horizontally and vertically.

Now that you've aligned the text, you will move the gridline to better fit the newly aligned text.

3 In the table, move the cursor over the gridline until the cursor resembles a double-headed arrow, and click the gridline between Tour and Duration in the top row. Move the gridline slightly to the right until the word *group* in the second to last row of the first column moves up.

4 Click the Save button on the Quick Access Toolbar.

Working with table styles and shading

A table style is a ready-made assortment of colors and border choices that you can choose from in the Table Styles gallery on the Ribbon. After you select a style, you can modify it by selecting table style options.

In this exercise, you'll use an alternate method to create a table and then apply a table style.

1 In Slide view, click slide 3 to see Hotels in full view.

2 On the Ribbon, click Insert and in the Tables group, click Table. PowerPoint displays the Insert Table menu.

You can select as many columns and rows in the Insert Table menu as you want.

3 Move the cursor over four columns and down five rows, and click at the ending location when you are done. The slide displays a four-column by five-row table.

You'll now change the style of the table to a plain table with only borders and grids, but no design.

4   With the table selected, on the Table Tools tab, click Design. In the Table Styles group, click the down-arrow to display the menu. In the Best Match for Document section, click No Style, Table Grid. The slide displays a simple table with borders and grid.

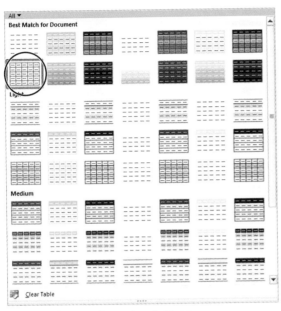

The Table Styles menu offers a variety of table styles.

5   Place the cursor in the top-left cell, type **Name**, and press Tab. The cursor moves to the next cell.

6   Type the following words in the remaining top cells and press Tab after each one.

   • **Location**

   • **Price**

   • **Rating**

   Now you'll apply shading to the top cells and a bold style to the font.

7   Click and drag to select the top row and press Ctrl+B to apply a bold style to the font.

8   In the Table Tools tab, click Design and then click Shading.

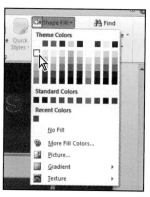

You can select shading in multiple colors.

9   Click the first gray color located in the second row to apply light-gray shading.

Merging cells

In this exercise, you will merge cells to create only one cell. You will then return to pp0302. docx and copy some text to paste into the table.

1   Move the cursor near the outside border of the table and to the left of the second row until you see a right-pointing arrow. Click to select the entire second row.

2   In the Table Tools tab, click Layout and then click Merge Cells.

3   In the Table Tools tab, click Design, click the Shading drop-down menu, and select Indigo Accent 6, the last color in the top row of the menu. The second row of the table is shaded deep blue.

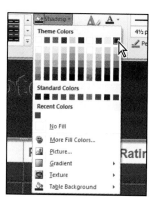

4   In the cell, type **Best Ratings Based on Customer Experience** and then press Ctrl+E to center it within the cell.

5   Select the last three rows of the table.

6   Press Alt+Tab to return to the Word document named pp0302.

7   Select the table under the word *Hotels* by clicking the small box in the upper-left corner of the table. On the Ribbon, click the Home tab and then click Copy in the Clipboard group.

8   Press Alt+Tab to return to the PowerPoint presentation. In the Clipboard group in the Home tab, click Paste.

9   In the Table Tools tab, click Design. Then click the Shading drop-down menu and select the light-blue color on the top row, second from the right. The bottom three rows are now shaded light blue.

10 Press Save on the Quick Access Toolbar.

11 You can toggle back over to the Word document by pressing Alt+Tab and select File > Close.

Working with charts

When you add a chart to a PowerPoint slide, numeric data is portrayed visually so your audience can quickly interpret and understand it. When you add a chart, PowerPoint launches Excel and opens a new Excel file that you can use to enter the chart data.

Choosing the right chart

The purpose of a chart is to present information across different categories, so when you select a chart, choose one that allows your audience to clearly make comparisons. Keep in mind that in a presentation, your audience sees the chart for only a brief period of time, so it has to be simple and make the point at one glance.

PowerPoint offers you 10 chart types and each type has an ideal use.

CHART NAME	DESCRIPTION
Area	Examine how values in different categories fluctuate over time and see the cumulative change in values.
Bar	Compare values in different categories against one another, usually over time. Data is displayed in horizontal bars.
Bubble	Examine data relationships by studying the size and location of the bubbles that represent the relationships. Bubble charts are often used in financial analysis and market research.
Column	Compare values in different categories against one another, usually over time. Data is displayed in vertical columns.
Doughnut	See how values compare as percentages of a whole.
Pie	See how values compare as percentages of a whole. Data from categories is displayed as a percentage of a whole.
Radar	Examine data as it relates to one central point. This kind of chart is used to make subjective performance analyses.
XY (Scatter)	Compare different numeric data point sets in space to reveal patterns and trends in data.
Stock	See how the value of an item fluctuates.
Surface	Examine color-coded data on a 3D surface to explore relationships between data values.

Creating a chart

When you decide on the type of chart that would best represent your data, you can create the chart in PowerPoint.

1 In the presentation, click on slide 4 in Slide view so that you can see the full view of the slide entitled *Flights to Rome*.

2 On the Ribbon, click Insert and in the Illustrations group, click Chart.

Click Chart in the
Illustrations group.

3 Select Bar and click OK. There are many bar charts that you can select from, but you'll use the default type for this exercise.

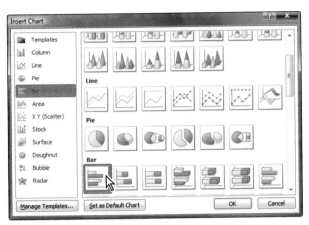

PowerPoint offers many chart types.

PowerPoint displays a sample of the chart type on the slide and the Excel window opens.

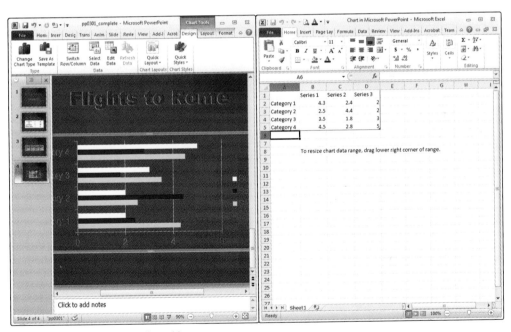

You can enter raw data into the Excel spreadsheet.

Now, you'll open an Excel spreadsheet and copy data from it.

4 In the Excel document, choose File > Open. Excel displays the Open dialog box.

5 Navigate to the OfficeLessons folder. Double-click the PPT03lessons folder, select the pp0303 Excel file, and then click Open. You'll copy the data from this spreadsheet into the spreadsheet that just opened with the chart in the presentation.

6 In pp0303, click the Select All box located to the left of column A. PowerPoint highlights the spreadsheet. Press Ctrl+C to copy the data.

Click the Select All box.

7 Click Chart on the status bar to return to the spreadsheet associated with the PowerPoint presentation.

Click Chart on the status bar.

8 In the Excel spreadsheet, click the Select All button and press Ctrl+V to paste the data. Notice that the PowerPoint slide reflects the data you entered on the spreadsheet.

9 Save the PowerPoint presentation by pressing Ctrl+S. Now you can close both Excel spreadsheets. If prompted, decline the option to have Excel save your copied information on the clipboard for later use, as you no longer need it.

Changing the chart type

In this exercise, you will change the chart type from a bar chart to a column chart.

1 In slide 4, click anywhere on the chart to select it. In the Chart Tools tab, click Design and then in the Type group, click Change Chart Type. PowerPoint displays the Change Chart Type dialog box.

2 Select Column from the menu and click OK. The chart changes from bars to columns.

3 Press Ctrl+S to save the presentation and then select File > Close.

You have completed the short presentation entitled Destined to Travel. As you can see, your presentations can be exciting and powerful. PowerPoint allows you to add elements like tables and charts to make your presentation effective.

Self study

1 Open pp0301_done and display slide 4, Flights to Rome from NY (RT), in the workspace. After selecting the chart, change the chart type to 3-D clustered columns, which is the fourth icon in the top row of the Change Chart Type dialog box.

2 In pp0301_done, in slide 2, add a row above and below Ancient Ostia Small Group.

3 In pp0301_done, select the row labeled Best Ratings Based on Customer Experience, and change the shading to a light tan color of your choice.

Review

Questions

1 How do you select a row in a PowerPoint table?

2 When would you use a table, and when would you use a chart?

3 Which two chart types are suitable to display values compared as percentages of a whole?

Answers

1 You place the cursor to the left of the row you want to select until the cursor changes to a right-pointing arrow, and then click. PowerPoint selects the row.

2 Tables are a good choice for side-by-side comparisons of measurable data, while charts allow you to present data visually for impact.

3 Doughnuts and pie charts are effective to show values compared as percentages of a whole.

What you'll learn in this lesson:

- Using the drawing tools
- Working with shape styles
- Inserting a picture and applying effects
- Creating a diagram
- Customizing and saving a theme

Working with Graphic Elements

In this lesson, you will discover how to dress up a presentation using pictures and graphic elements, such as effects, styles, and shapes. One way to make your slides more appealing is to insert photographs or clip art. After you insert a picture, you can resize, reposition, and perform other types of edits on it.

Starting up

You will work with several files from the PPT04lessons folder in this lesson. Make sure that you have loaded the OfficeLessons folder onto your hard drive from *www.DigitalClassroomBooks.com/Office2010*. See "Loading lesson files" on page XXIV.

See Lesson 4 in action!

Use the accompanying video to gain a better understanding of how to use some of the features shown in this lesson. The video tutorial for this lesson can be found at www.DigitalClassroomBooks.com/Office2010.

Using the drawing tools

When you work with pictures and illustrations, you will use the many tools that are available on the Ribbon. These tools help enhance your slides to make your presentation visually appealing to your audience.

When you insert a graphic or a graphic object, such as a shape or WordArt, PowerPoint displays the Drawing Tools tab on the Ribbon. With these tools, you can create shapes and apply styles to the shapes. You can also insert WordArt and arrange and resize your graphics.

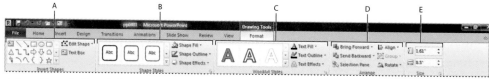

A. Insert Shapes. *B*. Shape Styles. *C*. WordArt Styles. *D*. Arrange. *E*. Size.

GROUP	DESCRIPTION
Insert Shapes	Inserts lines, rectangles, basic shapes, block arrows, equation shapes, flowchart shapes, stars and banners, callouts, and action buttons
Shape Styles	Applies shape styles, shape fills, outlines, and effects
WordArt Styles	Applies WordArt styles, shape fills, outlines, and effects
Arrange	Arranges, aligns, groups, and rotates
Size	Changes the height or the width of the shape or picture

Inserting a graphic as a background

In this exercise, you'll open a PowerPoint presentation and add graphic elements to it.

1   Choose Start > Programs > Microsoft Office > Microsoft PowerPoint 2010. A blank title page opens. You'll open an existing PowerPoint file for this exercise.

2   Choose File > Open.

3   Navigate to the OfficeLessons folder. Double-click the PPT04lessons folder, select the pp0401 file, and then click Open. A PowerPoint presentation opens entitled Willow Tree Farms.

4   Place the cursor to the left of the text *Garden Center*. The text is a very light color, so you have to look closely to see it. PowerPoint places an outline around the text box to indicate that it is selected. In the text box, you'll add a graphic as the background image.

5 Right-click within the selected text box. PowerPoint displays a shortcut menu and mini toolbar.

The shortcut menu and mini toolbar offer tools to format the text box and the font.

6 Select Format Shape from the shortcut menu.

7 In the Format Shape dialogue box, click Picture or texture fill, and PowerPoint changes the dialog box and displays tools to format a picture.

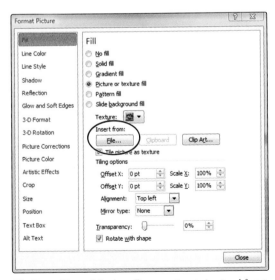

The Format Picture dialog box offers you options to insert and format a picture.

8 Be sure that the Tile picture as texture box is not selected and click Insert from File. PowerPoint displays the Insert Picture dialog box. Navigate to the OfficeLessons folder, double-click the PPT04lessons folder, select the pp0402 file, and then click Insert.

PowerPoint inserts the file. You should be able to see the words *Garden Center* at the top of the text box. Close the Format Picture dialog box.

Working with shape styles

Now, you'll add a shape style to the title text box.

1 In the presentation, click to the left of the title *Willow Tree Farms* and click the Drawing Tools tab.

2 On the Ribbon, click the More button which is also the down-arrow to the right of the Shape Styles group. PowerPoint displays the Shape Styles menu.

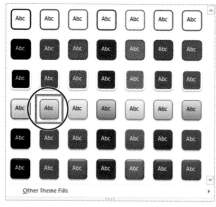

The Shape Styles menu offers you choices to add style to the shape.

3 Select the fourth style down in the green column, Subtle Effect Green Accent 1.

Inserting a picture and applying effects

In this exercise, you'll insert a picture into a slide and then add an effect to the picture.

1 In the presentation in Slide view on the left, click slide 2 to display the slide in full view.

2 On the Ribbon, click Insert and in the Images group, click Picture.

In the Images group, click Picture.

3   Navigate to the OfficeLessons folder. Double-click the PPT04lessons folder, select the pp0403 graphic file, and then click Insert. PowerPoint displays the picture in the presentation and the Picture Tools tab on the Ribbon.

You'll now add effects to the picture.

4   With the picture selected, click the More button which is the drop-down arrow to the right of the Picture Styles group and select Beveled Oval, Black from the menu.

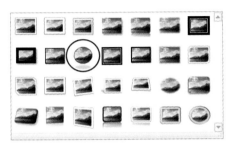

You can choose from many different styles for the picture.

5   Click File > Save As. The Save As dialog box appears. In the File name box, type **pp0401_completed**. From now on, when you want to save your changes, you just have to press Ctrl+S.

Aligning graphics

The Drawing Tools Format tab has the tools you need to align graphics. In this exercise, you'll select three WordArt objects and align them horizontally and vertically. You'll then group them so that they behave as a single entity.

1   In the presentation, click slide 3 in the Slide view to display it in full view.

2   Hold down the Shift key and click Annuals, Perennials, and Herbs to select them.

3   On the Ribbon, click the Drawing Tools tab, and then in the Arrange group, click the drop-down arrow to the right of Align.

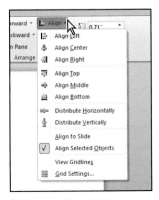

You can align the graphic objects in several ways, such as horizontally and vertically.

4   Select Distribute Horizontally from the Align menu, and then select Distribute Vertically.

Notice that PowerPoint moves the WordArt objects so that they are evenly distributed both horizontally and vertically.

5   With the WordArt objects still selected, click Group in the Arrange group to display the Group menu.

The Group menu allows you to group, ungroup, and regroup your selections.

PowerPoint places a border around the whole group. Now that the images are grouped, you can rotate, flip, move, or resize all shapes or objects at the same time as though they were a single shape or object. If you need to move or edit a single image in the group, you can always use the ungroup command to release the image from the group.

Ungrouping and regrouping graphic elements

Now, you'll place a graphic under the WordArt Annuals. You'll temporarily ungroup the WordArt objects that you just grouped so that you can align the picture of the pansy under the word *Annuals*. You will then regroup the WordArt.

1   On the Ribbon, click the Insert tab and in the Images group, click Picture.

2   Navigate to the OfficeLessons folder. Double-click the PPT04lessons folder, select the pp0404 file, and then click Insert. PowerPoint inserts a picture of a pansy on the page. Click the picture and drag it to under the word *Annuals*.

3   Click *Annuals*, and on the Ribbon, click the Drawing Tools tab. In the Arrange group, click Group and then select Ungroup from the Group menu. PowerPoint selects the other WordArt objects that were part of the group.

Using the Group menu, you can group, regroup, and ungroup items.

4 Click to the left of the word *Annuals*, and press Shift. Click the pansy picture and then in the Arrange group on the Ribbon, click Align. Select Align Center from the menu. PowerPoint centers the picture under the WordArt.

5 Click anywhere on the slide to ensure that there are no longer any selected items, and then click *Annuals*. Hold down the Shift key and select *Perennials and Herbs*. In the Arrange group on the Ribbon, click Group and select Regroup from the Group menu.

6 On the Ribbon, click Insert. In the Images group, click Picture. PowerPoint displays the Insert Picture dialog box. Click the pp0405 file and click Insert. PowerPoint inserts the file on the page.

7 Click the picture and drag it to under the word *Perennials* so that the right edge of the picture lines up with the end of the word *Perennials*.

8 Repeat the procedure to insert the pp0406 file, and drag the picture to under the word Herbs so that the right edge of the picture lines up with the end of the word *Herbs*.

The right edges of the pictures should align with the ends of the words.

9 Press Shift and click the pictures of both the perennials and the herbs. On the Ribbon, click Picture Tools, and then click Align. Select Align Left from the menu.

Creating a diagram

A diagram is a perfect union between pictures and words. PowerPoint diagrams are easy to create using SmartArt graphics. PowerPoint offers you 100 different diagram choices that fall into ten categories.

DIAGRAM TYPE	USE
List	Describes a block of related information and steps in a task, process, or workflow
Process	Describes how a concept or a process changes over time.
Cycle	Illustrates a circular progression without a beginning or end
Hierarchy	Describes hierarchical relationships between people, departments, and other entities
Relationship	Describes the relationship between different components
Matrix	Shows the relationship between quadrants
Pyramid	Shows proportional or hierarchical relationships
Picture	Creates diagrams that include photographs and pictures
Office.com	Downloads other types of diagrams from *Office.com*
Other	Creates custom diagrams

In this exercise, you'll use a diagram to illustrate the garden services available at Willow Tree Farms Garden Center.

1   Click slide 4 in the Slide view to display it in full view. On the Ribbon, click the Insert tab and then in the Illustrations group, click SmartArt.

2   In the Choose a SmartArt Graphic dialogue box, select Picture from the SmartArt menu and then select Picture Caption List, the third diagram from the left. Click OK. PowerPoint displays the Picture Caption List diagram for you to populate.

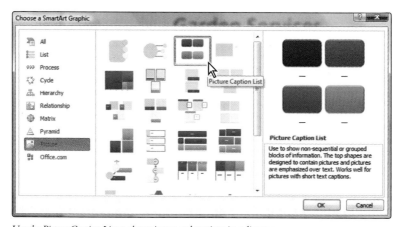

Use the Picture Caption List to show pictures and captions in a diagram.

3 In the Type your text here box, type the following text next to each bullet in the following order. After typing in each box, click in the next one to insert the next text. If you press Enter, it will create additional boxes. If you press Tab, it will create sub-categories.

- **Mulch and Soil**
- **House Plants**
- **Landscaping and Planting**
- **Container Gardening**

4 On the slide, click the graphic icon in the middle of the *Mulch and Soil* rectangle in the diagram. PowerPoint displays the Insert Picture dialog box. Select the pp0407 file, and then click Insert.

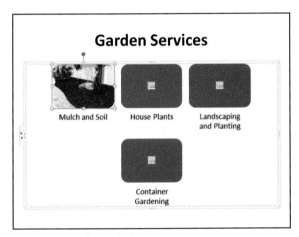

Insert the pp0407 file into the diagram.

5 Repeat the procedure in step 4 for the remaining bullets in the list:
- For House Plants, select pp0408
- For Landscaping and Planting, select pp0409
- For Container Gardening, select pp0410

6 In the slide, press Shift and click on each graphic to select them all. On the Ribbon, click the SmartArt Tools tab, and then the Design tab, click the drop-down arrow to the right of the SmartArt Styles group. Select Intense Effect, the last choice in the top row.

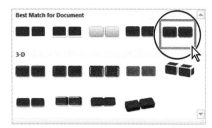

You can select effects for your diagram using the SmartArt Tools.

7 Click anywhere outside of the diagram to de-select it. Choose File > Save to save your work.

Customizing and saving a theme

In this exercise, you'll change the appearance of the presentation by customizing a theme. You'll then save the theme to use in future presentations.

1 In the presentation named pp0401_completed, click on slide 1. On the Ribbon, click the Design tab, and then in the Themes group, click Colors. PowerPoint displays the Colors menu.

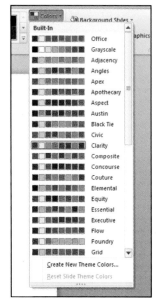

Use the Colors menu to select new theme colors.

2   From the Colors menu, select Grayscale. Notice that the banner around *Willow Tree Farms* changes to gray.

3   In the Themes group, click Fonts. PowerPoint displays the Fonts menu.

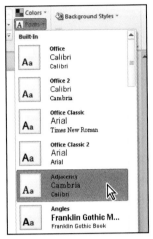

Use the Fonts menu to select new theme fonts.

4   From the Fonts menu, select Office 2. The font changes on all slides to the Cambria and Calibri style combination.

5   In the Background group, click Background Styles. PowerPoint displays the Background Styles menu.

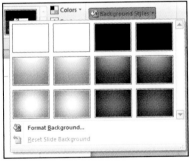

Use the Background Styles menu to select a new theme background.

6   From the Background Styles menu, select Format Background.

7   In the Format Background dialog box, click the drop-down menu for Color, and select White Background 2, the third color from the left.

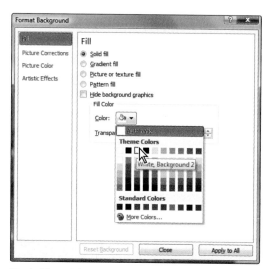

Use the Theme Colors menu to change the background color of the theme.

8   Click Apply to All and click Close.

9   On the Ribbon, click the Design tab. In the Themes group, click the drop–down menu to the right of the Theme Gallery. PowerPoint displays the All Themes menu.

The All Themes menu lists all the themes you can select.

10 Select Save Current Theme.

11 In the File Name box, type **MyGrayTheme** and click Save.

12 Press Ctrl+S to save your changes to the presentation and select File > Close.

You have completed the short presentation entitled Willow Tree Farms Garden Center. As you can see, your presentations can be detailed and colorful. PowerPoint allows you to add elements such as graphics and diagrams to make your presentation effective.

Self study

1 Open pp0401_completed and display slide 2, Window into Products and Services, in the workspace. After selecting the picture, change the picture style to Metal Oval, which is the last icon in the bottom row of the Picture Styles menu.

2 In pp0401_completed, display slide 4, Garden Services. Select Style 12 from the Background Styles menu.

3 In pp0401_completed, select a different color theme combination from the Colors menu.

Review

Questions

1 Which drawing tool changes the height and width of a shape or picture?

2 What menu can you use to distribute graphic objects horizontally?

3 What diagram type illustrates a circular progression without a beginning or end?

Answers

1 The Size drawing tool changes the height and width of a shape or picture.

2 You can use the Align menu to distribute graphic objects horizontally.

3 The Cycle diagram type illustrates a circular progression.

What you'll learn in this lesson:

- Introducing Access 2010
- Understanding the basics of database design and components
- Exploring the elements of the Access user interface

Microsoft Access 2010 Jumpstart

In this lesson, you will get a general introduction to Access 2010. You will learn some terminology and the basics of database design, and you will look at the user interface and some of the basic features. Finally, you will learn how to use the Help application.

Starting up

You will not need to work with any files for this lesson.

See Lesson 1 in action!

Use the accompanying video to gain a better understanding of how to use some of the features shown in this lesson. The video tutorial for this lesson can be found at www.DigitalClassroomBooks.com/Office2010.

What Is Access?

Access is an application that allows you to manage information in databases. It is available in certain editions of Microsoft Office and can also be purchased separately.

Access can handle databases ranging in complexity from a spreadsheet or text-filing system to those used by large organizations and companies. With Access, you can work locally on your computer or, if you have an account on a SharePoint Server, you can make your database available to the World Wide Web, and the data can be accessed through a web browser.

How can you use Access?

You can use Access to create, modify, and manage databases. Depending on the database's complexity and your needs, you can perform tasks such as the following:

- Create a database, either from a template or from scratch
- Establish relationships between types of information
- Add data to the database, either by directly editing fields of tables, or by using a form, which you can either design or choose from a selection of pre-made forms
- Import or link to external data sources
- Run filters and queries on the database to limit your display to relevant data
- Generate reports to present your results in an esthetically pleasing format

Database basics

In order to be able to work in Access, it's important to understand what a database is, and how it differs from a spreadsheet like those in Excel, which provide another common method for storing and managing data. A database is an organized collection of data that allows for storage, query, retrieval, and maintenance of information. A library's card catalog, a recipe box, and a company phone book are examples of databases, albeit using simpler technology. It's helpful to briefly compare and contrast databases and spreadsheets.

Both Excel and Access can be used to manage data. In fact, if your data can be easily entered, stored, viewed, extracted, and otherwise managed within a spreadsheet, your best option may be to use Excel, especially if you are already familiar with it. An example would be a small staff directory that includes items such as Last Name, First Name, Office, Phone Number, Department, and Start Date.

If, however, your data has relationships among certain fields, and you can see possibilities of duplication, which would mean extra maintenance and potential for errors, a relational database may be a better solution. For example, in a customer order database, you could have separate tables for customer names and their orders. A given customer can have many orders. This is an example of a one-to-many relationship, and is well suited for a relational database. Additionally, you might want to have another table for order details, as there may be several line items per order.

Basic database terminology

The following terms are frequently used when discussing databases, and it's useful to understand them before starting to work with an Access database.

TERM	DESCRIPTION
Table	A structured container for data about a particular item or purpose. Tables contain rows and columns, and therefore resemble a spreadsheet.
Record	A table row. Each record represents one instance of the subject of the table. For example, a record in an Orders table contains data about one particular order. Each record in a table should be unique.
Field	A table column, or attribute. For example, a FirstName field would likely be found in an Employees table.
Primary Key	The field (or fields), often an ID number, in each table that differentiates each record. This field is unique, permanent, and never empty.
Form	A graphical, user-friendly interface for managing information in a database.
Report	A method of presenting data to the user. Reports are highly customizable and are well-suited for printing.

Database design tips

Database design can be very complex, and advanced design skills often require months of classroom work. However, for basic design work, you can start with the following tips:

- Plan, plan, plan! You should never rush to create the components of a database. Rather, get as much information as you can from the database project stakeholders, such as your supervisor or client, before you start. Many experienced database designers have one or more conversations to determine what tables are needed, what their fields are, and how the tables are related.

- Diagrams can be very helpful in database planning. Sketch the tables on a piece of paper and use lines and arrows to show how they're related.

- Each table should have only one purpose, for example, to keep track of customers, orders, or employees.

- Avoid duplication of data. For example, you wouldn't want Customer fields in the Orders table. Redundant data not only increases the size and complexity of your database, but it also increases the likelihood of data entry or retrieval errors.

Quick tour of Access 2010

Before you can completely understand the capabilities of Access, you need to understand the components of the program. Let's begin by taking a quick tour to explore the program.

1 Choose Start > Programs > Microsoft Office > Microsoft Access 2010.

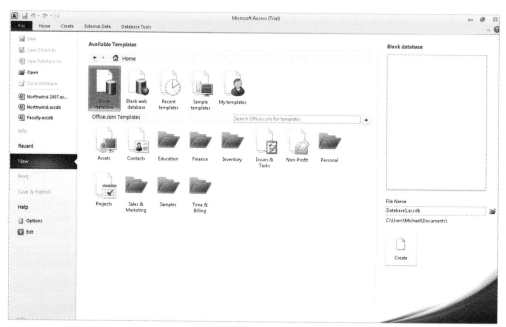

Backstage view of Access 2010.

Access 2010 opens in Backstage view, where you can create a new database, open an existing database, and view featured content from *Office.com*. Backstage view is described in more detail in the next section.

You can always access Backstage view, even when working in a database, by clicking the File tab.

Backstage view is new to Office 2010. Some of the user interface elements, such as the Ribbon and Navigation pane, were introduced in Access 2007.

Access 2010 components

The Access 2010 interface has the following main components:

- **The Ribbon**: This bar across the top of the interface contains several tabs. These tabs contain groups of commands, which are visible on all tabs except File.

- **Backstage view**: This view, which appears by default when you launch Access 2010, is the group of commands on the Ribbon's File tab.

The File tab always has a colored background, even when it is not the active tab. This may be confusing, so just remember that you can identify the active tab by the borders on either side of it.

- **The Navigation pane**: The area on the left side of the interface displays database objects when a database is open, or tabs in Backstage view.

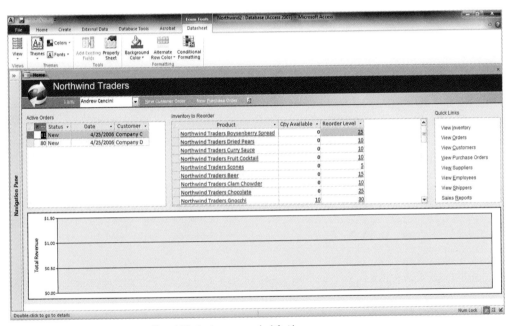

The Northwind database, showing a collapsed Navigation pane on the left side.

Let's examine these components in more detail.

The Ribbon

The Ribbon is divided into tabs, and within each tab there are groups. The Ribbon replaces traditional menus that existed across the top of the screen and toolbars which were found in older versions of Microsoft Office. The primary tabs of Access 2010 are File, Home, Create, External Data, and Database Tools.

The Access 2010 ribbon is divided into tabs.

The Ribbon's appearance changes depending on your current task. Some tabs, such as the Design tab, only appear in certain contexts. For example, when a database is open in Access 2010 and you click the External Data tab, the Ribbon displays groups of commands for importing, linking to, exporting, and collecting data.

You can hide and show the Ribbon by double-clicking the active command tab, making it easy to maximize your workspace as needed.

To hide or show the Ribbon:

1   In Backstage view, click the Home tab.

The Ribbon changes from a simple row of tabs to a group of commands. These commands are inactive because no database is open.

The Ribbon in full view, showing groups of commands.

2   Hide the Ribbon by clicking the Home tab.

The Ribbon with its command groups hidden.

3   Show the Ribbon by clicking the Home tab again.

You have successfully toggled the Ribbon by clicking the active tab. You can also toggle the Ribbon by clicking the Minimize/Expand arrow button in the upper-right corner.

Backstage view

Backstage view is the first view you see after you launch Access 2010.

It contains information and commands that affect an entire database, such as the following: opening and saving a database; a list of recently opened databases; and tabs for database information, recent databases, and database creation. You can also launch the help system and manage options in Backstage view.

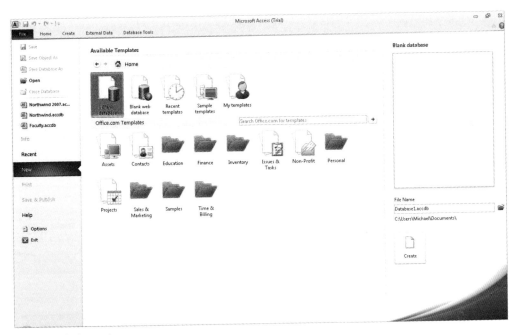

Access 2010 Backstage view.

Navigation Pane

The Navigation pane, which replaces the Database window of some older versions of Access, is located on the left side of the Access 2010 interface when a database is open.

The Navigation pane allows you to view and manage the database's objects, and is customizable.

 A database's objects include such items as tables, queries, forms, and reports.

As you did with the Ribbon, you can toggle the Navigation pane. Although the result is the same, the procedure is slightly different. You'll toggle and examine the Navigation pane in more detail after you've opened a database that contains some actual data.

Exploring a database

Now that you've covered some introductory information, you'll examine a database and discover how it works.

To open a sample template:

1   While in Backstage view, choose New and then Sample Templates.

2   Select *Northwind*, and then click the Create button located on the bottom-right of the screen.

3   You may see a Security Warning at the top of the screen. If so, click Enable Content.

Click Enable Content if a security warning is displayed.

3   In the Login Dialog box, leave the preset information in the Employee field and click the Login button to view the database.

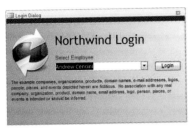

The Login window of the Northwind database.

As you open the database, the Ribbon expands and additional tabs appeared. The Datasheet tab is open and contains commands that are relevant to the content of the database.

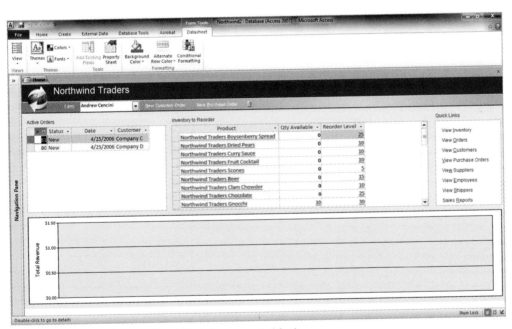

The Northwind database, showing a collapsed Navigation pane on the left side.

Let's explore the Navigation pane. Like the Ribbon, you can toggle the visibility.

To show or hide the Navigation pane:

1 Click the Open/Close button (») in the upper-right corner of the Navigation pane to view the contents.

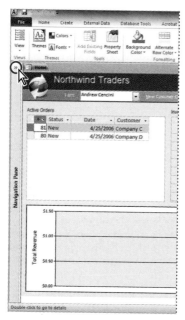

Click the Open/Close button to expand the Navigation pane.

2 Click the Open/Close button a second time to close the Navigation pane. It doesn't quite disappear, but it collapses to show only the title bar of the pane—this is called Shutter View.

3 Click the Open/Close button again to restore the Navigation pane.

You can alter the Navigation pane's width by clicking and dragging its rightmost edge.

The Navigation pane displays the database's objects. The default view shows all the main categories. Within each category are objects relating their headings.

Let's use the Search text box at the top of the Navigation pane.

To search for an object:

1   On each heading in the Navigation pane, click on the down arrow to show objects. You
will need to scroll down to access all the headings.

2   Type **customer** in the Search text box.

*The Search engine instantly finds objects
that match the text as you type it.*

As you type, objects that contain this text begin to appear. In the Northwind database,
there are two forms and two reports that contain the text *customer* in their titles.

3   Delete the text—either by clicking the Clear Search String icon (🗙) to the right of the
Search text box, or by using the Delete or backspace key—to show all objects.

Because you may not always want to use the default view of all objects, you can use
the Navigation pane to select from one of several different ways to display objects. For
example, there may be times when you want to see all objects of a particular type, such as
all the tables.

To arrange the appearance of the objects in the Navigation pane:

1 Click the down-arrow button in the upper-right corner of the Navigation pane.

The Navigation pane shows that the current category is the Northwind Traders database, and the group is Show All.

Use the Navigation pane to choose how objects are displayed and organized.

2 Change the Navigation pane to show tables by clicking Object Type.

All Access objects in this database now appear in the Navigation pane under the appropriate headings.

3 Scroll up to see the tables, which are listed at the top. You may need to open each category by clicking the down arrows located next to the headings to view results.

4 Click the down-arrow button again to change the display settings from Object Type. This time select Tables to display only the tables in this database.

You can double-click an object to open it. You can access more options by right-clicking an object.

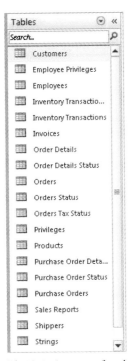

The Navigation pane configured to display only Tables.

To manage objects in the Navigation pane:

1 Right-click an object, such as *Customers*, to open a context menu.

The menu lists several options, depending on the object. For a table, these options include such items as Open, Design View, Import, and Export. Importing is covered in Lesson 2. The important thing to remember is that you can right-click objects to perform actions or to view information.

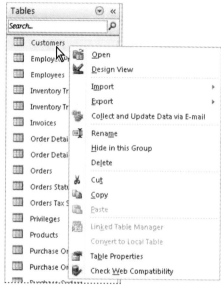

The contextual menu lists many options for managing items in the Navigation pane.

Working with records

Now that you've become familiar with database components, let's get a quick introduction to working with records. You'll use the Customers table in the Northwind database to search for, sort, add, and delete a record.

If necessary, open the Customers table from the Navigation pane, either by double-clicking it or by right-clicking it and selecting Open.

Searching for a record

To search a table for a record:

1 Press Ctrl+F or click the Find button (🔍) in the Ribbon to open the Find and Replace dialog box.

The Find and Replace window appears.

2 In the Find What text field, type your last name.

3 In the Look In drop-down menu, select Current Document.

4 Click Find Next.

If your last name did not appear, search for Lee, which appears twice.

Notice that the Table is sorted by the ID field in ascending order. You can easily sort by a different field.

5 When you are finished using Find and Replace, click Cancel in the Find and Replace dialog box.

Sorting records

To sort records:

1 Click the drop-down arrow on the Last Name column heading.

2 Select Sort A to Z.

The records are now sorted by Last Name, not by ID.

Adding and deleting records

Adding and deleting a record are similar processes. To add a record, it is not necessary to scroll to the end of a table.

Adding a record

To add a record:

1   Right-click the Record Selector (the leftmost square) of any row.

2   Click New Record.

Add a record regardless of your present location in a Table.

3   The ID field will change from "(New)" to an ID number that Access automatically assigns when you start entering information in the record's fields.

You can move to the next field by clicking either TAB or Enter, as well as by using the mouse.

4   Add 2 or 3 records, using names that you'll recognize.

Deleting a record

To delete a record:

1   (Optional) Use the Find command to locate the record you want to delete. You may use one of the records you just added.

2   Right-click the Record Selector (the leftmost square) of that record.

3   Click Delete Record.

Customizing the Quick Access Toolbar

Use the Quick Access Toolbar for convenient, one-click access to your favorite tools. Currently, the toolbar in the document displays the Save, Redo, and Undo options, and the Customize Quick Access Toolbar button.

Here you will customize the toolbar to include the Quick Print and Refresh All buttons. If you have completed the Microsoft Word lessons, you will already be familiar with this process.

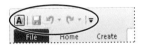

The Quick Access Toolbar.

To customize the Quick Access Toolbar:

1 Click the Customize Quick Access Toolbar button (▾).

2 In the drop-down menu, click Quick Print.

3 Click the Customize Quick Access Toolbar button.

4 In the drop-down menu, click Refresh All.

The Quick Access Toolbar now contains the Quick Print and Refresh All commands.

*The new commands are now added
to the Quick Access Toolbar.*

5 To remove a command, right-click it, and click Remove from Quick Access Toolbar.

Getting help

If you run into a problem or aren't sure how to perform a certain task, you can easily get help in Access by doing one of the following:

1   Press your computer's F1 key or click the Help button to display the help system.

2   In Backstage view, click the Help tab to display Support links for the help system, Getting Started resources, and a link to chat with, call, or e-mail Microsoft.

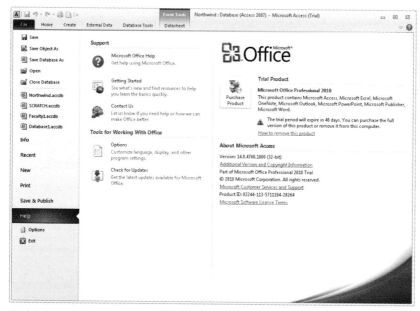

Get help by pressing F1 or clicking the Help tab in the Backstage view.

Ending an Access session

It is a good practice to save your work before closing Access. This can be accomplished by one of two easy methods:

- Click File Save, then File > Exit.

- Click Save on the Quick Access Toolbar, and then click the Close button located in the upper-right hand corner of the program.

The Close button exits the program.

Self study

1   Customize the Quick Access Toolbar beyond what you learned in the previous steps. Explore the More Commands option to discover the different customization options.

2   Customize the Ribbon by right-clicking on it. Make some changes to its functionality and appearance.

3   Explore the help system, including the Getting Started resources. Search the help system for Primary Key. Under Getting Started, watch the brief video entitled "Getting Started with Microsoft Access 2010" (you may need to scroll down to see it).

Review

Questions

1   What do records and fields correspond to in spreadsheets?

2   How do you customize the Quick Access Toolbar?

3   What does the Navigation pane show a list of?

Answers

1   In spreadsheet terminology, records and fields are called rows and columns, respectively.

2   You can customize the Quick Access Toolbar by clicking the Customize Quick Access Toolbar button.

3   The Navigation pane shows a list of all objects in a database.

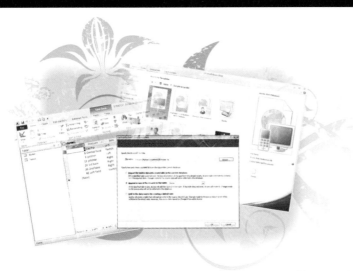

What you'll learn in this lesson:

- Introducing Access 2010
- Understanding the basics of database design and components
- Exploring the elements of the Access user interface

Getting Started with Microsoft Access 2010

In this lesson, you will discover how to create a database. You will also create basic tables while learning about data types. You will gain an understanding of how to bring data from Excel into an Access database.

Starting up

You will work with a file from the Access02lessons folder in this lesson. Make sure that you have loaded the OfficeLessons folder onto your hard drive from *www.DigitalClassroomBooks.com/Office2010*. See "Loading lesson files" on page XXIV.

See Lesson 2 in action!

Use the accompanying video to gain a better understanding of how to use some of the features shown in this lesson. The video tutorial for this lesson can be found at www.DigitalClassroomBooks.com/Office2010.

Access 2010 database types

Access 2010 has two types of databases: standard ("desktop") and Web. The exercises in this lesson involve the standard database type. A web database can be managed and viewed within a web browser, and requires that the host computer is running Server software. For Access, this would be SharePoint server. Users can use a web database in a web browser window, but you would still use Access 2010 to make design changes. This is different from a desktop database which stored locally on your computer or within your business network. A desktop database can be used and viewed on desktop machines, not over the Web.

Creating a simple database

In Lesson 1, you explored a database. Now you will create one. Access 2010 has two methods for creating a database:

- You can use one of the templates provided with Access 2010. A template is a database that contains several objects (such as tables, forms, and reports) needed to execute a particular task.

Even if a database is created from a template, you're not required to use objects as they are provided. Access 2010 allows you to customize objects. For example, if you feel that you have a better design for a form, or you need a different field name for a table (or a new table or two), you can make your own customizations.

- You can create a database from scratch, which is generally better suited for simple databases, expert users, or when you cannot locate a suitable template.

It is far likelier that your job will entail working on an existing Access database. You will probably enter information into the database and perhaps also be asked to edit or create database objects, such as forms, tables, and queries.

Creating a database using a template

1 Click File > New.

In Backstage view, several available templates appear, some of which are local (on your computer), and some of which are available for download from *Office.com*. The locally available ones are listed in the following table.

NAME	DESCRIPTION
Blank database	(Not a template.) This is a basic, empty desktop database.
Blank Web database	(Not a template.) This is a basic, empty Web database.
Recent templates	Contains templates that you have recently opened. There may be none available for you to select at this point.
Sample templates	Contains a dozen templates for various database types.
My templates	Contains any templates that you have designed.

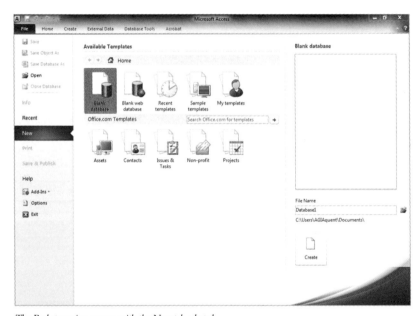

The Backstage view appears with the New tab selected.

2   Click Sample templates to display the different available templates. Several templates are available to help you design an Access database. Web databases have an Earth in the image background.

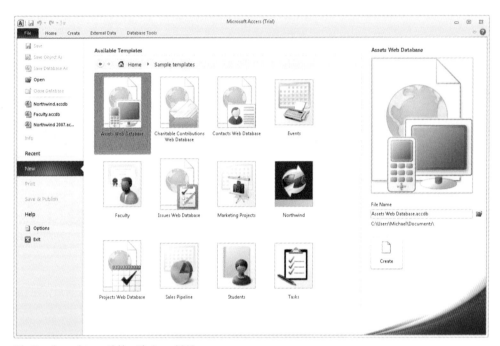

The Sample templates available with Access 2010.

3   Click Faculty and in the File Name text field on the right side, accept the default file name of Faculty as well as the default file location. Click Create. If a Security Warning dialog box appears, click Enable Content.

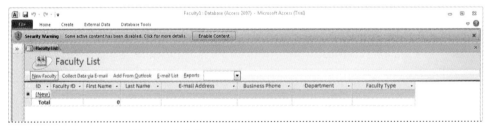

The Faculty List form appears, which may look similar to an Excel spreadsheet.

You have just created your first Access 2010 database. You can now enter data, explore the database's objects, or do any of several other tasks.

4   Click File > Close Database. This closes the database, but leaves Access running.

Even though you can have multiple databases open simultaneously, closing those databases that you don't currently need frees up your computer's resources to focus on the tasks that are most important to you.

Now you will create a database without using a template.

To create a database from scratch:

1 Click File > New > Blank database. This item, and its neighbor, Blank Web database, are listed under Available Templates, despite the fact that neither uses a template.

2 Type **SCRATCH** in the File Name text field, and then click Create.

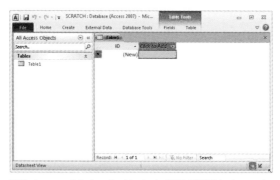

Table 1 appears. It is the only object in the SCRATCH database, and it awaits your input.

3 Click the Save icon (🔲), or click File > Save, and save the table, either with its default name of Table1 or with another name.

4 Click File > Close Database to close this database and leave Access running.

Tables, views, and data types

Tables are crucial to Access databases, and form the framework of relational databases. Next you will delve into various ways to view tables, and how to configure them to work with the data they will contain.

Access 2010 has two ways to view tables: Datasheet view and Design view.

Creating a table in Datasheet view

Datasheet view allows you to add tables and fields to your database. It resembles a spreadsheet, such as you would find in Excel. Datasheet view has evolved over the years to include some design features that had been exclusive to Design view.

1 Open the SCRATCH database by clicking on File > Recent > SCRATCH. (You may need to Enable Content again if a security warning appears.)

2 Click Create > Table. Table1 appears in Datasheet view. So far, this is all familiar from the previous exercise.

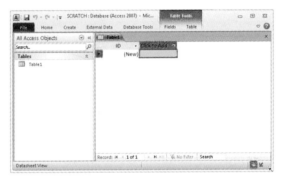

Table 1 in Datasheet view.

In Datasheet view you can examine the table more closely and notice the following:

• Datasheet view is displayed in the lower-left corner of the status bar.

• The Datasheet view icon is active in the lower-right corner of the status bar, and the Design View icon is inactive.

• In the Views group of the Ribbon's Home tab, the Design View command appears in color. By clicking the down-arrow, you can see that Datasheet view is active, but Design view is inactive. The Design View icon is active because it is the only other available option.

Although the Design View command is in color, Access is currently in Datasheet view.

Now, while still in Datasheet view, let's examine the actual datasheet.

Notice the following:

- The first column has a field name, ID, which is the primary key. A primary key is the unique record identifier for a table.
- The second column is ready to receive your input.

The light green color indicates the cell that is available for input.

While there are multiple ways to add fields to a datasheet, you'll assign the data type and then enter the name of the field. A *data type* determines what you can store and just as importantly, what you cannot store in a field. For example, you cannot enter letters, characters such as A, B, C, into a Funds field with a Currency data type, or into a Birthday field with a Date/Time data type.

Data types can have some unexpected properties. For example, the Text field can contain numbers, and numbers may have a data type such as Text, Number, and Currency.

For Table1, you will add fields for Last Name, First Name, and Date of Birth.

To add fields to a table in Datasheet view:

1 Click the *Click to Add* down arrow and select Text from the Data Type drop-down menu.

2 In the new column, replace *Field1* by typing **LastName**.

Field names cannot have spaces or symbols, but they can have underscores.

3 Repeat steps 1 and 2 to add a **FirstName** field.

4 Now to add Date of Birth, be sure to click Date & Time from the Data Type drop-down menu. Rename *Field1* by typing **DOB**.

Creating a Table in Design View

You can also use Design view to add tables and fields. Design view offers more control over field structure and properties. Design view is also well-suited for controlling field data types and descriptions.

When creating a table using Design view, create the table's structure in the Design view and then switch to Datasheet view to enter or import data.

To add a table to a database using Design view:

1 With Table1 of the SCRATCH database still in Datasheet view, click Create > Table Design (not Table).

The new table appears as a separate tab in Design view. Look at the status bar at the bottom of the window. *Design view* appears on the left side of the status bar, and the Design View icon is active on the right side.

Notice the Status bar shows the Design view icon when selected.

Adding fields to a table

To add fields to a table in Design view:

1 For each field, enter a field name, assign a data type, and enter a description as shown in the table below.

NAME	DATA TYPE	DESCRIPTION
ID	AutoNumber	Player's number
Position	Text	Preferred softball position
Bats	Text	Does the player hit right-, left-, or switch-handed?
Throws	Text	Does the player throw right- or left-handed?
AVG	Number	Batting average

For many fields, a description might seem unnecessary, but you should enter a description for any field that might have an unclear name. The description will appear in that table's status bar when the field is selected using Datasheet view; this can be helpful to others when entering data.

2   Right-click the ID field and select Primary Key.

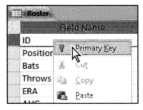

Selecting the Primary Key.

3   Right-click the table's tab and choose Save. Type **Roster** in the Table Name text field in the Save As dialog box and press OK.

At this point, you can enter data into the table cells by typing, copying and pasting, or importing.

Importing data from a Microsoft Excel spreadsheet

While spreadsheets can store data, databases are more powerful, expandable, and often easier when managing large amounts of data. You can import data from external sources such as text files, XML files, other database types, and spreadsheets into your Access 2010 databases. Here you will use the Import Spreadsheet Wizard to import data from an Excel spreadsheet into an Access table.

To import data from Excel:

1   Open the program Excel and choose File > Open. Navigate to the Access02lessons folder and double-click SB Roster to open the spreadsheet. The spreadsheet contains the following information:

ID	POSITION	BATS	THROWS	AVG
22	1st base	Right	Right	700
13	pitcher	Right	Left	250
23	2nd base	Right	Right	444
42	Left field	Switch	Left	333
8	Center field	Switch	Left	500
4	Catcher	Left	Switch	333
9	pitcher	Left	Left	198

2   Switch back to Access where your SCRATCH database is still active by clicking on the Access icon found on the Task Bar along the bottom of your screen.

3   In the Roster table select the External Data tab and click Excel located in the Import & Link group.

4   In the Get External Data window, browse to the Excel file and click Open so that it appears in the File name text field.

5 Click the second option (*Append a copy of the records to the table*), choose Roster, and click OK.

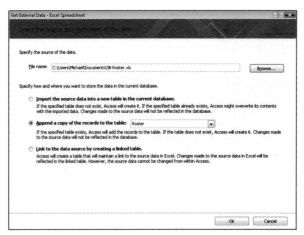

The Get External Data window.

 If the Roster table is not closed, you are asked to close it before proceeding.

6 Click Next, as your data is in Sheet1 of the Excel file.

7 Click Next again, as the first row of your Excel spreadsheet contains column headings.

8 Click Finish and then click Close.

9 In the Navigation Pane, double-click the Roster table to open it and see the imported data.

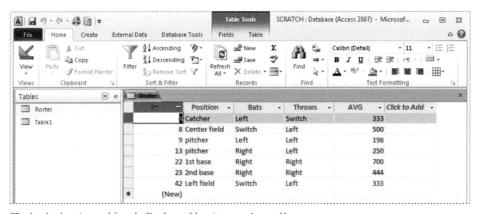

The data has been imported from the Excel spreadsheet into your Access table.

Importing and Linking

You may be familiar with this distinction if you've worked with other Office programs, especially Word and Excel. Importing is static. It's like taking a snapshot of the external data source (such as a spreadsheet) and bringing it into a database. Changes made to the external data source are not reflected in Access. In contrast, linking is dynamic. Changes to the external data source are automatically updated in Access.

Self study

1   Instead of importing the spreadsheet data, link to it. It's almost the same as the importing procedure you just completed. Start at Step 2 and follow the importing procedure, except on the first screen of the Get External Data window click the third option (*Link to the data source by creating a linked table*). The default Linked Table Name is Sheet1.

2   After Access creates the table, open the spreadsheet in Excel and make some changes. Give a few hitters much better batting averages!

If your linked Access table doesn't refresh when you change the Excel spreadsheet:

• In Access, make sure you're looking at the correct table (not Roster, in which you performed a static import).

• In Excel, make sure you saved your changes.

• Depending on your system, changes may take some time, either way, it should not take more than 30 seconds.

• If the link still appears broken, in Access, manually update the link by clicking External Data > Linked Table Manager. (This is especially important if you've moved the Excel file from its original location.)

Review

Questions

1   Name two ways to create a database in Access 2010.

2   True or False: When creating a table, the status bar indicates which view you're using.

3   True or False: Of the two views in this lesson, Database view offers the most control over field structure and properties.

Answers

1   You can either create a blank database or use a template.

2   True, both ends of the status bar indicate the current view.

3   False, the Design view offers much more control.

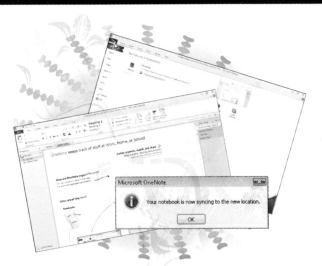

What you'll learn in this lesson:

- Discovering OneNote
- Working in Backstage View
- Customizing OneNote
- Getting help
- Ending a OneNote session

Microsoft OneNote 2010 Jumpstart

In this lesson, you will get a general introduction to OneNote 2010. You will become familiar with OneNote terminology, and you will look at the user interface and some of the main features, such as Search.

Starting up

You will not need to work with any files for this lesson.

See Lesson 1 in action!

Use the accompanying video to gain a better understanding of how to use some of the features shown in this lesson. The video tutorial for this lesson can be found at www.DigitalClassroomBooks.com/Office2010.

Discovering OneNote

OneNote has long been the "forgotten child" of the Microsoft Office suite. Most computer users know, or are at least familiar with, Word, Excel, PowerPoint, Outlook, and perhaps Access, the database program. In contrast, OneNote may be among the most widely distributed, yet least used programs. Furthermore, few of the computer users who are aware of OneNote (most likely due to either its presence on the Windows Start menu or having read the product packaging) have any idea of what you can actually do with the program.

OneNote allows you to collect and organize data in various formats, including:

- Text
- Images
- Audio
- Video
- Web pages
- Freehand sketches

OneNote is similar to the physical notebooks (such as three-ring binders) that you've undoubtedly used at work or school. For example, a OneNote Notebook contains Sections, which in turn contain Pages that you use to store your content. Like a physical notebook, you can rearrange a OneNote Notebook's Sections and Pages as you see fit. As a result, OneNote is designed to be much more user friendly than an Access database, even though both programs are designed to contain and organize information.

Working with OneNote

OneNote can help you manage notes in situations where you would normally use a physical notebook. Here are some examples:

PURPOSE	SECTION POSSIBILITIES
Trip Management	Maps, Things to See, Pictures, Videos
Recipe Organization	Types of Food, Events, Meal Ideas, Markets/Suppliers
Musician Planner	Songs, Videos, Pictures, Gig Calendar, Band Bios
Lab Inventory	Equipment, Suppliers, Possible Experiments
Student Notebook	Science, Algebra, Music, English
Car Service Log	Oil Changes, Major Repairs, Accident Photos, Customizations

No doubt you could think of several uses for one or several OneNote Notebooks.

Exploring the OneNote environment

OneNote has two main views that you will be concerned with: Notebook View and Backstage View. Notebook View appears after you open OneNote, so let's start with that.

Notebook view

OneNote comes with a sample Notebook. Let's take a closer look at the Notebook and its components, and also become familiar with the OneNote graphical user interface (GUI) or environment.

Open OneNote by doing one of the following:

- Click Start > All Programs > Microsoft Office > Microsoft OneNote.
- Click Start, type **OneNote** in the Search text box, and click on Microsoft OneNote 2010.
- If there is a desktop shortcut for OneNote, double-click it.

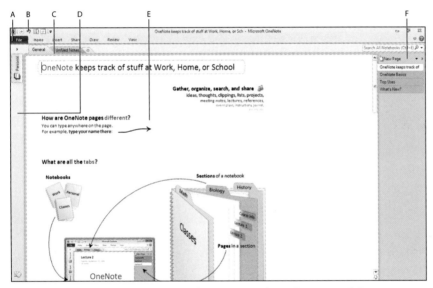

A. Ribbon. B. Quick Access Toolbar. C. Section tabs. D. Navigation bar. E. Content pane. F. Pages pane.

The OneNote window appears, displaying a page of the sample Notebook. The cursor is over the Expand/Collapse Navigation Bar button.

Notice the following components of the OneNote window:

Navigation bar. On the left side of the OneNote window, the Navigation Bar shows an icon and the title of each Notebook stored in the default Notebook location.

By default, the Navigation Bar's width is minimized. You can click the Expand/Collapse Navigation Bar button (the left-arrow at the top of the Navigation Bar) to make it wider. You can click it again to minimize the Navigation Bar.

Section tabs. To the right of the Navigation Bar and above the Notebook pane, Section tabs indicate the titles of the Notebook's Sections. These are analogous to plastic tab dividers in physical notebooks. For example, your high school Math notebook may have had separate sections for Lecture Notes, Problems, and Homework. You could create a OneNote Notebook for Math with these Sections.

Content pane. Most of the OneNote window is dedicated to the Content pane. This is the active page of the Notebook, in which you will add and view different types of content. The title of the active page appears at the top. For pages that you create, the date and time of the most recent update also appears.

Pages pane. On the right side of the Content pane, the Pages pane displays Pages and Subpages for the active Notebook.

Ribbon. If you have used other Microsoft Office 2010 programs, you may be surprised that the Ribbon seems to be missing from OneNote. It's actually minimized by default, like the Navigation Bar, to maximize the space available for the Content pane. You can click the Expand/Collapse Ribbon button (the down-arrow to the left of the Help button) to make it wider. You can click it again to minimize the Ribbon.

The following table gives an overview of the default Ribbon tabs in OneNote 2010.

TAB	MAJOR FUNCTIONS
Home	Clipboard functions, formatting text, managing tags, and e-mail
Insert	Inserting, linking, and otherwise incorporating media of various types
Share	Collaborating via e-mail, sharing Notebooks
Draw	Inserting and editing handwritten (or computer-drawn) content
Review	Spelling, researching, and translating text; working with linked notes
View	Modifying the appearance of your OneNote windows

You can sometimes perform opposite actions, such as expanding and then collapsing a tab, by clicking the same screen icon; this is called toggling. You can toggle the size of the Ribbon, Navigation Bar, and Pages pane in OneNote 2010.

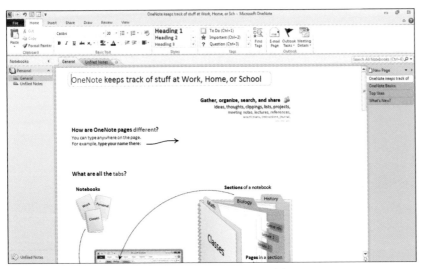

The OneNote window with both the Navigation Bar and Ribbon expanded

Quick Access Toolbar: Found in the upper-left corner of every Microsoft Office 2010 program interface, the Quick Access Toolbar contains buttons for selecting frequently used functions.

The Quick Access Toolbar.

The default commands on the Quick Access Toolbar are the Back, Undo, Dock to Desktop, and Full Page View buttons. Like the Ribbon, the Quick Access Toolbar is customizable; in fact, you will customize both later in this lesson.

Working in Backstage view

While Notebook View is where you do most of your work in OneNote, Backstage View is also important. If you've used other Microsoft Office 2010 programs, you may be familiar with Backstage View. Think of this view as the place where you can manage a Notebook's properties, or otherwise act on the Notebook as a whole, rather than manage or act on its content.

The File tab, which displays Backstage View when clicked, always has a colored background, even when it is not the active tab. This may be confusing, so just remember that you can identify the active tab by the borders on either side of it, as well as how it appears to be more a part of the Ribbon than its neighboring tabs.

1 Click the File tab to display Backstage View.

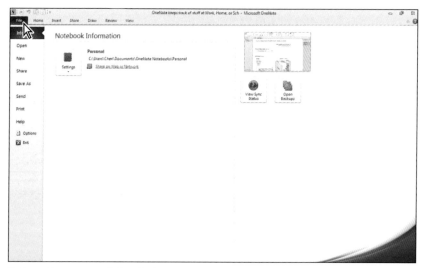

Backstage View appears, with the Info tab active.

The following table gives a brief overview of the tabs in Backstage View.

TAB	MAJOR FUNCTIONS
Info	Manage and view Notebook properties; share and view synchronization status (if applicable); and open backup Notebook copies
Open	Open a Notebook, either by browsing or selecting a recently closed Notebook
New	Create a Notebook to be stored on the Web, a network computer, or your computer
Share	Allow Notebook sharing by storing it on the Web, a network computer, or Microsoft SharePoint
Save As	Save the current Page or Section in various file formats, including XPS and PDF (A Notebook may also be saved as a OneNote Package, which is a distributable file)
Send	Send the current Page to Outlook, PDF, Word, or a Word-generated blog
Print	Print (and preview) a Page, Page group, or Section
Help	Obtain information about your copy of Microsoft Office; access the help system, Getting Started resources, and methods to contact Microsoft; and check for program updates

You will return to Backstage View later. Click the File tab to view the default Notebook.

Searching OneNote

One drawback of a physical notebook is that it can sometimes be difficult to find relevant information, despite the use of sections and tab dividers. Fortunately, OneNote has a powerful Search feature that you can use to quickly find the content you are looking for.

To search the initial Notebook:

1 If it is not already open, open Microsoft OneNote 2010

2 In the Search text field which is located in the upper-right hand corner, click the drop-down menu and select This Notebook.

The default Search Scope is All Notebooks. To limit it to the present Notebook, click the drop-down menu and click This Notebook, then click the drop-down menu again and click Set This Scope as Default.

3   Type **numbers** in the Search text field.

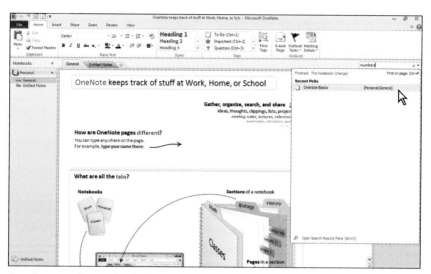

Pages that contain the query (numbers) appear as you type. The query is highlighted on the Pages.

4   Click on the search result to display the page that *numbers* was found on with the query text highlighted. In this exercise, the search result is called OneNote Basics which is a page in the General section.

Sharing a Notebook

OneNote lets collaborators share a Notebook simultaneously, and it automatically synchronizes edits to keep a Notebook current. If a user goes off the network (such as while traveling), the user can work on a local copy. Changes are resynchronized for all collaborators when the user reconnects to the network.

OneNote lets you share an existing Notebook.

To share an existing Notebook:

1   If it is not already open, open the Personal Notebook (its default location is \\Documents\OneNote Notebooks\).

2   Choose File > Share.

3   Under Select Notebook, select the Personal, if it is not already selected.

4   Under Share On, select Network.

5   Under the Network Location, browse to the proper location.

6   Click Share Notebook.

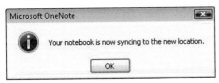

A confirmation dialog box appears for Notebook synchronization.

Customizing OneNote

Like all Microsoft Office 2010 programs, you can customize components to suit your individual preferences. The Quick Access Toolbar is a favorite customization candidate; you can use it for convenient, one-click access to your favorite tools.

As mentioned earlier, the default commands on the Quick Access Toolbar are the Back, Undo, Dock to Desktop, and Full Page View buttons.

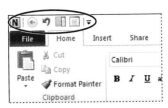

The default appearance of the Quick Access Toolbar, showing the Customize button at the far right.

Now you will customize the Quick Access Toolbar to include the Print and Format Painter buttons. If you have completed the Microsoft Word lessons, you will already be familiar with this process.

To customize the Quick Access Toolbar:

1   Click the Customize Quick Access Toolbar button.

2   In the drop-down menu click Print. The Print command appears in the Quick Access Toolbar.

3   Click the Customize Quick Access Toolbar button.

4   In the drop-down menu click More Commands. The OneNote Options Quick Access Toolbar window shows a lengthy list of popular commands.

5 Scroll down the list and click Format Painter.

6 Click Add. The Format Painter now appears on the list of Quick Access Toolbar commands, below the newly added Print command.

7 Click OK.

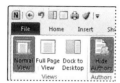

The Quick Access Toolbar now displays both new commands.

Getting help

If you run into a problem or aren't sure how to perform a certain task, you can easily access the OneNote help system.

- Press your computer's F1 key or click the Help button to display the help system.
- In Backstage View (click the File tab), click the Help tab to display Support links for the help system, Getting Started resources, and a link to contact Microsoft.

Ending a OneNote session

To end a session, you can either:

- Choose File > Exit; or
- Click the Close button located in the upper-right corner of the program interface.

While most other programs extol the virtues of saving early and often, OneNote saves every time you edit content or design. You'll learn more about this feature in the next lesson.

Self study

1 Customize the Quick Access Toolbar beyond what you learned in this lesson. Explore the More Commands option to discover the different customization options.

2 Customize the Ribbon by right–clicking on it. Make some changes to its functionality and appearance.

3 You saw how to share an existing Notebook. Use the help system to learn how to create a shared Notebook and store it on your computer.

Review

Questions

1 True or False? Both the Navigation pane and the Ribbon can be collapsed.

2 How do you customize the Quick Access Toolbar?

3 True or False? The OneNote Search feature is capable of searching only the present Section, Section Group, Notebook, or All Notebooks.

Answers

1 True.

2 You can customize the Quick Access Toolbar by clicking the Customize Quick Access Toolbar button.

3 False. It can search a Section.

What you'll learn in this lesson:

- Managing Notebooks
- Managing Sections
- Grouping Sections
- Saving a Notebook
- Managing Pages
- Adding Content

Getting Started with Microsoft OneNote 2010

In this lesson, you will learn how to create and manage Notebooks, as well as their components, Sections and Pages. You will also add several types of content to your Notebook, from text to multimedia.

Starting up

You will not need to work with any files for this lesson.

See Lesson 2 in action!

Use the accompanying video to gain a better understanding of how to use some of the features shown in this lesson. The video tutorial for this lesson can be found at www.DigitalClassroomBooks.com/Office2010.

Managing Notebooks

Now that you've become familiar with the OneNote working environment and have explored a Notebook, let's create one. Throughout this lesson you will see how a OneNote Notebook can store and manage information in various formats, including web page text and graphics, document files, spreadsheets, and multimedia.

To create a Notebook:

1 Open the OneNote program by clicking Start > All Programs> Microsoft Office > Microsoft OneNote if it is not already opened.

2 On the file tab, click New. To store the Notebook locally, click My Computer.

3 Type **My First Notebook** for the Notebook in the Name field.

Creating a Notebook in Backstage view.

4 Accept the default folder location unless you would like to place the new Notebook in a specific location.

5 Click Create Notebook.

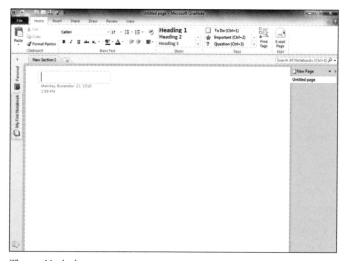

The new Notebook appears.

When the new Notebook is open, it's not obvious which one in the Notebook pane is the present Notebook. You're probably used to seeing the filename displayed in the title bar of a window (for example, a Word document's title). As you will see, OneNote is focused on the Page, and so the Page name, not the Document name, appears in the title bar of a OneNote window.

Although the above image was the first Notebook created from a fresh install of OneNote, sometimes previously used Notebooks are present in the Navigation Bar. If you want to close a Notebook, right-click it and select Close This Notebook.

Managing Sections

Now that you have a new Notebook, it's time to add Sections and Pages to it. Give some thought to how you will organize your Notebook's Sections, but don't worry—you can reorganize Sections later if necessary.

To create a Section:

1   In the Section Tab row, click the rightmost tab that currently displays a small star. This is found to the right of the New Section1 tab.

2   Repeat step 1 a few times so that your new Notebook has at least four Sections. You'll change their names in the following steps.

To rename a Section:

1   Right-click the first Section tab and click Rename.

2   Type **Set List** and press Enter to rename the tab.

3   Right-click the second, third and fourth tabs and rename them **Song Ideas**, **Gigs**, and **Gear**.

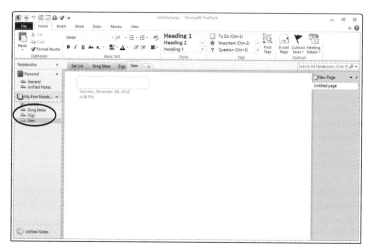

In this example, the Band Notebook contains the following Sections: Set List, Song Ideas, Gigs, and Gear. Each Section contains a default Page, currently named Untitled Page.

 If there are too many Sections to appear across the Section Tabs row, some will be hidden. Click the down-arrow to show the rest of the sections.

Grouping Sections

Your Notebook may include several Sections that are related in some way. You can group those Sections to make them easier to manage. The value of Section grouping becomes more apparent as the number of Groups increases to fill the Section tab row.

To group Sections:

1   On the Section tab row, right-click the area to the right of the tabs but to the left of the Search text field.

Creating a new Section group

2   In the drop-down menu, click New Section Group.

3 Type **Song-Stuff** and press Enter.

The new Section group appears.

4 Click the Set List tab and drag it to the newly created Song-Stuff group. If you hover your mouse over the new Section group, you can control the placement of the Section within the group.

5 If you are viewing the Song-Stuff group and would like to view the level above the group, click the arrow button to the left of the group.

6 Repeat step 4 and add the Song Ideas Section to the Song-Stuff group.

To move a Section from a group, drag it to the arrow button to the left of the group.

Saving a Notebook

Unlike other Microsoft Office programs, there is no Save icon that appears on the Ribbon by default. This is because OneNote constantly saves your work whenever you close a Section or Notebook, or while you take notes. If desired, you can save a copy of your Notebook, Page, or Section to a different location. In this example, you will save a copy of your Notebook.

To save a copy of the currently open Notebook:

1 Choose File > Save As.

2 Under Save Current, click Notebook.

3 Under Select Format, click OneNote Package.

4 Click the Save As button.

5 In the Save As dialog box, navigate to the location to which you want to save the file.

6 Accept the default name, or enter a new one and click Save.

Next you'll learn how to manage Pages, which will hold your content.

Managing Pages

A Notebook Section with only one Page is limited. As you might expect, OneNote allows you to create multiple Pages within a Section. If a Page becomes too large, you can create Subpages for it.

The easiest way to create a Page is to press Ctrl+N. When in the appropriate Section, you can also do one of the following in the Pages pane located on the right side of the screen:

• Click New Page.

• Click the down-arrow and select New Page.

• Right-click an existing Page in the Pages Pane on the right side, and select New Page.

• Hover your mouse over an existing Page (in the Pages Pane) to display the New Page icon. A small pointer movement up or down moves the icon above or below the existing Page. Click the icon to position the new Page.

Given that you can rename a Notebook or a Section by right-clicking it, it's somewhat surprising that you cannot right-click a Page to name or rename it. However, naming a Page is not complicated.

To create and name a Page:

1 Click on the Section labeled Gear from the Navigation Pane on the left side of the screen. We are going to add a page to this section of the Notebook.

2 Click New Page found in the Pages Pane on the right. You will notice that there are now two untitled pages listed in this pane.

3 In the Page Name text box, type **Bass Gear**. Notice how the Page name also appears in the Page pane on the right side of the screen.

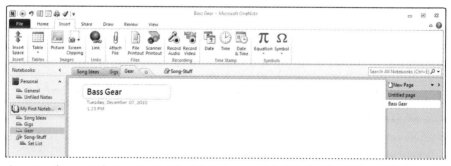

As you type the name in the Page Name text box, it instantly appears in both the OneNote title bar and the Pages pane.

4 Click on the Untitled page found above the newly created Bass Gear page. Type the word **Microphones** to name the page.

To rename a Page:

1 Click on the page named *Bass Gear* located in the Gear's section of the Notebook.

2 In the Page Name text box highlight Bass Gear and type **Extension Cords** to replace the name.

Adding content

One of the strengths of a Notebook is its flexible structure, which you can change as needed. Another key strength is its ability to let you collect and organize content of various types, in the following ways:

• Direct text entry (such as typing)

• Copying and pasting

• Creating a drawing using a mouse, touchpad, or electronic pen

• Adding audio and video notes

• Inserting web content

Let's add some content!

Direct text entry (typing)

1 Click anywhere on the Microphones Page and start typing.

This is typed text. It fits inside a container that expands as needed.

Typed text appears inside a constantly expanding container.

2 Apply some formatting to your text, such a change in font style, bold, or underline, as you would do in Microsoft Word by right-clicking in the text box or using the Home tab on the ribbon.

3 Click outside the note container when you have finished typing and formatting.

4 Move the container by clicking and dragging it anywhere on the Page.

Copying and pasting

1 From a source outside OneNote, select some text and copy it to the Clipboard, either by pressing Ctrl+C on your keyboard, or by selecting the text with your mouse, right-clicking, and selecting Copy.

2 Paste the text onto the Page either by pressing Ctrl+V on your keyboard, or by right-clicking to display the Paste options.

Pasting in OneNote by selecting a Paste option

Select one of the three Paste options:

- Keep Source Formatting: This maintains the selected text's original font size and style.
- Merge Formatting: This adopts the standard formatting used by OneNote.
- Keep Text Only: This removes any non-text items, such as images, and pastes text only.

You can examine how your text appears using all three Paste options. Depending on its original formatting, the results may be quite different.

Creating a drawing using a mouse, touchpad, or electronic pen

As with a physical Notebook, text usually isn't sufficient to convey meaning, and so drawing a map or figure may be necessary. You can use your computer's mouse, touchpad, or electronic pen to draw in OneNote.

To create a drawing:

1 Choose the Song Ideas Section and the Untitled page and then click the Draw tab, located in the middle of the ribbon.

2 Click on the drop-down arrow to the right of the drawing tools to view more option.

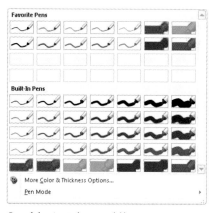

Several drawing tools are available.

3 Select the Dark Blue Pen (1.0 mm) which is the fourth over from the left and fourth down in the Built-In Pens section.

4 Draw anywhere on the Page by clicking and dragging the mouse.

5   Click the Select & Type tool in the Tools group and move the drawing's container to
    another location on the Page by clicking and dragging over the entire drawing first to
    select it.

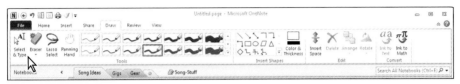

The Draw tab on the ribbon displays the drawing tools.

Adding audio and video notes

Words and pictures are usually all you need when taking notes. On some occasions, however,
you may want to also record audio, such as a melody, an odd pronunciation, or other sounds.

To record audio:

1   Choose the Set List Section located in the Song-Stuff folder and name the Untitled page
    Melodies. Now lets place an audio note on the Melodies page.

2   On the Insert tab on the ribbon, click Record Audio and begin humming a tune.

The Record Audio button is adjacent to the Record   The Audio & Video Recording tab appears, displaying playback controls.
Video button.

*It is not easy to tell when OneNote is actually recording. Look for the elapsed time; if it is
changing, then OneNote is recording.*

An icon for the audio file appears on the page.

3   Click Stop to end the recording.

4   Double-click the file icon to play it (or click Play in the Audio & Video Playback tab).

While audio is certainly useful, video (with audio) can be indispensable. The procedure for recording video in OneNote is very similar to recording audio.

To record video:

1   Choose the Gigs Section and name the Untitled page **Movements**. Now lets place an video on the Movements page.

2   On the Insert tab on the ribbon, click Record Video.

The Audio & Video Recording tab appears, displaying playback controls.

You can also see what your camera is recording. If you click Pause, it is not obvious that recording has stopped, as you continue to see the camera's video feed. An icon for the video file appears on the page.

3   Click Stop to end the recording.

4   Double-click the icon to play it (or click Play in the Audio & Video Playback tab).

Inserting web content

You may want to add content from the Web into your OneNote Notebook. The procedure is straightforward; however, you must use Internet Explorer as your web browser.

To insert a screen (Web) clipping:

1   In Internet Explorer, open the web page www.UsuallyNormal.com and scroll down to the photo of the band. We will insert this image into the OneNote Notebook.

This Explorer window contains a picture that would be good to import into OneNote.

2   Return to the current Notebook and click the Microphones Page located in the Gear section. We will insert the clipping here.

3   Click anywhere on the page and type **Here's a picture from a recent show**:

This is where the clip from Explorer will appear.

4   Choose Insert > Screen Clipping and the screen will show the currently opened web site with a faded screen.

5   In Internet Explorer, click the top-left corner of the image, drag to the bottom-right corner, and release the mouse button.

Here's a picture from a recent show:

Usually Normal - Official Web Site
http://usuallynormal.com/
Screen clipping taken: 11/3/2010 14:16

The screen clipping now appears in your OneNote Notebook.

Notice that OneNote also inserts the URL and timestamp.

Although importing an item from a web page is a nice feature, there may be times when you'd like to add an entire web page in your OneNote Notebook.

To insert an entire web page:

1   In Internet Explorer, with www.usuallynormal.com still opened, select Tools > Send to OneNote.

2   In the Select Location in OneNote window, select the Gigs Section and click OK. OneNote will place the web site on a new page.

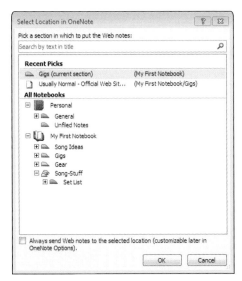

The Selection Location in OneNote dialog box appears.

The Web page appears as a new Page in your OneNote Notebook. (Note that its appearance in OneNote and in Internet Explorer may differ slightly.)

Congratulations! You have completed the lesson.

Self study

1 Add some shapes to a Notebook Page. Use the Select & Type feature, and note how it differs from the Lasso Select feature.

2 Create a new Notebook with two or three Sections, each with two or three pages. Add some content. Notice how little time it takes to do this.

3 Create a drawing using at least three drawing tools.

Review

Questions

1 True or false? A group of Notebooks is called a Section.

2 True or false? There are more than two ways to create a Page.

3 True or false? All text copied from an external source is always pasted as text only (that is, without formatting).

Answers

1 False. A group of Pages is called a Section.

2 True. There are at least five.

3 False. You can choose from one of three Paste options, depending on the final formatting that you want.

What you'll learn in this lesson:

- Introducing Publisher 2010
- Understanding the basics of creating publications
- Exploring the elements of the Publisher interface

Microsoft Publisher 2010 Jumpstart

In this lesson, you will get a general introduction to Publisher 2010. You will learn some terminology and the basics of publication design, and you will look at the user interface and some of the basic features. Finally, you will learn how to use the Help application.

Starting up

You will not need to work with any files for this lesson.

See Lesson 1 in action!

Use the accompanying video to gain a better understanding of how to use some of the features shown in this lesson. The video tutorial for this lesson can be found at www.DigitalClassroomBooks.com/Office2010.

What is Publisher?

Publisher is an application that helps you create professional-looking publications quickly and easily. It is available in certain editions of Microsoft Office and can also be purchased separately.

Publisher combines the power of a word processor and the creativity of a graphics package into one flexible and easy-to-use program. This combination lets you create unique and exciting documents such as newsletters, brochures, letterheads, and business cards without having to study for a degree in graphic design.

How can you use Publisher?

You can use Publisher to manage the creation and editing of publications. Depending on the publication's complexity and your needs, you can perform tasks such as the following:

- Create a publication, either from a template or from scratch
- Insert text boxes, and then type or import text from other sources
- Add pictures and crop them to the size you want
- Insert Building Blocks, which are reusable pieces of content that are stored in galleries
- Print your document to a local printer, or prepare it for e-mail distribution

Publication basics

Publisher 2010 allows you to create a publication from a template or from scratch.

A template is a document with preset formatting and placeholder text that lets you know what information you should enter. Publisher gives you access to hundreds of installed templates organized in different categories, including advertisements, greeting cards, labels, and invitations. After you select a template, you can modify the layout and select options in the right pane to help you customize the page.

If you can't find a suitable template among those provided, you can easily download templates from *Office.com*. You can create a publication for a specific job such as a special event or fundraiser, or create your own personal stationery. You can also create publications for print, Web, or e-mail.

While Publisher's preset designs can help you get started with a new publication, you may want to create a unique publication if none of the preset designs meet your needs. With a little knowledge of how to create and use frames, you can create a blank publication from scratch.

You will create a publication from scratch in the next lesson, "Getting Started with Microsoft Publisher 2010."

Quick tour of Publisher 2010

Before you can completely understand the capabilities of Publisher, you need to understand the components of the program. Let's begin by taking a quick tour of the Publisher interface.

1   Choose Start > Programs > Microsoft Office > Microsoft Publisher 2010.

Backstage view of Publisher 2010.

Publisher 2010 opens in Backstage view, where you can create a new publication, open an existing publication, and view featured content from *Office.com*. Backstage view is described in more detail in the next section.

You can always access Backstage view, even when working on a publication, by clicking the File tab.

Backstage view is new to Office 2010. Some of the user interface elements, such as the Ribbon and Navigation pane, were introduced in previous versions.

Publisher 2010 components

The Publisher 2010 interface has the following main components:

*   The Ribbon: This bar across the top of the interface contains several tabs. These tabs contain groups of commands, which are visible on all tabs except File.

*   Backstage view: This view, which appears by default when you launch Publisher 2010, displays a group of commands on the Ribbon's File tab.

The File tab always has a colored background, even when it is not the active tab. This may be confusing, so just remember that you can identify the active tab by the borders on either side of it.

- The Navigation pane: The area on the left side of the interface displays pages when a publication is open, or tabs in Backstage view.

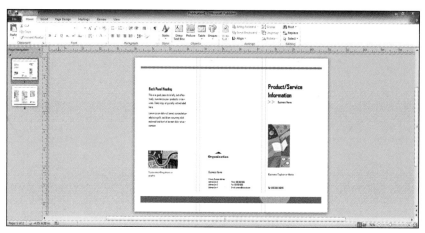

An open publication, showing the Navigation pane on the left side.

Let's examine these components in more detail.

The Ribbon

The Ribbon is divided into tabs, and each tab contains groups of commands. The Ribbon replaces menus that existed across the top of the screen and toolbars, which were found in older versions of Microsoft Office. The primary tabs of Publisher 2010 are File, Home, Insert, Page Design, Mailings, Review, and View.

The Publisher 2010 Ribbon is divided into tabs.

The Ribbon's appearance changes depending on your current task. Some tabs, such as the Format tab, only appear in certain contexts. For example, when a publication is open in Publisher 2010 and you draw a text box on the page, the Ribbon displays groups of commands for formatting the text in this box.

You can hide and show the Ribbon by double-clicking the active command tab; this makes it easy to maximize your workspace as needed.

To hide or show the Ribbon:

1 In Backstage view, click the Home tab.

The Ribbon changes from a simple row of tabs to a group of commands. These commands are inactive because no publication is open.

The Ribbon in full view, showing groups of commands.

2 Hide the Ribbon by double-clicking on the Home tab.

The Ribbon with its command groups hidden.

3 Show the Ribbon by clicking the Home tab again.

You have successfully toggled the Ribbon by clicking the active tab. You can also toggle the Ribbon by clicking the Minimize/Expand arrow button in the upper-right corner.

Backstage view

Backstage view is the first view you see after you launch Publisher 2010. It contains information and commands that affect an entire publication, such as the following: opening and saving a publication; a list of recently opened publications; and tabs for printing, saving, and sending a publication. You can also launch the help system and manage options in Backstage view.

Publisher 2010 Backstage view.

Navigation pane

The Navigation pane is located on the left side of the Publisher 2010 interface when a publication is open.

The Navigation pane allows you to view and manage the publication's pages, and is customizable.

Opening a publication

Now that you're more familiar with the interface, you'll examine a sample publication and perform some simple tasks in Publisher.

To open a sample template:

1 In Backstage view, click the File tab, and then click New.

2 Click the publication type you want to use; Brochures was chosen in this example.

3 Click the thumbnail that displays the design for the publication you want to create. Under the Informational section, Arrows is selected as the design template.

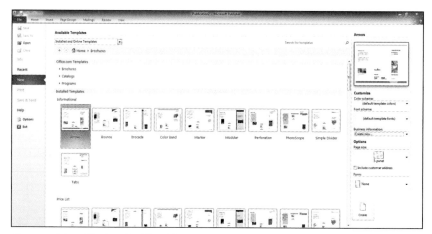

Open an existing publication using File > New.

4 Click the Color Scheme or Font Scheme list arrow, and then select how you want to customize the layout.

5   Select other options, such as page size. The options vary depending on the publication type. Click Create.

To open an existing publication:

1   In Backstage view, click the File tab, and then click Open.

2   In the left pane of the Open Publication dialog box, click the drive or folder that contains the file that you want.

3   In the right pane of the Open Publication dialog box, open the folder that contains the publication that you want.

4   Click the file and then click Open.

Changing your view

You can view the pages in your publication in a one-page or a two-page spread. A two-page spread mimics the way your publication would look lying open in front of you, with two pages facing each other.

To view a publication in one- or two-page view:

1   Click the View tab.

2   In the Layout group, click the Two-Page Spread button or the Single Page button.

     The selected view displays, and the button you clicked is now selected.

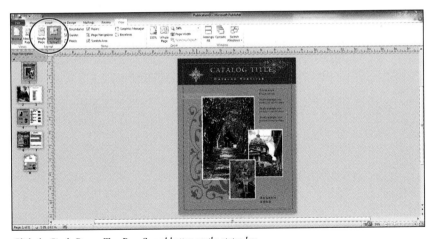

Click the Single Page or Two-Page Spread button on the status bar.

To change the view size of a page:

1   Click the View tab.

2   To select standard view sizes, in the Zoom group click any of the following buttons: 100%, Whole Page, Page Width, or Selected Objects.

Press F9 to toggle between current and 100% views.

1   To specify a custom view size, click the Zoom list arrow, and then select a view percentage.

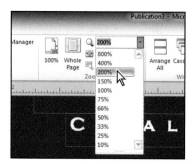

Choose a custom view size from the Zoom list.

Click the Zoom In or Zoom Out button or drag the Zoom slider on the status bar to change the view magnification.

Saving a publication

By default, Publisher saves a file in a working folder. If you want, you can specify a different location.

1   Click the File tab, and then click Save.

2   If you are saving a file for the first time, the Save As dialog box appears. Find the location you would like to save the file, click in the File name text field and type a name for your publication.

3   Click Save.

Customizing the Quick Access Toolbar

Use the Quick Access Toolbar for convenient, one-click access to your favorite tools. Currently, the toolbar in the document displays the Save, Redo, and Undo options, and the Customize Quick Access Toolbar button.

Here you will customize the toolbar to include the Quick Print and Refresh All buttons. If you have completed previous lessons in this book, you will already be familiar with this process.

The Quick Access Toolbar.

To customize the Quick Access Toolbar:

1   Make sure you are not in the Backstage view and click the Customize Quick Access
    Toolbar button (▾).

2   In the drop-down menu, click Quick Print.

3   Click the Customize Quick Access Toolbar button, again.

4   In the drop-down menu, click Print Preview.

    The Quick Access Toolbar now contains the Quick Print and Print Preview commands.

*The new commands are now added
to the Quick Access Toolbar.*

5   To remove a command, right-click it, and click Remove from Quick Access Toolbar.

Getting help

If you run into a problem or aren't sure how to perform a certain task, you can easily get
help in Publisher by doing one of the following:

1   Press your computer's F1 key or click the Help button to display the help system.

2   In Backstage view, click the Help tab to display Support links for the help system,
    Getting Started resources, and a link to chat with, call, or e-mail Microsoft.

Get help by pressing F1 or clicking the Help tab in the Backstage view.

Closing a Publisher session

When you're finished exploring Publisher, save your file and close the program by following these steps:

1 Choose one of the following methods to save your file:

- Select File > Save.
- Click Save (📙) on the Quick Access Toolbar.

2 Choose one of the following methods to close Publisher:

- Select File > Exit.
- Click the Close button located in the upper-right corner of the Publisher window.

Self study

1 Explore the selection of tabs and settings in the Ribbon, and then hide the Ribbon to give yourself more screen space to work with.

2 Practice opening, saving, and closing installed templates from the selection in Backstage view. Try downloading different templates from Office.com and explore the additional designs.

3 In the Help system, become familiar with the Options area, which contains settings for customizing language, display, and other program attributes.

Review

Questions

1   Which tab does NOT display the Ribbon when you click it?

2   Where can I go to download additional templates?

3   What is the advantage of viewing a publication in a two-page spread?

Answers

1   The File tab. The Ribbon tabs contain groups of commands that are visible on all tabs except File.

2   If you can't find a suitable template among those provided, you can easily download templates from *Office.com*.

3   A two-page spread mimics the way your publication would look lying open in front of you, with two pages facing each other.

What you'll learn in this lesson:

- Creating and configuring a publication

- Adding, formatting, and threading text

- Inserting and modifying images

- Preparing a document for printing or e-mail distribution

Getting Started with Microsoft Publisher 2010

In this lesson, you will discover how to create a basic publication from scratch. You will also learn how to bring text and graphics into a publication, as well as prepare it for printing or distribution via e-mail.

Starting up

You will work with several files from the Pub02lessons folder in this lesson. Make sure that you have loaded the OfficeLessons folder onto your hard drive from *www.DigitalClassroomBooks.com/Office2010*. See "Loading lesson files" on page XXIV.

See Lesson 2 in action!

Use the accompanying video to gain a better understanding of how to use some of the features shown in this lesson. The video tutorial for this lesson can be found at www.DigitalClassroomBooks.com/Office2010.

Creating a blank publication

In Lesson 1, you saw how Publisher's preset design templates can help you create a new publication. In this lesson, you'll explore how to create a new blank publication, for those times when the provided templates don't meet your needs.

To create a blank publication:

1　Start Publisher.

2　Click the File tab, if you are not already in Backstage view, and then click New.

3　Click on More Blank Page Sizes, and then Create New Page Size (under the Custom heading) to define a new size for your document.

You can click on Blank 8.5 x 11" or Blank 11 x 8.5" to quickly create a standard letter-sized blank publication, or choose from a selection of standard page sizes by clicking on More Blank Page Sizes.

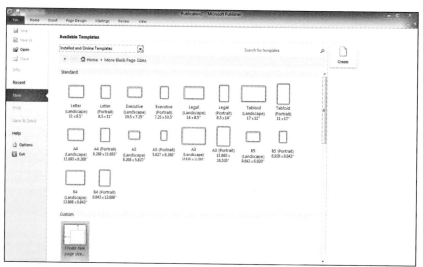

Define a new publication size.

4　In the Create New Page Size dialog box, name your document **Newsletter**. Then set the width to 9 inches and and height to 12 inches, respectively. Leave the margins at their defaults, and click OK.

5　In the Customize section to the right, click the Color Scheme down arrow, and choose the Civic scheme. Then click the Font Scheme down arrow, and choose the Equity scheme.

6　Click on the Create New down arrow under Business Information, select Create new.

7   Type your name, job position, and contact information in the provided fields. Click Save to attach this information to your file.

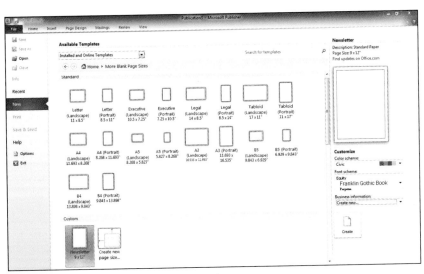

Customize your publication by choosing color and font schemes.

8   Click Create to accept the settings for your new blank publication.

9   On the Quick Access Toolbar, click the Save button (💾). In the dialog box that appears, navigate to the Pub02lessons folder, name the file Newsletter, and click Save.

Working with pages

The thumbnails in the Navigation pane correspond to pages in your publication. You just created a one-page document, but if you find it necessary to add or delete pages, you can do so one page or one spread at a time.

If you're working on a publication with multiple pages, you'll want to display the page before or after the one you want to insert. You'll be choosing whether to add a page before or after the current page.

To insert one or more pages:

1   Click the Insert tab, and then click the Page drop-down arrow in the Pages group. Choose Insert Page from the menu that appears.

To insert a single blank page, choose Insert Blank Page. To insert a duplicate page, choose Insert Duplicate Page.

2   In the Insert Page dialog box, change the settings so that you're inserting three new blank pages after the current page.

Insert new blank pages into your publication.

3   Click OK.

To delete, rename, or move a page:

1   Select the last page (page 4) in the Navigation pane.

2   Click the Page Design tab and in the Pages group, click the Delete button. This will remove page 4 from your publication. This may not be obvious because we are working with blank pages. However, you can see the change in the Navigation pane.

3   On the same tab and in the same group, click the Move button. In the Move selected pages section of the Move Page dialog box, click on the After radio button. Choose Page 1 from the This page section, and click OK to move page 3 to a position after page 1.

You can also drag a page icon in the Navigation pane to move it.

4   On the Page Design tab in the Pages group, click the Rename button, and in the Rename Page dialog box, rename Page Title to **Page 2**. Click OK.

Use the Page Design tab to delete,
rename, or move pages.

Setting page margins

The blue rectangle that appears within the boundaries of your page represents the page's margins. Publisher automatically sets the margins to one-half inch when you create a new document, but if you need to adjust the margin size, you can choose from several options in the Margins area of the Page Design tab.

The margins are only for guidance. It is possible to place text, graphics, and other objects outside the document margins in Publisher.

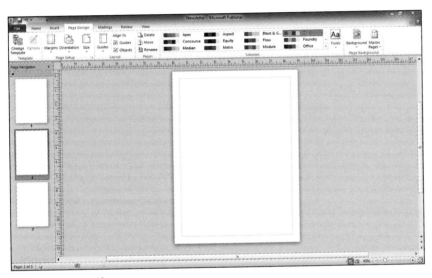

Use page margins to guide you.

Changing page orientation

As you work with your publication, you may want to switch the page orientation. So far, you've been working with a blank document in portrait format, but you can easily switch to landscape format (and back).

To change the page orientation:

1 Click on the Page Design tab.

2 Click on the Orientation button in the Page Setup group to reveal the options.

3   Choose the Landscape option to change the layout.

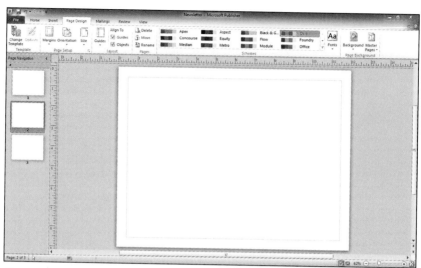

Change your page orientation to Landscape.

4   Repeat steps 1 and 2, but this time choose the Portrait option to return to the portrait orientation.

Changing page sizes

The publication you're building is currently formatted to fit on a 9 x 12-inch sheet of paper. Because this is not a standard document size, you'll want to change the size to Letter before you begin adding content.

To change page sizes:

1   Click on the Page Design tab.

2   Click on the Size button found in the Page Setup group.

3 Choose Letter (Portrait) from the Size menu to change the size of the current publication to that of a standard Letter.

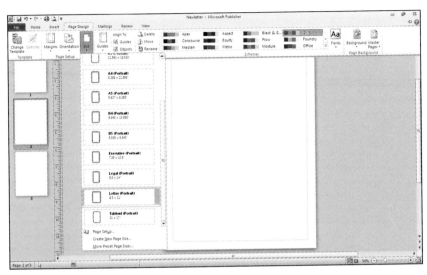

Change your page size to Letter.

Publisher does not allow you to mix page sizes and orientations within a single document. If you must use multiple page sizes or orientations, you will have to create separate documents.

Now that you have set up your publication's pages, margins, orientation, and size, you'll begin to add content to it.

Inserting a text box

Any text that you add to a Publisher document must be contained in a text box. To add a title to your newsletter, you'll first insert a text box and then enter your text inside the box.

If your text doesn't fit inside a text box, you can do one of the following:

- Make the text box bigger
- Reduce the size of the text
- Continue the text in another text box on the same page or on another page

To insert a text box:

1 Select the first page from the Navigation pane on the left of the screen. Click on the Insert tab in the toolbar, and in the Text group, click on the Draw Text Box button.

2 In your publication, move your cursor over the intersection of the left and top margins, and click and drag diagonally until you have a text box that stretches to the right margin and is 2 inches tall.

Draw a text box to hold your newsletter's title.

 You may have to display the publication's rulers to accurately measure the text box's height. Do this by right-clicking anywhere outside the current page, and choosing Rulers from the context menu that appears.

3 Click inside the text box and type the title, **Bike Hikes**.

Formatting text

The text you've inserted is obviously too small and light to be legible. You'll fix this using the Text Box Tools Format tab, which appeared in the toolbar when you added the text box.

To format your text:

1 Select the title by clicking and dragging over it inside the text box.

2 Click on the Text Box Tools Format tab, and in the Font section, choose Franklin Gothic Book from the Font drop-down menu.

3 Also in the Font section, use the Font Size drop-down menu to change the size to 72 points.

4 Click on the Bold button to make the title more visible, and the Italic button to give it more style.

5   Add some color to the title by clicking on the Font Color drop-down menu, and selecting Accent 2 from the scheme colors you chose earlier. Click outside the text box to de-select the title.

Format your text using options in the Font section of the toolbar.

6   Choose File > Save As and in the dialog box that appears, locate the Newsletter file you saved earlier, and click Save to replace it with your new file.

Next you'll insert some body copy into the publication, and learn how to thread it from text box to text box.

Flowing text

You've created a single text box, and added a small amount of text to it. However, if you want to continue a story from one part of a page to another, or even between pages, you can flow text between two or more connected text boxes. Publisher allows you to do this with the click of a button.

You can also connect text boxes prior to adding text to them. When you add your text, it will automatically flow from one text box to the next.

To flow text into your publication:

1   Open Microsoft Word, choose File > Open and navigate to the Pub02lessons folder. Double click to open the file called bikestory.

2   Highlight the text found in this document and press Ctrl+C to copy. Switch back over to the Publisher document.

3   Draw a text box on each of your three pages. You will need to click on the Draw Text Box button each time you want to draw a text box. Use your creativity to mix and match box shapes and sizes and make the layout more interesting.

4   Click in the first text box, and press Ctrl+V to paste your text.

5   Click on the Text In Overflow button (⊡) that appears to the right of the text box. The cursor changes to a pitcher icon, which informs you that the text is ready to "pour" into the next frame.

6   Click in the next frame on the second page, and the text flows into it automatically. If the Text In Overflow button appears again, continue clicking and *pouring* into additional text boxes until you have placed all the text.

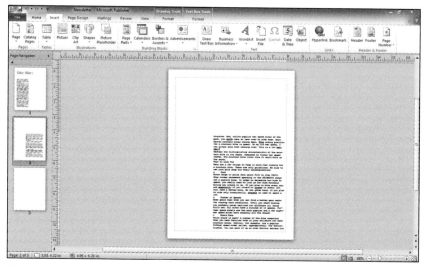

When you see the pitcher icon, you can flow text into the next frame.

You can use the Previous and Next tools in the Linking group of the Text Box Tools Format tab to view all the connected text boxes in your publication. Use the Break tool if you want to break a link from one text box to the next.

Continue inserting and formatting text in your Newsletter publication to fill the available space on all three pages. When you're satisfied with the look and feel of the text, you're ready to start inserting and modifying images.

Inserting and modifying images

Text-heavy publications lack visual appeal when compared to those that also incorporate images. Luckily, Publisher 2010 includes useful features for not only inserting, but also modifying those images in your publications. These tools enable you to adjust brightness and contrast, add various artistic effects, rotate an image, and even crop an image without having to leave the program.

To insert an image:

1   Return to the first page of your publication, using the Navigation pane on the left.

2   In the Illustrations section of the toolbar, found on the Insert tab, click on the Picture button.

3   In the left pane of the Insert Picture dialog box, navigate to the Pub02lessons folder, inside the OfficeLessons folder you loaded onto your hard drive earlier.

4   Select the image named biker.jpg, and then click on the Insert button.

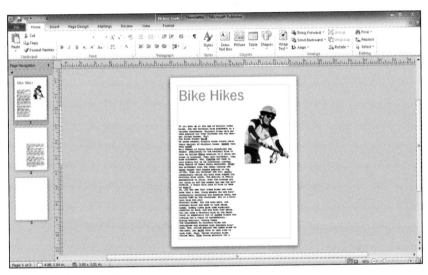

Insert a picture into your publication.

The image is imported into a picture box in your publication.

5   Click and drag on the center of the image to position it where you want on the page. Notice that the text within the text boxes shifts to accommodate the image.

You can't click and drag an image to another page in your publication. Use the Copy and Paste feature to move images between pages.

To modify an image:

1   Select the picture you just placed, and click on the Picture Tools Format tab.

2   You can roll your cursor over each of styles in the Picture Styles gallery to preview their effects. Click on the second choice to change the picture box to an oval.

3   In the Adjust group of the toolbar, click on the Brightness drop-down menu, and choose -10% to darken the image.

4 Click on the Contrast drop-down menu, and choose +10% to add clarity to the picture.

5 Click on the Recolor drop-down menu, and apply a vintage effect by choosing the Sepia color mode.

6 In the Arrange section of the toolbar, click on the Rotate drop-down menu (🔄), and choose Free Rotate to allow dragging of the picture in the direction you want to rotate it. To do this, click on the image and then click on the small green button found just above the picture box and drag to the left a quarter of an inch.

7 Click the Crop button (in the Crop section of the toolbar) to display handles on the image. You can then drag the handles until the image shows only the portion you want to keep. Click anywhere outside of the image to de-select it and accept the crop.

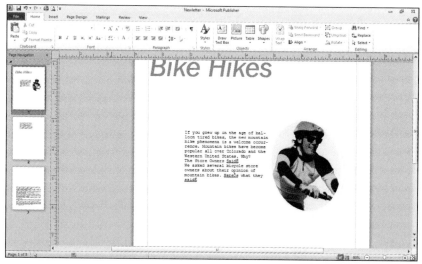

Use the Picture Tools Format tab to modify placed images.

8 Click Save in the Quick Access Toolbar to save your work.

Printing your publication

The ultimate goal of using of Publisher 2010 is to produce high-quality print publications. You can print these on a desktop printer, or send them out to a commercial print shop using a convenient packaging feature.

To print to a desktop printer:

1 Click the File tab, and then click Print.

2 In the Print section, enter the number of copies to print in the Copies of print job text box.

3 In the Printer section, make sure that the correct printer is selected.

The properties for your default printer appear automatically.

4   In the Settings section, do the following:

- Confirm that the range of pages is correct.

- Choose the format for imposing (or arranging) your pages on the printed sheet.

Choose settings to print your publication to a desktop printer.

Ask your printer if it's necessary for you to impose your pages for printing.

- Choose the paper size.

- Choose whether to print on one side of the sheet of paper or both.

- If your printer is capable of printing in color, choose color or grayscale printing.

5   When you're ready to print, click the Print button.

Using Pack and Go

Publisher's Pack and Go Wizard packages your publication and its linked files into a single file that you can send to a commercial printer. You can also take the packed file to another computer to be edited. Using the Pack and Go Wizard ensures that you have all the files necessary to hand off the completed publication to someone who can work with or view it.

To save for a commercial printer:

1   Click the File tab.

2   Choose Save & Send, and then select Save for a Commercial Printer.

3   Under Save for a Commercial Printer, you have the following options:

  •   File size and quality options that are similar to those available when saving to a PDF.

  •   Save PDF and/or Publisher files: You can save to both formats, or either, depending on your printer's requirements.

4   Click the Pack and Go Wizard button.

5   If you are prompted to save your publication, click OK. Locate the previous version and replace it with your new version.

6   In the next window, browse to select the Desktop as the location for saving your (packaged) files. Click Next and then OK to finish packaging the publication into a single file.

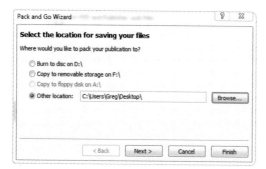

Use the Pack and Go Wizard to package your files for commercial printing.

In the Save & Send interface, you can also save your publication as an HTML file, a Microsoft Publisher 2010 template, or in a format compatible with Publisher 2000 or Publisher 98.

Sending a publication using e-mail

In addition to saving your publication, you can send it as either an e-mail message or an attachment.

In order to send a publication using e-mail, you must have one of the following programs installed on your computer:

  •   Microsoft Office Outlook

  •   Outlook Express (version 5.0 or later)

  •   Windows Mail

To send your publication using e-mail:

1   Click the File tab.

2   Choose Save & Send > Send Using E-mail

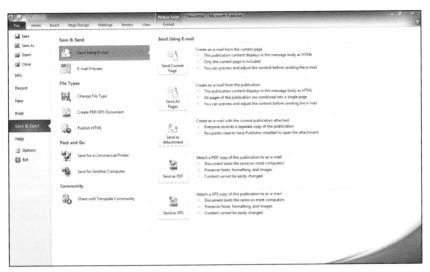

Use Save & Send to send your publication using e-mail.

3   Choose one of the following five options:

- **Send Current Page:** This sends the currently selected page from your publication as an HTML e-mail message, so the recipients do not need to have Publisher to view the publication. You can preview the e-mail in your default web browser, and adjust or cancel the message before you send it.

- **Send All Pages:** All the publication's pages are combined into a single page. You can preview the e-mail in your default web browser, and adjust or cancel the message before you send it.

- **Send as Attachment:** Every recipient receives their own copy of the publication, and each recipient must have Publisher installed in order to open the attachment.

- **Send as PDF:** This option preserves fonts, formatting, and images, but the recipients must have a PDF reader installed on their computer, such as Adobe Reader (available from Adobe Systems).

- **Send as XPS:** This option preserves fonts, formatting, and images, but cannot be easily modified.

4   When your e-mail program launches, enter the recipients' addresses, a subject line, and any other options, and click Send.

E-mail preview

This feature allows you to see what your publication will look like in an e-mail message by opening it as an HTML version in your default web browser.

Preview your e-mail publication in a web browser.

To preview an e-mail:

1 Click the File tab.

2 Choose Save & Send > E-mail Preview, and then click on the E-mail Preview button to the right.

3 Close out of the internet browser and then choose File > Close to close the current document.

Congratulations! You have finished this lesson, and you now have the basic skill set to create publications from scratch in Microsoft Publisher 2010.

Self study

1 Create a new, landscape-oriented publication, add and rearrange two more pages, and change the margins on each page to .75 inch.

2 Insert a text box into your new publication, import text from a Word document, and format the text using the Text Box Tools Format tab.

3 Insert an image into your new publication and use the Picture Tools Format tab to change its brightness, contrast, and cropping.

4 Save the publication as a PDF for commercial printing, using the Pack and Go Wizard.

Review

Questions

1 Is it possible to place text and images outside a publication's margins?

2 How can you get text to automatically flow from one text box to another as you import it?

3 What programs are needed to send a publication using e-mail?

Answers

1 Yes. Publisher's margins are only for guidance; it is possible to place text, graphics, or other objects outside the document margins.

2 You can connect text boxes prior to adding text to them. When you add your text, it automatically flows from one text box to the next.

3 In order to send a publication using e-mail, you must have Microsoft Office Outlook, Outlook Express (version 5.0 or later), or Windows Mail installed on your computer.

What you'll learn in this lesson:

- Using Outlook for email messaging
- Scheduling activities and sharing your calendar
- Maintaining and organizing contact information

Microsoft Outlook Essentials

You can use Outlook to communicate via email, maintain contact details for colleagues, and organize your schedule with robust calendar capabilities.

Starting up

You will not need to work with any files for this lesson.

See Lesson 1 in action!

Use the accompanying video to gain a better understanding of how to use some of the features shown in this lesson. The video tutorial for this lesson can be found at www.DigitalClassroomBooks.com/Office2010.

What is Outlook?

Regardless of your type of business or your role, you probably need to send and receive email for work, keep track of contacts, including office numbers, mobile numbers, and email addresses, and you also need to schedule meetings and appointments. Outlook helps you keep all these things organized. Many Outlook users would consider themselves lost without it because it does a great job of keeping you organized in today's fast-paced work environment. It reminds you of meetings, lets you send meeting updates, and, of course, keeps all your email organized.

Setting up Outlook

When you start using Outlook, you need to set it up for email communication. It needs to know your email address and email password so it can retrieve your email and display it for you. If you have an IT department that has already set up Outlook for you, you can skip this section and move on to Composing Email, a few pages ahead in this lesson. But if you are starting Outlook for the first time, you'll need to tell it where your email is stored and how it is sent. If you use a Microsoft Exchange server, this can be as simple as entering your email address and password, while other email servers may require a bit more work on your part. You'll start the configuration process of setting up a new email account in the Control Panels of your computer. While you can do this directly within Outlook, there are some email server configuration steps that are more efficient when you access them through the Control Panel. For this exercise, we'll have you configure Outlook via the Mail Control Panel, which is part of the operating system.

1 Make sure Outlook is closed.

2 Within the Windows operating system, click the Start menu, then choose Control Panel. Double-click to open the Mail control panel.

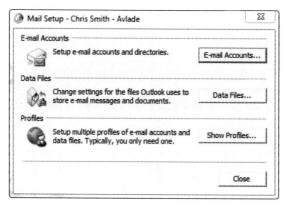

The Mail Setup control panel.

3 In the Mail Setup control panel, click the E-mail Accounts button. The Account Settings Window opens.

4 In the Account Settings window, using the E-mail tab, click the New... button, then click the E-mail account radio-button, and click Next. The Add New Account window is displayed.

5 In the Add New Account window, enter your full name as you would like it to appear when sending messages. Also enter your E-mail address, such as *me@mydomain.com*, and enter the password provided by your IT department or Internet service provider.

Outlook will attempt to locate your email server and configure your email for you. If it cannot locate your email server, it may ask you additional questions about the type of email account you are using. If necessary, obtain the additional information from your Internet service provider that hosts your email account, your IT department, or click the Help button (❷) in the main Outlook window.

Using more than one email account

If you have more than one email account and would like to use Outlook to send and receive email from your other accounts, you can do so. Repeat the steps above to set up Outlook to communicate with any additional email servers. Each email account functions similarly for sending, receiving, and managing messages. As such, the remaining sections of this lesson apply regardless of whether you are working with one or more email accounts.

Composing email, Adding recipients, and sending messages

To create a new email message, follow these steps.

1 Click the New E-mail button (🗐) in the Home tab of the ribbon. A new, untitled message appears.

2 In the field to the right of the To button, enter the email address of the recipient of the message. Separate additional recipients with a semicolon (;).

If the recipient of the message works at a different company or has a different domain—the part of the email address after the @ symbol, then you will need to enter the complete address. For example, to send an email address to Jennifer Smith at work you might enter, jsmith@company.com. If you work at the same company, you may only need to enter their email name and not the entire domain address.

3 Enter a subject for the message. It is useful to enter a short, descriptive subject that summarizes the content of the message.

4 Enter the body of the email message, and then click the Send button.

Adding attachments to email messages

You can send a file such as a Microsoft Word file or PowerPoint presentation along with your email message. You may want to do this so that you can share the document or have someone review your work. To attach a file:

1   With a new message open click the Attach File button (📎). The Insert File window appears.

2   Using the Insert File window, navigate to the file you wish to attach to the email message, then click the Insert button within the Insert File window.

   You can also click and drag a document into the body portion of an email message you are composing to attach it to a message.

When sending files as attachments, be careful not to send anything too large. Some email systems are not able to accommodate email messages more than a certain size. The upper limit tends to be near 10 MB, although this varies by the policies set by the recipient's email administrator, and could be lower.

Adding signatures

You may want to add your contact information and company name to the bottom of email messages you send. You can avoid needing to enter this information separately with every message by creating an email signature. You can use an email signature to apply a common, repeated set of information at the bottom of every email. To use a signature, you create and save it one time, then apply it as needed.

1   Create a new message, and then click the Signature button in the Message tab.

2   After clicking the Signature button, a menu appears; click to select Signatures. The Signatures and Stationery window appears.

3   In the Signatures and Stationery window, click the New button. Enter a name for the signature. For example, if you wish to have a work email signature and a personal signature, you would name this **work**. The name is for your use only and not visible to people to whom you send messages.

4 Enter the information you wish to have appear at the end of your messages. For example, if your name is Jennifer Smith, you might enter:

> Jennifer Smith
> All-Star Designs, Inc.
> 617 555-1212 ★ jsmith@digitalclassroombooks.com
> www.DigitalClassroomBooks.com

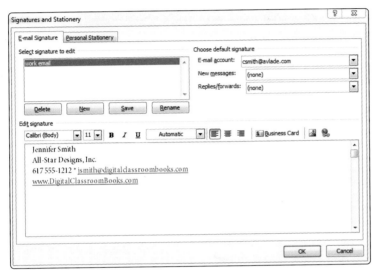

Creating a new email signature.

You can go to http://office.microsoft.com *and in the search field type Outlook Email Signature Templates to see a group of email templates that you can download and use.*

4 After entering the email signature information, under the Choose default signature section indicate which messages, if any, should use the email signature. To have the signature applied to new messages you create, select the signature name from the New messages drop-down menu. To apply your signature to your email replies and messages you forward, select the signature you created from the Replies/forwards drop-down menu. If you only want to apply the signature manually, not automatically, choose (none) from the default signature drop down menus.

5 Click OK. In the email message window, choose the signature you just created from the Signature drop-down menu at the top of the message window. If necessary, choose Signatures from this menu again to edit or modify the signature.

If you set your signature to apply automatically to your messages, create a new message to see the automatic signature.

Receiving email

After configuring Outlook, it will automatically attempt to receive email messages from your account at a specified interval. You can disable this option, and manually check for email more regularly. If you are connected to a Microsoft Exchange email server, your account will automatically update immediately upon receipt of a message.

1 To send and receive all email messages outside the regular schedule, click the Send/ Receive tab of the ribbon, then click the Send/Receive All Folders button ( ).

2 If you have multiple email accounts, you can send and receive only messages for one specific account by choosing the account to use from the Send/Receive Groups drop-down menu.

Organizing email

If you receive many email messages regarding a variety of topics, you can organize them to make it easier to locate and work with the messages. For example, you can put all the emails from a specific sender in one folder, or all emails regarding a certain topic in another folder. You can also have Outlook detect and remove junk email (spam) for you.

Using folders

Email folders act like folder on your computer or within a filing cabinet. Here you will create a new folder.

1 Along the left side of your Outlook main window, right-click your mouse on the name of your email account. Choose New Folder from the context menu that appears.

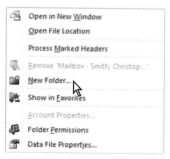

Creating a new folder to organize your email.

2 Name the new folder and drag it up or down to locate it in a convenient location.

3 Click and drag an email message into the new folder. Click on the folder to view its contents, click back on the Inbox to view your new mail.

4 Repeat this process to create as many folders as you need to effectively organize your email.

You can automatically route email messages to specific folders using Rules. From the File tab on the ribbon choose Manage Rules and Alerts, then create a new rule. For example, all email messages from a professional association to which you belong could be routed to a folder for you to keep them organized. When a rule is running, email messages can be routed directly to a specified folder, so be certain to look for them as they won't appear in your inbox if you asked them to be moved for you.

Avoiding Junk email, SPAM, and phishing

Unfortunately, some organizations abuse email to try and sell you things, or even to steal information from you. Outlook can help protect you from receiving some of the unwanted email. Outlook automatically filters suspected junk email and places it into the Junk E-mail folder. You can periodically check this folder to make certain that legitimate messages have not been placed into this folder, and then delete all other content.

Outlook also blocks email messages from displaying pictures. This is so that email senders cannot verify whether your email address is legitimate once an image is downloaded, and thus send you more junk email. You can download images for a single message by clicking the top of that message, or go choose File > Options then click Trust Center and click Trust Options.

Outlook may also disable links, including the ability to reply to some email messages to protect you from messages that may be disguised as being from a legitimate source, such as a bank or financial institution, when the sender cannot be verified. In these cases, it is best to delete the message and contact the sender separately to verify the legitimacy of the email message. You should never reply with personal information, as it may be a phishing attempt to illegitimately obtain personal information, and most businesses will never ask for personal information via email because it is unsecure.

Archiving old messages

If you have accumulated months worth of email, Outlook can put it aside for you so that you can focus on your current messages but still access the older messages later if necessary. This process is known as archiving. The contents of folders are archived at different intervals. Some folders are archived after two months, while others are archived after six months. You can change the period of time Outlook waits before archiving a folder, or specify that a folder is not archived at all. You can also have outlook delete old messages as well. If you work for a company you should check to see if they have a records retention policy before deleting messages, as some organizations have a need to keep messages for legal or compliance reasons. Note that an IT administrator can disable these settings if you are using an Exchange email server. If you do not see the settings below and work in a corporate environment, they may have been disabled because the settings have been applied for you.

To specify how often Outlook should archive your email messages:

1 Choose File > Options then click the Advanced tab. In the Advanced tab, click the Auto Archive Settings.

2 In the Auto Archive Settings window, specify how frequently the folder should be archived, how old items should be before they are archived, and whether the items should be moved or deleted. Click OK to close the Auto Archive settings window.

Specifying Auto Archive settings.

3 You can specify different Auto Archive settings for an individual folder. To do this, right-click the folder, then choose Properties from the context menu and make any necessary adjustments in the Auto Archive tab of the folder properties window.

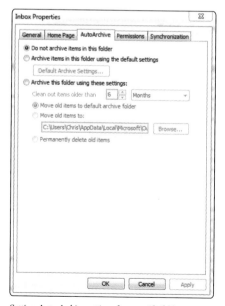

Setting Auto Archive settings for a specific folder.

Contacts and the Address Book

You can make it easier to communicate with colleagues, customers, and others by having Outlook keep track of contact information. If you use a Microsoft Exchange Server, Outlook will automatically locate contacts from within your organization.

Adding contacts

You can manually add contacts for individuals that Outlook has not automatically placed in your Contacts list.

1   Click the Contacts button at the bottom left corner of the Outlook window.

2   In the upper-left corner of the Home tab, click New Contact. Enter the information you wish to save, including email address and phone information.

3   Click Save and Close after entering the contact information.

Finding contacts

You can find a contact in the Contacts section of Outlook, or while sending an email or creating a meeting.

1   Click the Contacts button in the lower-left corner of the Outlook window.

2   At the top of the Outlook window, enter some or the entire name of the person you wish to locate.

3   When the person's name is displayed, double-click their name, then take the desired action such as sending an email message.

4   If you have not created a contact, but have previously communicated with the person, click Suggested Contacts along the left side, which keeps track of all email addresses to which you have sent messages.

Creating groups

If you frequently send messages to the same group of people, you can create a group to simplify the process. For example, if you frequently send emails to five colleagues in the sales department, you can create a single group and then only need to enter the group name to reach all five people. To create a group:

1   Click the Contacts button in the lower left corner of the window.

2   Click New Contact Group in the Home tab of the ribbon. An untitled contact group appears.

3   Enter a name for the group, such as **Sales Department**.

4   Click Add Members and locate members to assign to the group from your contacts or by entering a new email address.

5   Click Save & Close to save the new contact group.

Calendar

You can use Outlook to help organize your schedule, set-up meetings, and keep track of anything that needs to be done by a specific date or time.

Appointments and meetings

If you need to schedule time for yourself, Outlook considers it an Appointment. If you want others to participate, it becomes a Meeting.

Creating appointments and setting-up reminders

Follow these steps to create a new appointment in your calendar.

1   In the Home tab of the ribbon, click New Items > Appointment if you are in the Mail portion of Outlook, or New Appointment if you are in the Calendar portion of Outlook.

2   Enter a subject to display in your calendar, such as **Dentist Appointment**.

3   Enter the Location of the appointment, such as **123 Main Street, Anytown, NY**

4   Enter a start and end time for the appointment.

5   To receive a reminder of the meeting at some time before the meeting, click the reminders button ( ), then click Save & Close.

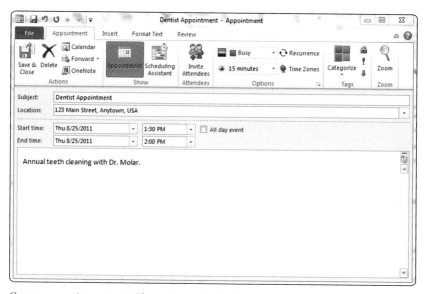

Create a new appointment to set-aside time in your calendar for an activity or event.

Setting-up meetings and inviting attendees

Follow these steps to create a new meeting and invite other participants. The process is almost identical to creating an appointment, except you invite other participants to the meeting.

1   In the Home tab of the ribbon, click New Items > Meeting if you are in the Mail portion of Outlook, or New Meeting if you are in the Calendar portion of Outlook.

2   Enter a subject to share with participants and to in the calendar, such as **Strategic Planning Session**.

3   Enter the Location of the appointment, such as **3rd floor conference room**.

4   In the To field, enter the email address or contact names you wish to invite to the meeting. If your colleagues share a group calendar such as Microsoft Exchange, click Scheduling Assistant to see times when prospective attendees are available for a meeting.

5   Enter a start and end time for the appointment.

6   To receive a reminder of the meeting at some time before the meeting, click the reminders button (☀), which will also remind others if they keep the default setting.

7   Click Send to send the meeting invitation.

    As those that you've invited respond to the meeting invitation, Outlook keeps track of who has accepted the meeting request. You will see individual notes indicating who has accepted or declined the meeting invitation.

Using tasks

You can create an electronic to-do list using Outlook's tasks.

1   From the Home tab of the ribbon click New Items > Task. An UntitledTask window opens.

2   Enter a subject for your task, such as **Gather paperwork for tax planning**.

3   Choose a priority, and enter the date you should start the work and the date the project is due.

4   Click Save & Close. The task is displayed in the task list, along the right side of the Mail window. You may need to click the small arrow (<) at the top-right side of the window for the Tasks to display.

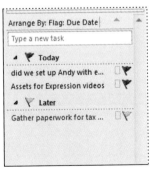

Tasks are listed along the side of the mail window so you can easily keep track of them.

Congratulations, you have finished this lesson!

Self study

1   Enter frequently contacted individuals into your Contact list.

2   Attach pictures and phone numbers to contacts.

3   Create a new meeting and invite participants.

Review

Questions

1   Is Outlook limited to connecting to only certain types of email servers?

2   Are you limited to working with one email account using Outlook?

3   What are the three main functions of Outlook?

Answers

1   Outlook connects to almost any email server. It can connect to Exchange servers, and popular online mail servers such as Hotmail.

2   No, Outlook can connect to multiple email accounts. The different accounts are displayed independently along the left side of the Mail window.

3   Outlook is used primarily for sending, receiving, and organizing Email communication; scheduling and organizing meetings and appointments; organizing contacts with whom you communicate.

Index

X

Z

Wiley Publishing, Inc.
End-User License Agreement

READ THIS. You should carefully read these terms and conditions before opening the software packet(s) included with this book "Book". This is a license agreement "Agreement" between you and Wiley Publishing, Inc. "WPI". By opening the accompanying software packet(s), you acknowledge that you have read and accept the following terms and conditions. If you do not agree and do not want to be bound by such terms and conditions, promptly return the Book and the unopened software packet(s) to the place you obtained them for a full refund.

1. **License Grant.** WPI grants to you (either an individual or entity) a nonexclusive license to use one copy of the enclosed software program(s) (collectively, the "Software") solely for your own personal or business purposes on a single computer (whether a standard computer or a workstation component of a multi-user network). The Software is in use on a computer when it is loaded into temporary memory (RAM) or installed into permanent memory (hard disk, CD-ROM, or other storage device). WPI reserves all rights not expressly granted herein.

2. **Ownership.** WPI is the owner of all right, title, and interest, including copyright, in and to the compilation of the Software recorded on the physical packet included with this Book "Software Media". Copyright to the individual programs recorded on the Software Media is owned by the author or other authorized copyright owner of each program. Ownership of the Software and all proprietary rights relating thereto remain with WPI and its licensers.

3. **Restrictions on Use and Transfer.**

    (a) You may only (i) make one copy of the Software for backup or archival purposes, or (ii) transfer the Software to a single hard disk, provided that you keep the original for backup or archival purposes. You may not (i) rent or lease the Software, (ii) copy or reproduce the Software through a LAN or other network system or through any computer subscriber system or bulletin-board system, or (iii) modify, adapt, or create derivative works based on the Software.

    (b) You may not reverse engineer, decompile, or disassemble the Software. You may transfer the Software and user documentation on a permanent basis, provided that the transferee agrees to accept the terms and conditions of this Agreement and you retain no copies. If the Software is an update or has been updated, any transfer must include the most recent update and all prior versions.

4. **Restrictions on Use of Individual Programs.** You must follow the individual requirements and restrictions detailed for each individual program in the "About the CD" appendix of this Book or on the Software Media. These limitations are also contained in the individual license agreements recorded on the Software Media. These limitations may include a requirement that after using the program for a specified period of time, the user must pay a registration fee or discontinue use. By opening the Software packet(s), you agree to abide by the licenses and restrictions for these individual programs that are detailed in the "About the CD" appendix and/or on the Software Media. None of the material on this Software Media or listed in this Book may ever be redistributed, in original or modified form, for commercial purposes.

5. **Limited Warranty.**

    (a) WPI warrants that the Software and Software Media are free from defects in materials and workmanship under normal use for a period of sixty (60) days from the date of purchase of this Book. If WPI receives notification within the warranty period of defects in materials or workmanship, WPI will replace the defective Software Media.

(b) WPI AND THE AUTHOR(S) OF THE BOOK DISCLAIM ALL OTHER WARRANTIES, EXPRESS OR IMPLIED, INCLUDING WITHOUT LIMITATION IMPLIED WARRANTIES OF MERCHANTABILITY AND FITNESS FOR A PARTICULAR PURPOSE, WITH RESPECT TO THE SOFTWARE, THE PROGRAMS, THE SOURCE CODE CONTAINED THEREIN, AND/OR THE TECHNIQUES DESCRIBED IN THIS BOOK. WPI DOES NOT WARRANT THAT THE FUNCTIONS CONTAINED IN THE SOFTWARE WILL MEET YOUR REQUIREMENTS OR THAT THE OPERATION OF THE SOFTWARE WILL BE ERROR FREE.

(c) This limited warranty gives you specific legal rights, and you may have other rights that vary from jurisdiction to jurisdiction.

6. Remedies.

(a) WPI's entire liability and your exclusive remedy for defects in materials and workmanship shall be limited to replacement of the Software Media, which may be returned to WPI with a copy of your receipt at the following address: Software Media Fulfillment Department, Attn.: *Microsoft Office 2010 Digital Classroom*, Wiley Publishing, Inc., 10475 Crosspoint Blvd., Indianapolis, IN 46256, or call 1-800-762-2974. Please allow four to six weeks for delivery. This Limited Warranty is void if failure of the Software Media has resulted from accident, abuse, or misapplication. Any replacement Software Media will be warranted for the remainder of the original warranty period or thirty (30) days, whichever is longer.

(b) In no event shall WPI or the author be liable for any damages whatsoever (including without limitation damages for loss of business profits, business interruption, loss of business information, or any other pecuniary loss) arising from the use of or inability to use the Book or the Software, even if WPI has been advised of the possibility of such damages.

(c) Because some jurisdictions do not allow the exclusion or limitation of liability for consequential or incidental damages, the above limitation or exclusion may not apply to you.

7. U.S. Government Restricted Rights. Use, duplication, or disclosure of the Software for or on behalf of the United States of America, its agencies and/or instrumentalities "U.S. Government" is subject to restrictions as stated in paragraph (c)(1)(ii) of the Rights in Technical Data and Computer Software clause of DFARS 252.227-7013, or subparagraphs (c) (1) and (2) of the Commercial Computer Software - Restricted Rights clause at FAR 52.227-19, and in similar clauses in the NASA FAR supplement, as applicable.

8. General. This Agreement constitutes the entire understanding of the parties and revokes and supersedes all prior agreements, oral or written, between them and may not be modified or amended except in a writing signed by both parties hereto that specifically refers to this Agreement. This Agreement shall take precedence over any other documents that may be in conflict herewith. If any one or more provisions contained in this Agreement are held by any court or tribunal to be invalid, illegal, or otherwise unenforceable, each and every other provision shall remain in full force and effect.

The on-line companion to your Digital Classroom book.

DigitalClassroomBooks.com

Visit DigitalClassroomBooks.com for...

 Updated lesson files

 Errata

 Contacting the authors

 Video Tutorial samples

 Book Samples

DIGITAL CLASSROOM

For information about the Digital Classroom series visit www.DigitalClassroomBooks.com

You have a personal tutor in the Digital Classroom.

978-0-470-56802-6

978-0-470-60776-3

978-0-470-52568-5

978-0-470-60777-0

978-0-470-60781-7

978-0-470-59524-4

978-0-470-60774-9

978-0-470-57777-6

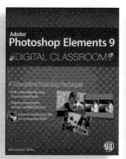

978-0-470-93230-8

978-0-470-60779-4

978-0-470-60783-1

DIGITAL CLASSROOM
A Complete Training Package

For more information about the Digital Classroom series, go to www.digitalclassroombooks.com.

Available wherever books are sold.

WILEY
Now you know.
wiley.com

Wiley, the Wiley logo, and Digital Classroom are trademarks or registered trademarks of John Wiley & Sons, Inc. and/or its affiliates.